THE KINGDOM OF CHARACTER

The Student Volunteer Movement for Foreign Missions (1886-1926)

Michael Parker

1998

American Society of Missiology
and
University Press of America,® Inc.
Lanham • New York • Oxford

Copyright © 1998 by
University Press of America,® Inc.
4720 Boston Way
Lanham, Maryland 20706

12 Hid's Copse Rd.
Cummor Hill, Oxford OX2 9JJ

Library of Congress Cataloging-in-Publication Data

Parker, Michael
The kingdom of character : the Student Volunteer Movement for
Foreign Missions (1886-1926) / Michael Parker.
p. cm.
Includes bibliographical references and index.
1. Student Volunteer Movement for Foreign Missions—History. 2.
College students in missionary work—History 19th century. 3.
College students in missionary work—History—20th century. I.
Title.
BV2360.P37 1998 266'.023'0601 —DC21 97-46435 CIP

ISBN 0-7618-1012-9 (cloth: alk. ppr.)
ISBN 0-7618-1013-7 (pbk: alk. ppr.)

For my parents.

TABLE OF CONTENTS

Preface

My interest in missions began while I was a student at Fuller Theological Seminary. A number of seminarians there were committed to going into the mission field whose level of commitment and enthusiasm I found nearly irresistible. Soon I was doing a three-month internship as a missionary in Pakistan as a way of testing my own growing interest in the missionary enterprise. Though profoundly impressed by the quality of the missionaries I encountered and the importance of the work, I concluded that my own skills and aptitudes were better suited to more strictly scholarly pursuits. Still, my interest in the field had not so much waned as taken a different direction. The germ of that interest eventually issued in a Ph.D. dissertation at the University of Maryland on the Student Volunteer Movement, which has here been subsequently honed to its present shape.

It is my pleasure to gratefully acknowledge those people whose assistance helped to make this book a reality. Although this is the first scholarly history of the Student Volunteer Movement, no scholarly product is ever the work of a single mind, and I am, first of all, keenly aware of the large debt I owe to those historians who have gone before me, whose insights and understandings have informed this work throughout, and who have rightly received copious acknowledgment in the endnotes and bibliography. Almost all of the material necessary to do the research for this book was available in the archives of the Yale Divinity School Library, and so I am very grateful to Martha Smalley and the staff in the Mott room at YDS, on whose cheerful and friendly help over many months I could always rely. My Ph.D. supervisor James Gilbert gave invaluable guidance at every step of the research and writing process, and David Grimsted and Robin Muncy read the dissertation and contributed many helpful suggestions. My sister-in-law, Rachel Parker, copyedited the final manuscript, enhancing its final appearance. Finally, I want to thank Linda Sargent without whose perseverance, during my absence abroad, this book might never have found a publisher. Naturally any errors in judgment or fact contained in the text are my own responsibility and should in no way reflect on the limitations of anyone but myself.

In telling the story of the Student Volunteer Movement perhaps an unintended consequence will be that others will be moved to follow in their footsteps. This has been my own case; and although I have striven to write a balanced and objective history, I would be less than candid not to admit that I have approached the story of the student volunteers with sympathy and appreciation, not only for their sakes but for the cause on which they have left an indelible and very American mark.

Michael Parker
Khartoum, Sudan
1997

INTRODUCTION

The nineteenth century was the heroic age of missions in modern Christian history. In the fin de siecle period, Christians looked back on the preceding century of missionary activity with boundless admiration for those who pioneered the early missionary enterprise. It was an age when missionaries were heroes and their stories were closely followed in the press and trumpeted in the pulpit. William Carey's work in India, Robert Moffat's in Africa and George Boardman's in Burma never ceased to inspire. The greatest of them all, David Livingstone, was the idol of the age. Luther Wishard, a leader in the American missionary movement in the late nineteenth century, upon reading *The Personal Life of David Livingstone* gushed that it was "the greatest missionary biography in all literature of this age or any age."[1]

Yet, despite the mounting enthusiasm, by 1870 America had sent out a total of only about 2,000 Protestant missionaries, and by 1890 there were only 934 American foreign missionaries then in the field, a feeble effort for a nation with the population, wealth and pretensions that America had in the nineteenth century. By the turn of the century, however, there were 5,000 American missionaries, by 1915 there were 9,000, and by the end of the 1920s there were 14,000.[2] The transition from heroic if nominal efforts to a determined and concerted program to evangelize the world occurred in the last quarter of the century and blossomed in the last decade of that century through a variety of new organizations, the most influential being the Student Volunteer Movement for Foreign Missions.

Generally known as simply the Student Volunteer Movement, or merely the SVM, this new missionary effort grew out of the collegiate YMCA. It was formed in 1886, and over the next three decades it became the most successful missionary recruiting organization in the nation. On a missionary tour of colleges in 1887-8, Robert Wilder and John Forman recruited 2,200 student volunteers, nearly as many missionaries as had been sent from the U.S. in the entire preceding century. During its first decade, other SVM organizations were created in nations around the globe, and they were linked by another new organization, The World Student Christian Federation (WSCF), which was an important forerunner of the Twentieth-Century ecumenical movement. The SVM reached the apogee of its success in 1921 when 637 student volunteers were sent out as missionaries, but in the 1920s and 30s it experienced a variety of problems that undermined its effectiveness.[3] During the Great Depression it became moribund, but limped along for several more decades until it finally dissolved in 1969.

The SVM should be seen as both a culmination and a radical departure from the long history of missionary effort in America. In the Sixteenth Century, when the settlement of North America was first considered by Englishmen, high on the priority list of Elizabethan propaganda for colonization was the need to convert Native Americans. Later, some of America's greatest names were enlisted in this cause, including John Eliot, the Mayhews, David Brainard and Jonathan Edwards. While sending missionaries to the indigenous population, the largely dissenter-colonists were themselves viewed by the Church of England as generally unchurched, and therefore fit subjects for missionizing. Consequently, in 1697 the Church of England established the Society for the Propagation of the Gospel, whose task ostensibly was to Christianize the Indians, but whose major efforts were in establishing Anglican churches in Puritan New England. Other churches were equally active in the effort to export Christianity to North America, and thus the Eighteenth Century proved to be a period of phenomenal church growth.

In the middle decades of the Eighteenth Century, during what was called the Great Awakening, a distinctly American style of religion was born – revival-centered, evangelical and arguably democratic in that it caused laymen to question established authorities – whose effects are still felt today. The Awakening produced in some an expansive vision of America's role in the world to which a later generation would give tangible expression in the missionary enterprise. At one point Jonathan Edwards, the leading intellectual spokesman for the Awakening, was so enraptured by the possibilities of the movement that he believed that it might be the beginning of the millennium.[4] Later, in considering an American-centered evangelization of the world resulting from the Awakening, he foresaw "that then many of the Negroes and Indians will be divines, and that excellent books will be published in Africa, in Ethiopia, in Tartary, and other now the most barbarous countries."[5]

In the nineteenth century these emphases in religion were confirmed and elaborated in the Second Great Awakening. Like Edwards before them, many saw this newest awakening as the possible beginnings of an American-centered world evangelization that would usher in the millennium.[6] The democratic emphasis of this second awakening was particularly apparent, as music, worship styles and even doctrines were reshaped to appeal to the common people.[7] Furthermore, the democratization of religion helped to spawn a variety of Christian organizations, largely run by laymen, known collectively as the "Benevolent Empire." It was at this time, buoyed by their own successes and dreaming of world evangelization, that American Protestants became interested in foreign missions.

Some of the largest of the new benevolent organizations formed in the early nineteenth century were concerned with missions. The American Board of Commissioners for Foreign Missions (ABCFM), formed in 1810, was the second largest of the benevolent societies, following behind the American Bible Society. By 1860 there were 16 mission societies in the U.S. and by 1890 the number of mission societies had grown to 90.[8] By the time the SVM was formed in 1886, America was poised for the greatest period of missionary activism heretofore in its history.

During its heyday, the SVM was a mainstream organization of late Victorian American culture, if only because Protestant missions were such a highly visible and central part of that culture. Although missions were probably embraced by only a minority of Americans, they were given official endorsement at the highest levels. For example, the Ecumenical Missionary Conference in New York in 1900 was conspicuous for its political ornaments, including among its speakers former President Benjamin Harrison, then President William McKinley, and future President Theodore Roosevelt. In fact all American Presidents from McKinley to Wilson gave the Protestant missionary effort their blessing, as did other prominent Americans, such as William Jennings Bryan. The SVM was at the center of this missionary movement and was supported by all of the mainline Protestant churches, which looked to it to supply many of the foreign missionaries that their mission boards sent abroad.

By 1920, then at the height of its recruiting success, the SVM had supplied about half of all the American missionaries of the previous three decades.[9] The ideas expressed by the leaders of the SVM and the traditions they represented ran the gamut of American Protestant religious emphases, from pre-millennialism and revivalism to the Social Gospel and ecumenism. That the SVM was able to give expression to these varying views and still receive the support of all the mainline denominations suggests the overriding missionary consensus that characterized American Protestantism in the Victorian era. Beyond the context of American religiosity, the movement's optimism and expansiveness as well as its provincialism and ethnocentrism typified the dominant stream in the broader American culture in the several decades preceding World War I.

Historians have advanced a variety of explanations to account for the remarkable missionary upsurge that occurred at this time. Missions historian Kenneth Scott Latourette, who at one time was a member of the SVM, believed that late nineteenth century Anglo-American missions paralleled "the spirit of enterprise and adventure" that led other Europeans at that time to geographical exploration, imperial expansion, and scientific discovery. Moreover, he believed that nineteenth-century Protestantism experienced a "surge of vitality" and an impulse "which was as old as Christianity itself and which came through Jesus."[10] In contrast to Latourette's Christian idealism, Sidney Ahlstrom believed that the sudden interest in foreign missions in the late Victorian period was attributable to the churches' desire to avoid conflict on a variety of fields that were then confronting religion: higher criticism, evolution, liberalism, urbanization and its attendant social problems.[11] Robert Handy, in a less expansive vein, explained the missions boom as a direct extension of the volunteerism that began in the 1830s.[12] Similarly, Valentin Rabe saw the upsurge in turn-of-the-century missions as a largely lay effort. Focusing on the lay professionalization of the missionary movement that occurred in this period, Rabe argued that missions mirrored the Progressive Era's emphasis on organization and experts, as it attempted to replace "spontaneous enthusiasm and spiritual dynamism" with "businesslike planning, organization, and promotion to achieve the same result."[13] More recently, William Hutchison saw American missionaries as essentially cultural imperialists. In his estimation, Americans began with an "errand into the wilderness" that by the end of the nineteenth century became an "errand to the world." Americans, he argued, believed that they had a special obligation as God's chosen emissaries to Christianize the world, His "new Israel."[14]

Often brilliant, sometimes mundane, usually partial, historian's interpretations are often simply a matter of emphasis. I will not quarrel with any of the interpretations of my predecessors. Indeed, they have informed my work throughout. However, I intend to present an interpretation that has not heretofore been made for the understanding of American missions. The usual plot line for missions in the late Victorian period traces the evolution of missionary thinking from a missions philosophy reflecting late nineteenth-century American provincialism to one reflecting the more sophisticated vision of "world missions" in the 1920s. I have embraced this narrative because it is perfectly reflected in the experience of the SVM. The essential contribution I hope to make to this traditional analysis is to place the SVM in the context of the broader culture of Victorian America. I will interpret the missionary upsurge as a working-out, by men and women with a heightened Protestant commitment, of the Victorian motif of character. My principle assertion will be that the Victorian concept of character, a concept especially important to the middle classes and one rich in social, philosophical and theological associations, was the central organizing principle of the movement. As important as the concept of grace was to the Protestant reformers or the concept of virtue in classical republicanism was for the generation that fought the American Revolution, so the concept of character was for the ideology of middle-class Victorians. What Victorians meant by character, how that term was developed and used by the Student Movement, and how new ideas and events in the Twentieth Century came to make the concept of character outmoded by the 1920s, is the larger story to be told here.

Throughout this tale of colorful personalities, war-time disruptions, competing theologies, and cultural transitions, the SVM can be best understood in how it answered one question. Francis Greenwood Peabody, a Social Gospel writer, asked this deceptively simple and perhaps timeless question in his 1905 book, *Jesus Christ and the Christian Character*: "Does the world make the person or does the person make the world?"[15] The SVM's answer, which emphasized the power of individuals both to shape themselves and their environment, is a powerful indication of how the world of today differs from the world that our great-grandparents knew. It also provides a number of the key underlying assumptions of the more than 10,000 SVM missionaries who carried in tandem to nearly every nation on earth the twin evangels of the Christian gospel and the Victorian ideology encapsulated in the word character. The history of the SVM that follows is an attempt to give in detail the SVM's answer to Peabody's question and to show the implications and internal development of that answer in the changing social and cultural matrix of late Victorian society.

Chapter One

THE MOUNT HERMON 100

> For a long time, it was supposed by the church, that a revival was a miracle, an interposition of Divine power which they had nothing to do with, and which they had no more agency in producing, than they had in producing thunder, or a storm of hail, or an earthquake. It is only within a few years that ministers generally have supposed revivals were to be promoted, by the use of means designed and adapted specially to that object.
>
> ---Charles Grandison Finney[1]

Dwight L. Moody, the greatest revivalist of the age, presided over the meeting with a great deal of earnest intensity and a robust give-and-take with the students. "If you want to ask a question, speak out," he bellowed. "That's what we are here for, to get all the cobwebs swept away, and go back to our college mates inspired with the truth."[2] So began the student conference at Mount Hermon, Massachusetts, whose story was told many times in the speeches, pamphlets, articles and books of the SVM, until its recitation became a ritual evoked as a divine imprimatur on the self-proclaimed providential origin of the movement.

While the main speakers in the daily session continued in their course of Bible study and conservative theological pronouncements, the students were beginning to organize a missionary "gusher."[3] Sometime early in the conference Robert Wilder, a recent graduate of Princeton, called together everyone interested in missions. Twenty-one students, some of whom had already signed a missionary pledge written by the Princeton students, attended the first meeting. John Mott, the future leader of the movement, later recalled that the students prayed "that the spirit of missions might pervade the conference, and that the Lord would separate many men unto this great work."[4] After two weeks, when their movement had gained some momentum, they asked Dr. Arthur T. Pierson to address the group on the issue of missions. Pierson, a well-known missionary enthusiast and future editor of the *Missionary Review of the World*, spoke on the theme "Christ means that all shall go, and shall go to all."

One week later, on the Saturday night of July 24, what was later known as "The Meeting of the 10 Nations" occurred. Because Moody, the sponsor of the conference, had not planned to have any addresses on missions delivered during the morning sessions, Robert Wilder requested that 10 students be allowed to speak on this theme. After conferring with the conference leaders, Luther Wishard and Charles Ober, who assured him of Wilder's competence and reliability, Moody agreed to his request. Ten students arose to speak on behalf of their native lands. The nations represented were Japan, Persia, Siam, Germany, Armenia, Denmark, Norway, China, India, and one representative of the American Indians from the Santee agency in the Dakotas. Three of these countries were represented by the sons of missionaries sent there, such as Wilder who represented India. Each student spoke for three minutes, delivering a Macedonian call to the audience, and at the conclusion each spoke the words "God is love" in his native language.[5]

The meeting was concluded by a brief address from Dr. William Ashmore, who had just arrived. Ashmore was a Baptist China missionary of 36 years from the Fuchu district, who, although uninvited, read about the conference in the *Springfield Daily Republican* and arrived with the aim of gaining missionaries for China. Ashmore further stirred the crowd with a report on the needs of China and a summons to Christian duty. "Be willing to be brave, to bear the hardship," he exhorted the students. "Show cause if you can why you should not obey the command of Christ, `Go ye forth and preach the gospel to every creature.' The Burden of proof is on you."[6]

"The Meeting of the 10 Nations" was the unplanned emotional high point of the conference. Wilder later wrote: "Seldom have I seen an audience under the sway of God's spirit as it was that night. The delegates withdrew to their rooms or went out under the great trees to wait on God for guidance."[7] During the eight days that remained of the conference, the number of delegates pledged to become missionaries swelled from 21 to 100. And so it was that in the summer of 1886 on the gently rolling hills overlooking the Connecticut River at Mount Hermon, 100 students launched the most geographically far-reaching missionary drive in world history.

Moody and the YMCA

The SVM was part of what was called the Student Movement in Victorian America and Britain. A river of activity fed by many tributaries, the Student Movement was an uprising of college students for Christian service. Channeled and controlled largely by the Young Men's Christian Association (YMCA) and its college manifestation the Intercollegiate YMCA, the students were influenced by a variety of traditions: evangelist religion, revivalism, the holiness movement, as well as the growing missionary impulse in the last decades of the century.

The most important influence on the origins of the movement was the revivalistic tradition in America, and for its immediate inspiration and founding, the SVM is perhaps most deeply indebted to Dwight L. Moody. It was under Moody's auspices that the Intercollegiate YMCA sponsored the famous Mount Hermon summer conference where the SVM was born. But to understand Moody and the SVM, the YMCA must first be examined. It was the medium in which Moody did much of his work and the organization that supplied the ethos for all of his Christian endeavors.

At the world's fair held in London in the summer of 1851, Americans were exposed for the first time to the increasingly successful London YMCA established by George Williams in 1844.[8] The movement quickly crossed the Atlantic, and in December of 1851 the Boston YMCA was founded. This association became a model for others across the country.[9] The revival that swept the nation in 1857-8 gave further impetus to the idea, and by 1860 there were 205 YMCAs in the U.S., one located in all of its major cities. Moody joined the Boston association in 1854. In the 1860s and early 1870s Moody was a successful one-on-one evangelist for the YMCA among the youth of Chicago's poor. He was also a mission Sunday school director, lay-pastor of the 800-member Illinois Street Church, and finally president of the Chicago YMCA. It was not until the early 1870s, however, that he became a mass evangelist.

A bearded, portly man, with boundless energy and the air of a modern take-charge type of businessman, Moody was the heir of George Whitefield and Charles G. Finney, who in their times were the greatest practitioners of American revivalism.[10]   Whitefield's appeal during the first Great Awakening in the colonial period was non-denominational and broadly pietistic, much like Moody's.   In effect, both men eschewed fine theological points and spoke to a felt need for a personal relationship with God and to a desire for moral, upright living.[11]   As the heir of Charles G. Finney, Moody was a superb technician of revivalism.   Finney was the greatest revivalist of the Second Great Awakening, who in the 1820s and 1830s pioneered or perfected the "new measures" of American revivalism.[12]

In previous days it was assumed that a revival was the work of the Holy Spirit, and therefore it should be brought about by prayer, not human agency. Jonathan Edwards ascribed to this view when he attributed the success of the First Great Awakening to a "shower of divine blessing."[13] But Finney's successful use of techniques changed the popular understanding of revivalism. Like Finney, Moody was able to "work up" rather than "pray down" a revival.[14] Moody took the revival techniques of Finney and further adapted them to the modern city, engineering revivals through energetic promotion, careful organization, and a practical approach to revival meetings that aimed at bringing people to make an immediate decision for Christ. His revival meetings were bathed in the sentimental religious hymns and simple gospel songs of his singing partner, Ira Sankey. Whenever a prayer got too long, or a crowd too raucous or bored, Moody signaled Sankey to work his magic over the meeting.

Moody appealed to the new urban, middle-class, businessman. His portly build, no-nonsense manner, and authoritative pronouncements that reinforced Victorian values of family and the work ethic made him, in the words of one biographer, "the incarnation of a middle class businessman, both in body and mind."[15] He was also the religious embodiment of the entrepreneurial spirit in the Victorian era. When the height of his evangelistic career had passed in the early 1880s, Moody could already be found lavishing more and more of his attention on the construction a permanent legacy. He founded the Northfield School for Girls (1879), the Mount Hermon School for Boys (1881), and the Bible Institute in Chicago (1886), which was later renamed the Moody Bible Institute. He also published a number of periodicals and pamphlets and began a series of summer Bible conferences first at Mount Hermon and then at Northfield, which in 1886 spawned the Student Volunteer Movement for Foreign Missions.

The immediate antecedent to the SVM was the establishment of the Intercollegiate YMCA, an effort which became known as the Student Movement. Parallel to the growth of urban America in the nineteenth century was the growth of colleges and universities, which was particularly accelerated in the last third of the century. In the 1870s there were only about 23,000 undergraduates and 350 colleges in the U.S. But by 1900 there were 100,000 students attending more than 500 institutions of higher education.[16] During these years, U.S. colleges were also in a period of transition. Standards were raised, the age of students increased, and civilizing influences such as fraternities, libraries, literary and music societies and activities such as debating and athletics were encouraged.

Onto this stage the YMCA easily stepped. Several collegiate YMCAs were formed following the revivals of the 1850s, and several more were formed in the 1860s. But the first major growth period for collegiate YMCAs began in the 1870s, when YMCA secretary Robert Weidensall began to promote them, and by 1874 he could report that there were then 32 associations.[17] By 1877 the Student Movement was large enough that a union of the college YMCAs was formed, and the YMCA leadership appointed its first intercollegiate secretary, Luther D. Wishard.

Not satisfied with organizing a mere domestic movement, Wishard began to think of promoting missions among the students. At the 1879 YMCA Convention, Wishard helped to organize the missionary department of the Collegiate YMCA, which then sought to promote missions on college campuses by means of mission speakers, and organizing mission studies. He also commenced the *College Bulletin*, which became the major outlet for missionary news and promotion on American college campuses. In this student publication, Wishard chronicled what he believed to be a missionary "uprising" among college students in the 1880s.

Writing in the *College Bulletin* in November 1880, Wishard was nearly beside himself with excitement and struggled to find ever greater superlatives to describe a new inter-seminary organization. He declared that "such a turning to Mission fields ... has not been witnessed since the days of the Apostles..."[18] The American Inter-Seminary Missionary Alliance ran from 1880 to 1898. Its annual conventions were the first student conventions to deal exclusively with missions, and they were the largest student meetings ever held until the SVM Quadrennial Conventions of the 1890s.[19] By 1886, the year of the formation of the SVM, there were 33 seminaries represented at the Inter-Seminary Alliance Convention with 235 delegates present. Of the 102 evangelical seminaries in the nation, 53 eventually became alliance members.[20]

In 1883 Wishard moved to duplicate the success of the Inter-Seminary Alliance among medical students. He organized a series of Medical Students' Missionary Conferences, the first being February 2-4, 1883, at Lake Forest, Illinois, included only 28 students, half of whom were undergraduates. Over the next two years, Wishard organized five more conferences, some of which were considerably more successful. More than 800 people attended a conference in Chicago, at least 600 of them medical students. At the sixth conference, held in Philadelphia in March, 1885, Wishard reported that 500 students attended.[21]

During the 1885-86 school year, the missionary enthusiasm among students received further stimulation by the college tour of J.E.K. Studd, the brother of the famous English cricketer C.T. Studd. An interesting example of the cross-fertilization of the Anglo-American Christian community, both J.E.K.'s brother, C.T. Studd, and his father were energized in their faith by attending one of Moody's London revival meetings. J.E.K., joined by six other recent college athletes, formed the famous "Cambridge Seven," who in 1883-84 stunned the British nation by pledging themselves to become missionaries to China, and then toured England to promote missions. J.E.K. Studd's tour of American college campuses, which he undertook to tell the story of the "Cambridge Seven," heightened the growing interest about missions in the American student world of the mid-1880s.

As Wishard slowly organized the Student Movement, his thoughts turned to how he could enlist Moody into his cause. In the summer of 1885, Wishard and Charles Ober, who had become the second secretary for the Intercollegiate YMCA in 1882, and two others in the student work were staying on the Moody grounds in Northfield, where Moody lived and where his boys and girls schools were located. Studd and his wife were also guests of the Moodys' at the time. One day Moody stopped by to ask if the group would join him and his wife and daughter and the Studds for a drive up to Mount Hermon in the "carryall." They agreed, and as they were passing some "shacks on a grove" Moody proposed to the College Secretaries that "If you fellows will get together a company of Association General Secretaries next summer, we can entertain them on these workman's houses and I'll give them a Bible reading every day."[22]

In April of 1886, when Moody was visiting Atlanta for a series of meetings, Wishard suggested to Moody that his summer school idea might be used for college students. Moody responded that the college boys would probably not be interested in interrupting their vacation for a Bible conference. Wishard countered that "the river and the hills and such ball games and races as we could arrange would afford them the vacation of their lives." He might have added, as he later advertised in the *College*

Bulletin, "A month's contract and companionship with Mr. Moody, a man who has been so wonderfully used by God in extending His kingdom is in itself a very great attraction."[23]   Moody deferred the question for the moment, but later consented, saying simply, "Well I guess we had better try it."[24]

With less than three months to organize the conference, Wishard and Ober devoted all their time to visiting the college associations to encourage the students to attend. Ober made a visit to Cornell to invite one of the future leaders of the SVM, John R. Mott. Born in 1865 of pioneer stock, Mott grew up in Postville, Iowa.[25] His father was one of the leading citizens of the community, while his mother was a quietly religious woman. From 1881-85 Mott attended Upper Iowa University in Fayette, excelling in debate and oratory while becoming an increasingly devout Christian. In his sophomore year, Mott transferred to Cornell University, where he immediately joined the college YMCA and was so well received that he was elected its vice-president that December. In January of 1886 J.E.K. Studd arrived for a one week stay at Cornell. Mott was profoundly influenced by Studd's talk and sought a personal interview with him, later deciding to enter the ministry. Due to Ober's invitation, the following summer he attended the Mount Hermon conference.

Wishard visited Princeton before the conference, where he met Robert Wilder, probably for the first time, and so corralled another important future leader of the movement.

Wilder's heart and mind were well prepared for Wishard's entreaty. His father, Royal Wilder, went to India as a missionary under the American Board of Commissioners for Foreign Missions (ABCFM) in 1846. The fourth of five children, Robert was born on August 2, 1863 in Kolhapur. In 1876 Royal Wilder decided to return to the United States. His health was poor, and the two youngest children, Robert and Grace, needed to begin a more formal education. His interest in missions, however, did not wane. He soon founded *The Missionary Review*, which he edited single-handedly for 10 years. He and his wife, Eliza, had also successfully instilled in both Robert and Grace a commitment to missions. When Robert was 10 and Grace 12 years of age, they prayed together and one day solemnly dedicated themselves to the service of their God, pledging themselves to return to India to work as missionaries.[26]

Robert attended the Princeton Preparatory School and then spent a year at Williston Seminary, at Easthampton, Massachusetts, before beginning his college work at Princeton in 1881. In the autumn of 1883 he and two other students were invited to attend the Inter-Seminary Missionary Alliance meeting at Hartford, where they heard a memorable address by A.J. Gordon on empowerment by the Holy Spirit. The three students returned to Princeton greatly inspired. An immediate result of Wilder's religious quickening was the establishment of the Princeton Foreign Missionary Society. The three original auditors of Gordon's address, plus two other students, formed the nucleus of this missionary band. They wrote a constitution and bylaws into a hard covered notebook that still survives in the SVM archives. The notebook includes a list of 40 students who signed the charter, and above the names is the following pledge, which the constitution refers to as a covenant: "We the undersigned declare ourselves willing and desirous, God permitting, to go to the unevangelized portions of the world."

The group met on Sunday afternoons in the Wilder home at 12 Stockton Street, Princeton, where Royal Wilder would often speak to the earnest band about his own experiences in India and of the Scriptural injunctions to go to the heathen. While these meetings were going on, Grace Wilder would be in an adjoining room praying for the work of missions. Grace later became a missionary to India, and in her own right was an organizer of missions work and enthusiasm on the home front. While a student at Mount Holyoke Seminary, she founded the Mount Holyoke Missionary Association (MHMA), which met from 1878 to 1884. Mary Matthews, a member of the MHMA, wrote years later "that Grace Wilder told her brother Robert to go to the Conference at Northfield and organize the SVM and she would be praying for him at home in Princeton, N.J."[27] Wilder recalled, though this was many years later and may reflect the unintended distortion of a pious mind, that Grace prophesied that there would be 100 volunteers to emerge from the conference.[28]

Mount Hermon

In the minds of the SVM leaders, the Mount Hermon conference always held an important, and perhaps crucial, place in providential history because of its association with the goal of world evangelization. Reflecting 50 years later on the pivotal "Meeting of the 10 Nations" at the Mount Hermon conference, John Mott offered that it "may occupy as significant a place in the history of the Christian Church as the Williams Haystack Prayer Meeting."[29] This is high praise indeed. Few events in American religious history have been as hallowed as the famous "Haystack Prayer Meeting" of 1806, which four years later resulted in the organization of the ABCFM, the first missionary society in North America.

The famous Mount Hermon summer Bible study meeting lasted four weeks, from July 7 to August 1, 1886. The events at the meeting were copiously recorded for posterity by a reporter for the nearby *Springfield*

Daily Republican, which devoted nearly its entire August 2 issue to recapitulating the meeting. The original plan was to invite one delegate from each of the 225 institutions of higher education with a YMCA on campus. Instead 251 young men arrived, representing 89 colleges and universities across the country, but with a heavy concentration from the east coast.

Moody presided over the meetings, but much of the work fell to the conservative evangelical ministers, missionaries and seminary professors who agreed to assist in the preaching and teaching. The most important of these were the Reverend Dr. Moorhead, a professor at Xenia theological seminary in Ohio; the Reverend Dr. James H. Brooks, pastor of a Presbyterian church in St. Louis; the Reverend Dr. Arthur T. Pierson, a Presbyterian pastor of Bethany Church in Philadelphia and noted writer of mission articles; and the Reverend Dr. A. J. Gordon, the Baptist pastor of the Clarendon-Street Church in Boston whose preaching had so inspired Robert Wilder.

The morning after the "Meeting of the 10 Nations," Ashmore had been asked to deliver a formal address. "As soon as we found a live missionary among us," Wilder later explained, "we asked him to address some of the delegates."[30] Ashmore made the imagery of conquest the center-piece of his talk. The Bible, he averred, was replete with the language of Christ as a king with a world dominion, but the church had lost the concept of a "world conquest." At the close of the address, Moody asked Ira Sankey, his famous singing partner, to sing "Tell it to all the nations that the Lord is king." Moody then followed with a prayer that some of the delegates would receive the missionary spirit.

The volunteers held two final meetings before their departure. Mott wrote of these meetings much later, but with a vividness and even tenderness that suggests an experience of profound consecration. At dusk on the final evening of the conference, the delegates met, each volunteer standing before their peers to explain why he had decided to sign the missionary pledge. By this time 99 had signed. The following morning at a farewell prayer meeting, Mott recalled a solemn ceremony:

> It was in a room in Recitation Hall. There were not seats enough and some had to stand. We knelt, however, all of us, and while we were kneeling in that closing period of heart-burning prayer the hundredth man came in and knelt with us."[31]

The missionary upsurge at Mount Hermon had many causes. The missionary tempo in America had been quickening for sometime, and the

missionary enthusiasts at the conference had their arguments well
marshaled and their appeals finely honed. But what made their calls for
missionary volunteers so compelling at the conference? Certainly the
personal magnetism of Moody and the persuasive powers of Pierson and
Ashmore should not be underestimated. Yet the missionary impulse at
Mount Hermon did not originate from the platform, but from the small
missionary meetings organized by Robert Wilder, which steadily grew
until they became the dominant theme of the conference. Twenty-five years
later Mott remembered that the missionary enthusiasm spread from person
to person until, "You could hardly go anywhere without somebody crossing
your path and presenting this great missionary message."[32]   After the
students themselves had taken over the agenda of the conference, the
power of a group dynamic became nearly irresistible. No one, it seemed,
wanted to quench the Spirit or miss the calling of a lifetime, and
consequently 79 people in the space of eight days dedicated themselves to
becoming foreign missionaries.[33]

To a large extent their decisions to become foreign missionaries have to
be attributed to the revival-like atmosphere of the conference. Intended as a
way to energize campus leaders of the collegiate YMCA, the Mount
Hermon conference got away from its sponsors, with the result that all the
heavy artillery developed for modern revivalism – group pressure,
emotional appeals, celebrity speakers, etc. – was trained on college students
for the purpose of gaining recruits for the mission field. Now, not only
could revivals be "got up" rather than "prayed down," but so could
missionaries. More important, the effort did not result in merely gaining
100 new missionaries, but in initiating a movement.

Manipulated or not, the recruits themselves were sincere and devout
Christians. Prayer was one of the most commented upon features of the
conference, with students frequently found alone and in small groups
making supplication to their Lord. Inspiration, not manipulation, was
what they felt characterized their proceedings. Students at the conference
were leaders in their college associations and would not have been new to
missionary appeals or to the power of religious conferences. By merely
coming to the conference they deliberately placed themselves in a position
where their emotions could be built up and played upon, because they
undoubtedly wanted a religious experience.

Launching a Movement

In the last days of the Mount Hermon conference, Wishard and Ober,
recalling the missionary tour of the "Cambridge Seven," suggested to the

student volunteers that a similar band be formed from those present, who would tour the colleges to spread the missionary enthusiasm and to form missionary bands on college campuses. Four students were selected for the task, which included Robert Wilder and John Mott. All but Wilder eventually backed out of the band. Mott was to begin his junior year at Cornell in the fall of 1886, and felt, upon further reflection, that finishing school was more important than proceeding with the band. Wilder also had a good reason to withdraw; his father was dying and needed him to help in the editing of the *Missionary Review*. Royal Wilder, however, closed off this rout of escape, telling Robert, "Son, let the dead bury their dead. Go thou and preach the kingdom."[5]

Wishard and Ober planned the tour for the 1886-87 academic year, and to pay for it they enlisted Daniel W. McWilliams, a leader in the Brooklyn Association and the secretary and treasurer of the Manhattan Elevated Railway Company. Accompanied by John N. Forman, a member of Wilder's Princeton band and a son of missionaries in India, Wilder visited 162 colleges, universities and seminaries. Many of these were either woman's colleges or coeducational institutions. YWCAs on these campuses generally provided the access to women students that the YMCAs did to men. The two missionary recruiters were successful beyond their wildest imaginings, enrolling 2,106 volunteers before the year was out, about a quarter of whom were women. Each recruit signed a pledge card modeled on the Princeton pledge, and missionary bands were generally established on the campuses at which they spoke. Profoundly impressed by the success of the movement, James McCosh, the President of Princeton and a Wilder supporter, asked a rhetorical question that would be quoted for years by the SVM leaders: "Has any such offering of living men and women been presented in this age – in this country – in any age, or any country, since the day of Pentecost?"[35]

At the end of the 1886-87 academic year, Wilder decided to attend Union Theological Seminary. Forman, who had originally intended to go to Union, decided instead to return to India as a missionary, which he did in the company of Wilder's sister and mother after the death of Royal Wilder. Consequently, with Forman in India and Wilder in seminary, there was no official campaign to promote the SVM during the academic year of 1887-88. Wilder, however, continued to travel to schools and churches to promote the movement on an informal and ad hoc basis. In 1888 Wishard had gone on a world tour for the YMCA, and so Ober was now the head secretary for the collegiate YMCA and arranged all of Wilder's speaking engagements. With 2,000 volunteers now enlisted, a number of them also spoke in colleges and churches on behalf of the movement.

Letters from these recruiters and from the volunteers themselves were sent to Wilder, and lists were kept of the new volunteers. A fellow seminarian at Union, William H. Hannum, agreed to help Wilder with the mounting demands of record-keeping and correspondence. Hannum kept a record of the names and addresses of the recruits under his bed and frequently sought out help from other students, which may have compromised his popularity on campus. Hannum recalled that "One classmate asserted that when I got to Heaven I should be making lists of the angels."[36]

At the end of the SVM's second year of activity some 600 more volunteers had signed the pledge. Nevertheless, by the summer of 1888 it was clear to the leaders of the movement that it was in danger of fragmenting, and that the initial enthusiasm on the campuses was ebbing. The fear at Mount Hermon that the movement would become independent of the YMCA was also in danger of being realized. Some of the missionary bands on the campuses were calling themselves "Wilder Bands," and asserting their independence of the association.

At the 1888 Northfield student summer conference, student leaders discussed these problems and decided that a committee should be formed to organize the volunteer movement. It is not clear who was on this committee, but Ober, Wilder and Mott were present at the conference, and their membership on the committee was probably automatic. It was suggested that Wilder should take another year off from his seminary studies to make a second tour of the campuses, revisiting all the institutions he had spoken at in 1886-87, coaxing the independent bands back into the student association and encouraging the bands to be missionary recruiters. Wilder agreed to this, even though it meant he would not graduate from seminary until 1891. The leaders also decided to confine the movement to students and to give it its official name, the Student Volunteer Movement for Foreign Missions. Moreover, they developed a plan for a three-member executive committee to represent the four student organizations that were already supplying student missionaries: the Intercollegiate YMCA and YWCA, and the Inter-Seminary Missionary Alliances, American and Canadian. It was not until the end of the year, however, that these plans began to be put into action.

Richard C. Morse of the YMCA's International Committee believed that Ober was the logical choice to represent the men's association and that Ober also ought to chair the committee. Ober objected. He wanted Mott for the job and prevailed. No longer a student, but an employee of the YMCA, Mott first came to the attention of Student Movement leaders at the Mount Hermon Conference. His subsequent highly successful presidency of the Cornell YMCA, which culminated in the dedication of a new association building in 1888, set him apart as a future leader in the Student Movement. With Wishard leaving on his world tour, Ober sought out Mott for role of the college secretary. Mott hesitated, but eventually agreed to take the job on a one-year trial basis. Thus he began on September 1, 1888 a lifetime of work in the Student Movement. In December of 1888 Mott had only been a college secretary for about three months, but he had been diligent in visiting colleges, re-organizing their associations and energizing them. Ober later claimed that in insisting on Mott as the head of the SVM, he was only concerned to promote the young man's future.[37]   The organization of the SVM was finalized on December 6, 1888 in New York City, with the Executive Committee to be made up of Mott representing the YMCA, Nettie Dunn the YWCA, and Wilder the two inter-seminary missionary alliances. Wilder would be the organization's first traveling secretary, continuing his work for the remainder of the 1888-89 academic year. There was also to be an advisory committee made up of older and more experienced missionaries and church leaders.[38] The purpose of this committee was to show the denominational mission boards that, despite the youthful leadership of the organization, the SVM would be steadied by seasoned hands. To avoid splintering the movement at the college level, it was further agreed that the SVM bands on campuses would be the missionary departments of the college associations. The single unifying watchword of the movement was also officially adopted, "The Evangelization of the World in this Generation."

Organizational Structures

Five years after its founding at Mount Hermon, there were missionary bands in 350 educational institutions in Canada and the United States. There were also 6,200 volunteers, who had taken the missionary pledge, and about 320 volunteers who had actually sailed as missionaries to foreign countries.[39] By 1898 the SVM had reached 839 institutions of higher education, held about 4,000 current volunteers, and seen 1,173 of its missionaries sail to 53 different countries under 48 different denom-inations.[40]   By 1906, the 20th anniversary of the Mount Hermon conference, the SVM leaders boasted that 2,953 volunteers had gone to the foreign mission field, under the auspices of nearly 100 missionary agencies, to every part of the globe, doing medical, educational, and traditional evangelistic work.[41]

The phenomenal growth of the SVM and of the missionary enterprise in general must be attributed to a variety of factors, but among the most important were the organizational structures and promotional techniques used by the SVM. The simplicity of the organization, its emphasis on student participation, and its total commitment to the promotion of missions were strong measures of the movement's vitality. The SVM created a structure that fostered rapid expansion and employed techniques that appealed successfully to thousands of college students and many thousands more of their co-religionists who stayed at home, but who supported the missionary enterprise financially.

The traveling secretaries of the SVM were probably the key to its success. They were generally former college band members who had recently graduated and agreed to spend a year promoting the movement before traveling to the mission field. Among the most famous and influential of the early traveling secretaries was the trio of Sherwood Eddy, Horacy Pitkin and Henry Luce. Eddy was an eloquent speaker for the SVM throughout his career; Pitkin was the movement's first notable martyr, a victim of China's Boxer Rebellion; and Luce is best remembered today as the father of the founder of Time Magazine.[42] Traveling secretaries journeyed from college to college engendering enthusiasm, organizing bands, trouble-shooting, recruiting delegates for the national conventions, offering practical advice and giving spiritual direction.

SVM speakers carried with them a set of pledge cards to be signed by the volunteers. Probably inspired by Moody's famous "decision cards," the SVM pledge cards read simply, "We are willing and desirous, God permitting, to become foreign missionaries." In a pamphlet published in 1890, Wilder listed the benefits of having volunteers pledge themselves to becoming missionaries.[43] The pledge cards, he argued, were necessary to put the question of missionary service in a tangible form so that it could not be easily avoided; and they were invaluable as a way to secure laymen for missionary service as undergraduates, because later on the lure of worldly occupations in the United States would generally be too great to resist. This was true too of seminary students, because they could often be persuaded that an invitation from a prominent domestic church was their actual calling. An early decision also had other advantages. It allowed the volunteers a greater preparation time for the study of the language and culture of the country to which they might be sent; and they could make a missionary appeal for both money and volunteers more effectively than someone who had not so dedicated their lives. Finally, a pledge card gave the SVM the names and addresses of volunteers, who could then be strengthened and encouraged in their commitment.

Despite its apparent virtues, some objected to the pledge card on the grounds that immature students should not be committing themselves so rigidly to missions. Should some volunteers later hear a more urgent call to a non-missionary vocation, the pledge might place them in the position of resisting the leading of Providence. To accommodate this objection, in 1892 the SVM changed the pledge to "It is my purpose, if God permit, to become a foreign missionary." This wording left plenty of maneuvering room for Providence to intervene. To further soften the volunteer commitment, in 1900 it was no longer called a pledge, but simply a declaration.

Once students had made the decision to become volunteers, they were expected to joined the SVM band on their campus. The student bands of the SVM were the fundamental units of the organization. Robert Wilder's Princeton band was the model: a small group of earnest, prayerful students, encouraging one another, studying the various mission fields, keeping the subject of missions alive in their hearts, on their campus and in their college association. Finally, they were to spread the movement by taking every opportunity to persuade other students to become missionaries.

In addition to bands, there were also regional unions that volunteers could join whose meetings were an opportunity for isolated volunteers or those from institutions with lethargic bands to associate with like-minded mission enthusiasts. In the New York Union, the major organizing thrust of each year was a city-wide campaign to spread the missionary gospel, which was held in the late fall or early winter months.[44] Also student volunteers were recruited to speak throughout the year to local churches about the movement and the mission fields. Unions in the second decade of the new century organized annual regional or state conventions, which often included several hundred delegates and were generally credited for much of the recruitment success of the movement.[45] Unions organized slowly in the 1890s. In 1897 there were only10, but their numbers grew steadily, reaching 27 by 1914. After the First World War the union idea finally caught on, with the number of unions growing to 41 by 1922, where they stayed for several years. By the 1920s the unions were an established intermediate level of the SVM organization and provided representatives to the Executive Council at the national headquarters.

In addition to gathering in bands and unions, representatives at every level of the movement in Canada and the U.S. assembled for four or five days every four years to attend the famous international conventions of the SVM. A convention was a non-controversial means to popularize the SVM and to advance the cause and unity of the missions community. Like the YMCA conventions that they were modeled after, the SVM conventions succeeded in heightening the enthusiasm and commitment of the volunteers to its cause. Delegates heard addresses about faraway people and places and attended fact-laden seminars on missionary work and issues. The conventions were both dramatic and educational, setting the intellectual and spiritual tone of the movement as well as providing the emotional apogee in the college careers of the young people who would experience them only once as students.

Five years after the creation of the SVM at Mount Hermon, and only two years after its formation as an organization, the movement organized its first convention in Cleveland, Ohio. In all, 558 students, representing 150 educational institutions, were present, as well as 126 others.[46] The SVM's report on the convention, a 200-page document, boasted that it was the largest student-attended missionary convention ever held.[47] Each successive quadrennial convention tended to be larger and more elaborate than the ones that preceded it. The Second International Convention, held at Detroit in 1894, was nearly twice as large as its predecessor, having 1,082 student delegates and 243 others.[48] By 1906 there were 4,235 delegates, and in 1914 there were 5,031 delegates.

The Toronto Convention in 1902 was particularly well-covered in the religious press because the SVM made a point of inviting 50 religious journalists to Toronto to report on it. The reporters noted what was a commonplace at SVM conventions: on the platform in Massey Hall a large map of the world was displayed, over-hung with a banner with the watchword of the movement. The YMCA reporter observed that the meetings "were characterized by a serious dead-in-earnestness that is seldom noted in a gathering of college men. There was no froth, college yelling, Chautauqua salutes or horse-play."[49] In large measure this was due to Mott's management of the convention. He discouraged applause after addresses, although it did sometimes occur. He also avoided having committee reports presented or mundane SVM business conducted on the platform. He ran the convention like a consecration meeting, as speaker after speaker urged on students the seriousness of the calling they were being asked to consider and the great need of their efforts in the world.

Mott began a tradition at the 1891 convention that he followed at every convention that he presided over. He told the students that the organization needed a certain sum of money per year in order to meet the needs of the steadily growing missionary movement. At the 1891 convention he asked the students for an annual pledge of $3,000 for four years. At the 1894 convention he doubled the figure to $6,000 and in 1898 more than doubled it to $16,000. The students never failed him. By the 1906 convention they were pledging $21,000.

Compared to the budgets of other Christian organizations, such as the YMCA or the various missionary boards of the denominations, the budget of the SVM was quite small. The 1904 annual budget provides a general overview of the expenses of the movement. In total $10,650 went for salaries with an additional $3,360 for traveling secretaries. The remainder of the budget was for overhead and other expenses, with the total budget coming to $19,855. Through the next 15 years the SVM budget increased to keep pace with the growing number of volunteers and its own bureaucratic expansion until by 1919 the budget had tripled to $60,000.[50]

In hindsight the major weakness in the SVM's approach to finance was in relying so heavily on student pledges of annual contributions for four years. It became apparent that this was not the best long-term strategy to fund the organization in the 1920s when students started to become ambivalent about the movement. At that time it became increasingly hard to collect their pledges. But Mott did not rely completely on students for financing the organization. He also collected donations from a small group of supporters, but this base of support was probably too narrow for the long-term best interests of the movement. In the 1930s when budgetary constraints were quite tight due to the depression, E.F. Campbell of the WSCF in a letter to Jesse Wilson of the SVM rued the reliance on a small number of givers, a policy he blamed on Mott.[51] But this is getting ahead of the story.

The first quarter century of the SVM was marked by mounting success as the movement broadened and deepened its organizational structure. It developed its own periodical and then published a journal jointly with the YMCA. It continued to work closely with the denominational missionary boards, dropping the old Advisory Committee in 1902 when it was no longer needed to lend gravitas to the increasingly well-regarded organization. In 1907 the SVM established The Candidate Department, which coordinated the specific needs of the missionary boards of the denominations and the student volunteers, to facilitate the placement of missionaries. What had begun in a fiery burst of enthusiasm among 100 students at an obscure spot in western Massachusetts in the summer of 1886, and threatened to flicker out as early as 1888, had become by the early years of the Twentieth Century the nation's major recruiter of foreign missionaries.

This reputation was well-supported by missions statistics. The American contribution to the missionary output of the West by 1900 was about 9,000, and of this 4,500, or about one-half, were student volunteers. By 1906, the 20th anniversary of the SVM, there were 19,000 European and American Protestant missionaries in the world. About 6,000 of them, or one-third, were student volunteers from around the world. Between 1886 and 1920 the SVM records indicate that the SVM's 8,742 missionaries were represented on every continent except Antarctica, and that they had traveled to most of the countries of the world. Primarily, however, they went to countries under European colonial domination, as these countries were most open to missionaries and could provide them the greatest protection. Nearly one-third went to China, by far the most popular destination for American missionaries.

The Volunteers

The SVM gathered a variety of statistics on its volunteers. Of the 33,726 who had volunteered by 1920, only about 26.5 percent eventually sailed.[52] The aggregate numbers of men and women sent were almost equal by 1920. At the beginning of the movement, however, women constituted only about one-third of the volunteers, but the proportion of women grew steadily until by the 1920s they constituted about two-thirds of the volunteers. Not surprisingly the bulk of the students who signed the SVM declaration cards were people in their early 20's. One study done by the SVM of 3,801 of the volunteer application forms, which every volunteer was asked to fill out, showed that 18- to 25-year-olds constituted 64.7 percent, 26- to 30-year-olds equaled 25.2 percent, and those over 30 years of age constituted only 7.2 percent of the movement. Those under 18 represented the smallest age group, forming only 2.9 percent of the total number of applicants.

Records from the 1891 convention report and the *College Volunteer Enrollment Directory*, which include the years 1891-1904, provide the volunteer enlistments by state, and in Canada, by province. These records indicate that, although there was a large number of volunteers in Massachusetts and New York, the bulk of the volunteers came from the Midwestern states and the Canadian provinces around the Great Lakes. The directory also shows that the overwhelming majority came from small Christian colleges and seminaries. It is important to note, however, that volunteers came from all over the country. For example by 1904, 397 had volunteered in Virginia, 381 in Tennessee, 237 in California, and 133 in Texas. Also, although the majority of volunteers were from small Midwestern institutions, prestigious Eastern universities were also represented. For example, the three SVM conventions of the 1890s showed a total of 57 delegates from Yale University, 27 from Princeton University, and 21 from Harvard University – and this does not include delegates from their seminaries or medical schools.[53]

Identifying the volunteers statistically does not explain the turn-of-the-century missionary impulse. This requires a more intimate look at the missionaries themselves. Fortunately the archives of the SVM include some 48,000 volunteer application forms, referred to as "blanks," that can help shed some light on who the volunteers were and something of their motivations.[54] The "blanks" were filled out by volunteers after they had signed a declaration card. For purposes of record keeping and future effectiveness, the SVM queried students about how they came to make their decision, who influenced them, and what literature they found most influential.

After selectively reviewing a number of the 48,000 forms, some patterns did emerge. Not surprisingly most seemed to be raised in pious Christian homes. Many had striking spiritual experiences, and some decided quite early that they would be foreign missionaries. Some experienced deaths in their family, which led them to consider a religious vocation. Others were driven primarily by humanitarian reasons to help the less fortunate in other lands, usually by providing medical or educational opportunities. Often people who had early leanings toward becoming a missionary were brought to a crisis of decision by a missionary speaker, a missions book they had read, or a friend presenting an argument for missions. But despite the often glowing accounts of conversions and decisions for the mission field, about three-quarters of them would never make it to the field. The reasons given on the "blanks" for what might prevent them from going abroad included health, the expense of education, the opposition of parents, and the need to care for those parents as they grew old.

The language and ideas used in the "blanks" suggest that the missionary impulse involved a mixture of timeless Christian values and values especially emphasized by Victorians – personal heroism, lofty humanitarianism, self-sacrifice, and Christian dedication. Potential volunteers struggled with their consciences, grappled with the meaning of Christianity and the demands it made, felt for the "unfortunates" in the non-Christian lands, and wrestled Jacob-like with God's plan for their lives. In the end, thousands of them sailed abroad as missionaries, with 300 becoming martyrs by 1924.[55] What explains this extraordinary phenomenon? As Perry Miller wrote of the Puritans, the student volunteers at heart were of an Augustinian spirit, an intensely pietistic group of individuals who dedicated themselves to living out their most profound spiritual convictions.[56]

Still, looking beneath the language of spiritual experience, lofty humanitarianism, and Christian idealism that are rife in the "blanks," the volunteers often seem to be reluctant and conflicted saints. A religiously passionate but anxious and introspective group of people, the volunteers agonized over their decisions to become missionaries. Were they throwing their lives away on a will o' the wisp? Were they abandoning family responsibilities heedlessly? Were they being spiritually presumptuous to become missionaries? Did they need to wait for a specific call?

The spiritual intensity as well as anxiety reflected in these questions was given its classic treatment in Max Weber's *The Protestant Ethic and the Spirit of Capitalism*.[57] Weber noted that Protestants were a people torn from the institutional security of the Catholic faith. Salvation for them was no longer guaranteed by practicing rites and ceremonies, but could only be based on the individual's own relationship to God. This created a people anxious to produce the signs indicating a blessing from God as proof of their salvation, thus easing the religious tension in their lives. Although the relationship between the spirit of capitalism and Protestantism is problematic in Weber's thesis, the evidence in the SVM "blanks" suggests that religious anxiety often compelled conscious-stricken Protestants to become spiritual over-achievers by working out their salvation according to the highest and most demanding ideals of their culture – going to the mission fields.

Their culture, however, sent them mixed signals, lauding at one time high-minded altruism and at another the acquisitive spirit. Consequently, in nearly every case the decision to become a missionary was a victory in the individual for the demands of faith over the lure of worldly success and comfort. The anxiety of being middle-class Americans was therefore also important, and was reflected in the "blanks."[58] The cluster of personal values necessary for a smooth-running capitalist society is so closely associated with this status group that they are often simply denoted as "middle class." Yet unlike Weber's classic Protestants, who could work out their salvation through a rigorous and world-affirming application to business, middle-class Americans accepting a missionary career would have to work out their salvation through the world-denying life of personal self sacrifice and the pursuit of spiritual goals. The abandonment of worldly ambition, the shame of poverty, the fear of being declassed, and the guilt of appearing to escape the rigors of the business world for the missionary life were sometimes expressed openly in the "blanks" but more often in such vague words as "sacrifice" and "surrender." It is little wonder, then, that this decision, because it violated so many middle-class sensibilities, was often accompanied by a spiritual crisis.

The SVM helped volunteers to deal with these fears by depicting missionary life as fraught with difficulties and hardships, and filled with endless possibilities for practical humanitarian projects. Moreover, it depicted the successful missionary as practical, down-to-earth, organized, task-oriented, self-disciplined and self-sacrificing. In effect, the more the SVM made the missionary life appear to be demanding, the more they made it acceptable to the middle class as a career possibility. Admittedly, this approach might also have scared off some potential volunteers, but the SVM's success in missionary recruitment speaks for itself. In conflating the practical, success-driven middle-class capitalist with the ascetic, spiritually minded, evangelistic Protestant, the SVM created an ideal missionary type that simultaneously eased middle-class anxieties, tapped into potent middle-class virtues, and appealed to traditional Protestant idealism.

*　　*　　*

Conceived in the heart of Luther Wishard, the SVM was born at the Mount Hermon Summer Conference of 1886. In many respects this conference was a culminating event in America's growing missionary enterprise in the nineteenth century. Yet its inspiration was at least equally attributable to the revivalistic impulse of the period, which itself was fully embodied in the person of Dwight Moody and given organizational expression in the YMCA. The new religious style inherited by the SVM from these various sources was highly democratic in its emphasis on lay leadership and a practical business-like approach to the spread of the Gospel in the urban environment.

The growth of the SVM in the late Victorian Era can be attributed to many factors, but not least among them was its organizational efficiency. Like John Wesley a century and a half before, the founders had a genius for creating structures that preserved and advanced their cause. From the small bands – a Methodist term – to the regional unions and international headquarters in New York City, the SVM had a lean but effective organization that cost surprisingly little and could be adequately staffed by as few as a dozen salaried people. That these austere arrangements worked, and worked so well, underscores what every SVM leader knew: The engine of their success ultimately lay not in money or organization, but in the enthusiasm of the volunteers. And they were enthusiastic. Burying their anxieties under the language of duty and devotion, filling their minds with visions of exotic lands and useful service, the volunteers steeled themselves to be missionaries in distant lands where life might well be lonely, dangerous and heartbreaking, but also, just possibly, sublime.

Chapter Two

THE MASCULINIZATION OF CHRISTIANITY AND THE FORMATION OF MANLY CHARACTER

The world's great need today is for men. In every walk of life, in every land, in the face of every great human need, and before every open door of opportunity, men are wanted. Real men are always in demand and they are rare. Men of character and leadership were never more needed that at this hour of the world's history.

George Sherwood Eddy[1]

In seeking to make religion appealing to men, Christian leaders of the late nineteenth and early twentieth centuries spoke in the language of "muscular Christianity." It was a language that resonated with the practical, down-to-earth businessman, for whom religion had often become associated with effeminacy. Missionary leaders easily adopted the vocabulary of this movement, appealing to potential volunteers by depicting missionaries as decisive, heroic and virile men.

The emphasis on manliness was also one aspect of an even larger Victorian motif: character formation. Good character was an especially important theme for the vast American middle class, which stood without the communal props of the peasant or the ample resources of the wealthy. The middle class was the creature of the new producer-oriented culture of the early nineteenth century, which rose or fell based largely on its own efforts. Although the rise of corporate capitalism toward the end of the century undermined much of the relevance of this individual ethic, it would continue to have cultural significance for years to come.

Student Movement leaders combined these ideas into a concept of manly Christian character, which pictured the businessman as the ideal Christian. They then made the virtues of the businessman essential for achieving the highest levels of Christian spirituality. For the leaders of the SVM the secret to personal spiritual vitality lay in combining worldly practicality with an emphasis on personal holiness. Worldly practicality meant a disciplined business-like approach to spirituality, as well as embracing the ethos of the masculine business world to achieve specific religious goals. Personal holiness meant "practicing the presence of God;"[2] that is, adopting the theology and techniques of the Holiness or "higher life" movement, as it was developed and understood in the last quarter of the nineteenth century, in order to achieve spiritual empowerment.

The SVM leaders never denied, indeed they extolled, the necessity of divine providence for the success of their movement. But they also stressed the practical steps necessary to harness divine power to achieve their immediate ends. The intrinsic appeal of merging the power of modern business techniques with the power of the Holy Spirit was hard to resist. In the minds of the SVM, the combination of supernaturally empowered missionaries, utilizing the latest developments in communication and travel techniques, was so potent as to make possible the achievement of world evangelization in a single generation.

Jesus and the Development
of Manly Character

Religious people have long been subject to at least two cruel barbs: either they were castigated as too worldly, or they were dismissed as impractical, other-worldly idealists. American ministers during the colonial period were certainly not immune from harsh criticism and occasional witticisms at their expense – Benjamin Franklin immortalized Cotton Mather in literature as "Silence Dogood" – but they were generally regarded as pillars of the community and respected for their learning and sagacity. In the nineteenth century, however, ministers seemed to have come under increasing attack. American writers lamented and lampooned the irrelevance of the ministry. To the practical American, the learned parson's head was all too often filled with theoretical distinctions and an ossified Calvinism that left the auditor cold. For Ralph Waldo Emerson the formalist in the pulpit was a pathetic figure: "He had lived in vain. He had no one word intimating that he had laughed or wept, was married or in love, had been commended, or cheated, or chagrined."[3] Oliver Wendal Holmes's poetic comment on Puritan thought styled it a "One Hoss-Shay." Built in the year Jonathan Edwards published *On the Will,* the shay simply collapsed in a heap a century later. Mark Twain in *The Adventures of Tom Sawyer* was amazed at how boring ministers could be despite the gravity of their subject matter:

> The minister gave out his text and droned along monotonously through an argument that was so prosy that many a head by and by began to nod – and yet it was an argument that dealt in limitless fire and brimstone and thinned the predestined elect down to a company so small as to be hardly worth the saving.[4]

To this already deprecatory image, Victorian culture added yet another indignity to the nineteenth-century pulpit: the feminization of Christianity. In a study of the liberal Protestant ministers of the northeastern United States in the period 1825 to 1875, Ann Douglas shows that the clergy had given up their formerly "masculine" Calvinist theology for a "feminine" theology of sentimentalism.[5] She attributes this in part to the disestablishment of the churches following the Revolution, which left the clergy completely dependent on their congregations and therefore less willing to expound unpopular doctrines. This reinforced the liberal shift from a Calvinist theology, which emphasized a harsh doctrine of predestination, to a liberal theology, which emphasized private devotion, and personal and family matters.[6]

The clergy were increasingly seen to be a part of what in the Victorian world was defined as the women's sphere of activity as they, in Douglas's phrase, moved from the "exercise of power to the exertion of 'influence.'"[7] Similarly, the Christ of the new liberal theology did not conquer sin and death in an act of moral heroism on Calvary, but rather He exerted a moral influence. The new theology, then, was not concerned with the rigorous exposition of truth, but with a sentimental religion that was a superficial trivialization of Christianity, which pictured heaven as an American suburban home, as in Elizabeth Stuart Phelps's *The Gates Ajar.*

The Victorian concept of the separate spheres burdened society with gender-based dichotomies that extended beyond the simple demarcation of the marketplace as an arena for male activity and the home as an arena for female activity. For example, E. Anthony Rotundo in *American Manhood* has contrasted the Victorian view of lawyers and ministers in a way that shows how easily the ministry might have been dismissed as irrelevant to the broader world. Although both were learned professionals, masters of an arcane body of knowledge, and at their best masters of public persuasion, the law was seen as essentially masculine and the ministry as essentially feminine. The law promoted the male passions of aggression, self-seeking, conflict, and worldliness. The ministry symbolized the female virtues of morality, spirituality, love and concern for others.[8] By placing religion so thoroughly in the feminine sphere, Victorian culture may have helped to alienate some men from the church. The eighteenth- and nineteenth-century church was in fact composed of about two-thirds women; and, as they became increasingly visible due to their growing involvement in church-related voluntary societies, the image of religion as part of the feminine sphere was greatly reinforced.[9]

With religion now largely relegated to the women's sphere, holy men, including Christ, were depicted in literature as effeminate. In the Victorian world view, women alone were the depositories of society's moral virtue. Fictionalized paragons of virtue and innocence appeared in such characters as "Little Eva" in *Uncle Tom's Cabin*, while in the same book, the rough hewn masculinity of Simon Legree was the epitome of all that was wrong and most debased in society. One of the best-selling novels of the nineteenth century, Lew Wallace's *Ben-Hur*, depicted Christ as "a man with a woman's face and hair," with long auburn hair, large dark blue eyes, and "lashes of great length sometimes seen on children, but seldom, if ever, on men."[10]

Toward the end of the nineteenth century men began to reexamine their definition of manhood. The traditional notion of a man being independent and self-reliant was untenable in the new corporate world that was quickly developing. Also the increasing presence of women as secretaries tended to feminize what was the traditional male sphere, the work place. Men had to remove spittoons and watch their language, and consequently perceived that the genteel world of the home and the hearty, untamed world of the marketplace were now irrevocably mixed. In response, men began to redefine masculinity in ways that fit the modern world. They began to engage in wilderness recreation and spectator sports. Reacting to the perceived threat to traditional concepts of masculinity, Theodore Roosevelt espoused "the strenuous life" and William James searched for "The Moral Equivalent of War."

If the generation that lived around the turn of the century experienced a crisis of gender, Christians of that time were far from immune to its effects. There was long an undercurrent of thought that objected to the characterization of religion as feminine and asserted a Christianity that was practical, vigorous, this-worldly, and non-denominational. The attempt to masculinize Protestant Christianity became most overt in 1911-12 with The Men and Religion Forward Movement, a nation-wide attempt of Protestant organizations to alleviate the 3-million member disparity between men and women in the churches by specifically appealing to men to become church members.[11] The masculinization of Christianity was most memorably popularized, long after its emergence in the culture, in the 1924 biography of Christ by Bruce Barton *The Man Nobody Knows*. Interpretations of the life of Christ, because He stands at the center of the Christian religion, are a good measure of the impact that larger cultural currents are having on religion. Barton was notable because he finally succeeded in closing the gap between the separate gender spheres of business and religion by depicting Christ as a virile, manly man, and a practical businessman, who used modern techniques to build a mass following. This "muscular Christianity," a position sometimes associated with the imperialism and militarism of the nineteenth century, was nevertheless a Christianity that appealed to men of the world: salesmen, tradesmen, businessmen, professionals, entre-preneurs.[12]

The origins of "muscular Christianity" are generally traced to two mid-century British writers, Thomas Hughes and Charles Kingsley, who like many other writers of the nineteenth century attempted to translate antiquated notions of aristocratic chivalry into a more modern and democratic concept of manliness. Kingsley's most famous book *Westward Ho!* (1855) is a tale of the Elizabethan "sea dogs," who despite their common origins demonstrate the patriotism, heroism and knightliness that embody a primitive version of nineteenth-century middle-class Christian manliness.[13] Hughes's most famous book *Tom Brown's School Days* (1857) linked a masculine Christianity to vigorous sports and outdoors activities. Physical activities, properly pursued, Hughes believed, would help to form good Christian characters in boys. This idea became especially popular around the turn of the century and can be seen to have influenced Pierre de Coubertin in establishing the modern Olympic Games in the 1890s, James Naismith in creating basketball for the YMCA in 1891, and Robert Baden-Powell in founding the Boy Scouts in 1907.[13]

When it was pointed out to Hughes that the YMCA was incapable of reaching many young men because it made Christianity appear to them to be inconsistent with manliness, he was inspired to write a biography of Christ to counter what he believed to be a fallacious interpretation. It was the principle assertion of *The Manliness of Christ* (1880) that the founder of Christianity had passed every test of courage presented to him during His Earthly life.[15] As a boy and young man "the power and manliness of the character of Christ" are shown by His patience in waiting for the right time to begin his ministry. During the wilderness temptations, Jesus persevered "with patience and manly courage." As a poor itinerant preacher Jesus never compromised His message to gain a following, nor did he choose His 12 disciples from the higher ranks of society, nor did He shrink from attacking the religious leaders of His day. Rather, He spoke the truth to all who would listen, and He endured all the ingratitude, anger, and uncertain loyalty of those who claimed to be His followers. And finally, Jesus endured His passion "with great dignity and calmness."[16]

Hughes wrote the first of many biographies of Christ that would attempt to present Him as a "muscular Christian." However, his was not the first biography of Christ, nor the most popular interpretation of His life. In his famous book *The Quest of the Historical Jesus* (1906) Albert Schweitzer summarized the passion of many nineteenth-century biblical scholars to recover the historical Jesus from the Christ of the ancient creeds. Moving beyond what history alone could reveal, some writers attempted full bio-graphies, filling in the missing gaps of history with offerings from their own florid imaginations. Ernest Renan wrote the first popular biography of Jesus, *La Vie de Jesus* (The Life of Jesus) in 1863. It combined many of the insights of the German critical scholars with the saccharine sentimentalism of French novels. "Tenderness of heart was in him transformed," Renan wrote of Jesus, "into infinite sweetness, vague poetry, universal charm." Jesus was depicted as a "lovely character," surrounded by "good Galileans," whose "preaching was sweet and gentle," and who rode around Israel on a mule.[17] It was primarily against Renan, as well as the generally accepted version of a feminine Christ in the popular culture, that those who wrote for the Student Movement railed.

The Student Movement embraced the subcurrent of thought within the Christian world that rejected a feminized religion. Writers for the YMCA and SVM developed a concept of manly Christianity, which, though sharing much with British thinking at that time, reflected the American cultural context. David Leverenz has written in *Manhood and the American Renaissance* that there was, in addition to patrician- and artisan-class concepts of manliness, a concept of manliness that accorded with middle-class needs.[18] The new middle class of entrepreneurs, rising with the advent of the industrial revolution in America, defined manliness as success in the relentless competition between men in the marketplace. Men in this new venue valued ambition, social mobility, risk-taking, and self-control.

Those who wrote biographies and studies of Christ for the Student Movement, such as Robert Speer, Harry Emerson Fosdick and T.R. Glover, depicted Jesus with the personality traits and beliefs that marked the successful middle-class entrepreneur. He valued human energy, "energetic thinking," "decisive action," and detested "slackness," "the life of drift," and those who could be characterized as "easy-going" or "compromisers."[19] Glover, especially, emphasized the importance of the will in the human psychology. "Indecision," he believed, "is one of the things that in his [Jesus'] judgment will keep a man outside the kingdom of God, that make him unfit for it."[20] Crucial to the thought of the Student Movement leaders in their biographies of Christ and also in their writings on character is the psychological assumption that placed the will at the center of the human personality. They believed that if Christians achieved self-mastery, which is to say that their wills were dominant over their appetites, then they could re-invent themselves. They could in effect become whatever they wanted. In this conception of the mind, the will is like a muscle that can become stronger if properly exercised.

Aside from biographies of Christ, the Student Movement produced countless tracks urging young men to resist sinful temptations, a theme that is incomprehensible outside of their understanding of human psychology. Christians confronted with temptations, they believed, have an opportunity to exercise their wills. But if Christians give in to temptation, then their wills become weaker. Temptations therefore have to be fought vigorously, and are often depicted as battles. In this formulation, a strong will is essential to a strong character; hence the importance Glover's Jesus places on decisiveness and his loathing of "compromisers" and the "easy-going."

The fascination with the character of Jesus, so apparent in these biographies, reflects not only the nineteenth and early twentieth centuries' preoccupation with "The Quest," but also the Victorian concern with character itself. Warren Susman has referred to the nineteenth century as a "culture of character." He saw the Western fascination with character appearing as early as the seventeenth century. By 1800, he argued, the concept of character defined a model type of person, a person imbued with the values of self-control, honor, manhood, self-sacrifice, the Protestant ethic, all of which were essential to the social order of a producer-oriented society.[21]

The classical education offered by most colleges and universities through at least the first three-quarters of the nineteenth century reinforced this theme. Clergymen, who tended to be the presidents of colleges, generally taught the course in moral philosophy, which was comprehensive of all human life and which culminated the four-year program of the students.

One of the main purposes of classical education was to provide a regiment for character-building.[22] Armed with their character-producing liberal arts education, students could then take their place as leaders in pre-technical society.

In the post-Civil War period, American colleges were often denigrated as mere "ministry factories," because the education they provided students was not commensurate with the skills they needed. Consequently, between 1870 and 1920, colleges and universities underwent a transition. They slowly limited the number of courses required in the classics so they could become modern secular institutions that would provide the technical skills for students to meet the needs of an emerging corporate society.

Alert to the apparent moral crisis resulting from this shift in educational philosophy, the Student Movement adopted the role of producing Christian leadership in the colleges and universities, which those institutions were rapidly abandoning.

In its role as the unofficial guardian of the Victorian devotion to character-building in youth, the Student Movement emphasized character not only in its biographies of Jesus, but also in books, pamphlets and addresses that were specifically focused on the need for manly character in its young readers. Sometimes Student Movement paeans to character were so excessive as nearly to become parodies of themselves. For example, professor Henry Churchill King of Oberlin, Ohio, addressed the Northfield Student Conference on July 4, 1901 with the sermon "How to Make a Rational Fight for Character." King presented a number of common-sensical ideas to avoid common temptations, but for King the secret by which a Christian could avoid or overcome temptation was character. For King character was everything. Salvation itself was based on character.

> Men have come to see that to be saved is to share the life
> of God, and to share the life of God is to share His
> character, and so to share His blessedness; that means to
> save us to character, and that there is therefore, no way out
> for any man except by coming into character. Christ
> means to save us into character, into likeness of character
> with God. There is no other salvation.[23]

King believed that the secret of character was self-control, and the center of self-control was the will. Christians therefore should steel their wills with adequate sleep, exercise, associations with other Christians, and by seeking God's presence through prayer and Bible reading. He urged the Christian student to become "saturated with the spirit and teaching of Jesus until he has caught his convictions of God and the spiritual world."[24]

Examples of the literature on character are nearly endless. One more will be added, however, because it so clearly links the Student Movement's emphases on character formation and the character and character-producing power of Jesus. George Sherwood Eddy in *The Maker of Men* expounded the theme of Jesus as the preeminent exemplar and maker of manly Christian character. He showed this by asserting first that Jesus made his own character. As fully human, Eddy wrote, Jesus achieved his own sublime character not by divine endowment but by growing "into the full stature of his human personality, thought by thought, act by act, choice by choice, by means that were simple and natural and within our own reach."[25] Jesus saturated himself in the Scriptures, led a life of prayer, served others, and taught the people. He never allowed himself to become "a victim of circumstance." Despite being born in a simple village of humble parents, with a limited education in a small insignificant and despised country, with only three years of active ministry, Jesus became the center of subsequent Western culture. The gospel of Jesus, in Eddy's hands, had become a Horatio Alger story. Jesus, the poor ignorant boy of obscure origins, achieved rapid social mobility and lasting fame through a careful series of will-strengthening, character-building exercises.

In addition to making himself, Jesus also made men; thus satisfying the American predilection for re-inventing the self. The unreliable Peter was re-invented by the man-making Christ, and became a rock. John, originally nick-named one of the "sons of thunder," became the writer of "those matchless epistles of love." The publican Zacchaeus became "the first philanthropist." Paul the persecutor of Christians, became the great apostle "as tender as a woman, gentle as a little child, writing his epistles with many tears."[26] Eddy did not end with the immediate followers of Jesus, but traced the prominent Christian men of history down to George Williams, the founder of the YMCA. And Eddy concluded that Jesus continues to be a maker of men.

To sum up, the Student Movement leaders and writers presented a Christianity that reflected the nineteenth-century concern for gender definition and character formation. In their hands the personality of Jesus and Christianity itself were redefined to reflect more masculine traits, as Victorians conceived masculinity. Women still had a role to play, but now so too did men. Moreover, the role of men reflected the middle-class values of a carefully channeled male aggressiveness, self-mastery, and integrity that were necessary to the maintenance of the nineteenth-century producer culture. And finally, their beliefs about character were based on a psychology that emphasized the will.

Manliness and the Business Ethos

The links between the new middle class business culture and a masculine Christianity were more than coincidental and were clearly noted at the time. The appeal to young men through the new conception of Christian manly character was often expressed using the practical, no-nonsense, worldly businessman as an ideal type. This appeal can be seen in the personalities and approaches of the leaders of the YMCA and SVM. The YMCA, from which the SVM originated, was established specifically to appeal to practical, urban, young men on the make, and Dwight Moody, the leading star of the evangelical world, epitomized the new approach. He was never ordained and eschewed denominational affiliation and established theological schools of thought. He presented himself as a layman and a practical man. He sought to win souls through a clear presentation of the facts as he saw them, availing himself of all the modern techniques of mass urban evangelism, and avoiding controversial theological points. Although a theological conservative, he was in fact an ecumenist, who embodied a practical business-like approach to religion.

The Intercollegiate YMCA inherited this business ethos. Luther Wishard indicated the appropriateness of this approach when he described the average college student as "rollicking, unsanctimonious, [and] cant-hating" – the very antithesis of the other-worldly religious.[27] For similar reasons, Charles Ober as a college senior was greatly impressed upon meeting Robert R. McBurney, the general secretary of the New York Association. "Then I knew that a new thing had arisen within the general achene of Christian ministry that called for the consecration of talents ordinarily relegated to business, engineering and statecraft."[28] Ober, though originally planning to enter the ministry, was attracted to the businessman as an ideal type of Christian man.

> The business men, the Association laymen, impressed me much more strongly [than the local secretaries of the YMCA]....[they] were all very able men and manifested as I had never seen it before, the spirit of Christian brotherhood, undiluted by self consciousness or sectarian bias. It was something of which I had dreamed but that I had never expected to see incarnated in hard-headed, success-compelling men of affairs."[29]

The SVM was born under the inspiration of Moody, coached from the sidelines by Wishard and Ober, and drew its initial membership from the student members of the Intercollegiate YMCA. Of the four most notable

leaders of the SVM -- John Mott, Robert Speer, Robert Wilder, and George
Sherwood Eddy -- all but Mott had attended seminary, but none ever felt
the need to become ordained. Although outstanding Christian leaders, they
valued their status as laymen and conceived of themselves as down-to-earth
professionals. Consequently the SVM embraced the potent marriage of
evangelical Christianity and the American business ethos, which resulted
in an explosion of missionary activity.

The leaders of the SVM, because of the techniques they employed and
the spirit they exuded, were part of a new phenomenon in American
history that Alfred D. Chandler described in *The Visible Hand: The
Managerial Revolution in American Business.*[30]   Chandler argues that
Adam Smith's notion of the invisible hand of market forces that regulated
production was increasingly antiquated in the second half of the nineteenth
century as a new class of managers, college-educated business experts,
increasingly controlled every aspect of the economy. This new class was
made up of business managers, technicians, engineers, accountants, and
others. By the Progressive Era they had taken over, regularized, and
routinized the great empires built by the Captains of Industry who emerged
after the Civil War.

The SVM leaders were part of this new managerial class. They saw
themselves not only as evangelicals, but also as practical, business-like,
efficient, hard-working, virile Christians, who had the organizational
skills, technical ability, and practical know-how to take the gospel of Jesus
Christ around the world in a single generation. Unlike other generations,
the current generation, Mott believed, was particularly duty bound to
attempt to evangelize the world because of its demonstrably greater
knowledge, opportunity and ability than any generation that had preceded
it.

> The apostles were sent into an unknown world. We know
> that world-wide field and its peoples, together with their
> religions, philosophies, customs and languages. This
> could not be said of any other generation. We also have a
> larger opportunity, due not only to greater knowledge, but
> also to the fact that ours is the first generation to whom the
> whole world has been made accessible. Moreover, we
> have larger – ability than preceding generations
> possessed.[31]

As the new managerial class replaced the invisible hand in control of
the market place, so the new Christian managerial class manifested in the
SVM was in danger of usurping the invisible role of the Holy Spirit. In
effect their managerial skills were put to the use of "working up" rather

than "praying down" the movement. Yet the leaders always strove to keep the two concepts in balance. As traditional evangelicals they professed complete dependence on the Spirit, and trumpeted the efficacy and indispensability of prayer. Yet their reliance on and fascination with the accoutrements of the business world – statistics, organization, conventions, money-raising, communications – seems contradictory. Arthur Pierson at the 1891 SVM convention struck the balance. He proposed that the supernatural basis for the successful evangelization of the world was the presence of Christ and the Great Commission, but that the natural basis consisted of three great elements, "Men, Money and Methods."[32] Warming to his theme, he emphasized the limitless possibilities of marrying the relentless nineteenth-century entrepreneurial drive with traditional evangelism:

> Why should not we show a spirit of enterprise in the Church such as the world shows in all business schemes? What is the matter with the Church, that in this nineteenth century she has scarcely one of those great master agencies which men use to carry their inventions to the ends of the earth?   Why should we not have a great Church exploration society, and go forward and pioneer the way into destitute fields? Why should we not have a great transportation society to carry missionaries to other fields without cost?[33]

Historian Valentin Rabe saw the fulfillment of Pierson's dream in the professionalization of missions that occurred in the Progressive Era.[34] Relying on business methods such as high-pressure promotions and solicitation, groups such as the Layman's Missionary Movement relied more on technique than piety. According to Rabe, missions at this time became less a spontaneous movement, than a collection of highly efficient organ-izations. Rabe, however, overstates his case. Certainly missions became highly organized and more professional, but the techniques developed did not create the religious sentiment upon which missions were based. Professionalization simply harnessed the latent Christian commitment that was already present in the population.   That many Protestant leaders came to rely too heavily on secular promotionalism was obvious from the over-reaching that occurred with the Interchurch World Movement following the First World War, but this does not show that missions were not based on a foundation of piety. At the very least, the SVM is a good example, as Rabe concedes, of an association of missions-minded people that was both an organization and a movement.

Moreover, in many respects the business approach of the SVM had more style than substance. The actual management of the SVM was in fact quite simple, even primitive by late nineteenth-century standards. For example, while the great industrial giants were in the process of inventing cost accounting, the SVM had not yet advanced to double-entry bookkeeping. Yet the management of the SVM itself was not important as long as it did its job adequately. What really mattered was the image projected by the movement. After all, the SVM was only interested in recruiting missionaries, not in sending them abroad or organizing great missionary expeditions. Their task was primarily to inspire others. To this end their greatest asset was probably John Mott.

In the extensive reporting of the Toronto Convention of 1902, as noted previously, a common theme the reporters shared was their estimation of Mott's leadership and executive ability. One paper noted his military bearing: "With the mind of a general, and able to command an army, he has that gentleness of spirit and that grace of manner which compel obedience without the necessity of orders."[35] Another reporter marveled that he might have become "a captain of industry or a learned professor or a successful statesman."[36] Still another said that "he might easily control the House of Representatives.[37] The *American Friend* was perhaps the most laudatory of Mott's masculine and business qualities:

> The man above all others who made his presence felt, was
> Mr. J.R. Mott, the chairman of the convention, a strong,
> healthy man, a fine specimen of Christian manhood,
> whose deep conviction impresses all who hear him, and
> one who can convey his personal magnetism to his
> audience, a man, withal, who has great business qualities,
> and whose grip on the business in hand is steady and
> sure.[38]

As a speaker Mott was neither unctuousness nor flamboyant. To be sure he spoke with vigor and conviction, but his was the rock-steady style of the business executive, general, or statesman. *The Baptist Union* noted of Mott and Robert Speer, another regular SVM speaker, that neither were orators in a traditional sense, "but their facts, and their deductions from the facts, are marvels of excellence in their presentation."[39] Mott may have epitomized this style but the article concluded that it characterized all the speakers at the convention. Mott and the other SVM speakers represented a new type of Christian leader. Neither popes nor presbyters, they were unabashedly laymen, with the pragmatic perspective that characterizes successful leadership in the secular world.

The Holiness Movement

Although the SVM's emphasis on masculinity and business-like practicality might be thought to have excluded fervent spirituality from the movement, this was not the case. SVM leaders largely followed the contemporary teachings of the holiness movement as it was taught again and again at Moody's Northfield conferences. The evangelicals who spoke at Northfield, and the SVM leaders who promoted their cause there, emphasized the holiness movement teachings primarily as a means to achieve spiritual empowerment for service – and by service they generally meant evangelism.

While holiness might appear on its face to aspire to the kind of religious and moral purity that might normally have been associated with traditional female propensities, the emphasis on power for service gave it a masculine covering. Historian George Marsden points out that in the late nineteenth century the leadership of the "holiness movement was male-dominated and masculinity was equated with power and action."[40] Consequently, despite biblical prophecies that emphasized the gender inclusive nature of spiritual gifts,[41] the holiness movement helped to subordinate women and to pro-mote a masculinized and action-oriented evangelical Christianity.

The holiness movement was a distinctly Protestant form of spirituality that appealed especially to the middle class. Part of the genius of the Protestant Reformation was the creation of a popular form of piety centered on the Bible. With the invention of the printing press, the Reformation principle of *sola scriptura,* and the printing of the first authorized English Bible in 1539, a Bible-centered devotionalism became possible in the Protestant English-speaking world. Avoiding the asceticism of the monastery and the time-consuming and demanding nature of mysticism, devotional reading of the Bible appealed to the educated, worldly and time-pressured laity. Eventually knowledge of the Bible came to be seen as so crucial to salvation and personal spiritual growth that a hallmark of English Puritanism came to be literacy, with the New England Puritans of the seventeenth century creating the most literate society in the world at that time.[42]

One of the most controversial theological motifs of Pietism was contained in a book by John Wesley, *Christian Perfection.* Wesley believed that given that Jesus in His Sermon on the Mount called for perfection, such a state must be possible. He conceded that all sin could not be eliminated from human life, but, if sin were defined as willful disobedience, he believed sin in this attenuated sense could be eliminated by God's grace. Furthermore, grace could break the power of sin so that a Christian could achieve a state of "entire sanctification." In the second half of the nineteenth century, Methodist Holiness teachers spoke of a second blessing or "Baptism of the Holy Ghost" that was necessary to attain sanctification.[43]

Calvinists objected to Methodist Holiness because of their belief in human depravity and humanity's total dependence on God's grace. American revivalism in the nineteenth century went a long way in mollifying Calvinists, and in the 1840s the Oberlin Theology of Charles Finney was an attempt to modify holiness theology for a Calvinist audience. But this approach remained controversial.   However, the religious conferences held at Keswick (pronounced Kess-ic) in England beginning in 1873 created a strain of holiness teaching that did eventually become acceptable to Calvinists. The new teaching maintained that sin could not be eliminated, but that through consecrating self to Christian service and Christ-likeness, by "yielding" or "surrendering" the direction of one's life to God, Christians could be so "filled" with the Holy Spirit that they would rise above the tendency to sin. Thus it was now possible even for Calvinists to attain the "higher life."

This "Keswick" version of the holiness movement was largely popularized in America through the efforts of Dwight Moody. Not only did he write two books on holiness and make it the subject of many of his sermons, but holiness also became the central theme of the Northfield conferences. Conference speakers emphasized the Keswick themes of consecration, yielding, being filled with the Holy Spirit, victory over sin, and most especially, spiritual power for Christian service.[44] The leaders of the SVM who spoke regularly at the Northfield conferences, when not speaking on mission themes, invariably joined the swelling chorus of holiness speakers.

John Mott, who had no formal theological training, was heavily influenced by the Holiness movement, and, indeed, his religious thinking is inexplicable without it. Mott was reared in a Methodist family, and his mother was a devotee of holiness literature. When Mott attended Cornell, he joined the Aurora Street Methodist Church, which he described as "a warm-hearted Holiness congregation." At Mott's request his mother began sending him the *Guide to Holiness*, a Methodist holiness journal. He became increasingly drawn to the idea of total consecration, and, after his interview with J.E.K. Studd, he flew into a frenzy of religious activity. He began early morning Bible reading, organized a Bible class, held religious services at the local jail, and became very active in his church. Finally one morning during his regular Bible study he achieved the vaunted goal of all holiness Christians, the "second blessing."[45]

While the holiness movement called for a profound spiritual consecration, the means to the spirit-filled life were imminently practical. Mott recommended the study of the scriptures, especially the gospels. A certain level of knowledge about Christ, he believed, was fundamental for understanding the Christian message and the demands of Christ as Lord in the private life of the believer. The center-piece of this approach was the "morning watch." Mott recommended that the first 30 to 60 minutes of every day be devoted to individual Bible study and "secret prayer." To underscore his point, he used traditionally masculine sports metaphors. The moral and spiritual faculties need to be disciplined and exercised if spiritual atrophy was not to set in, he explained, for "the price we must pay for growing Christlikeness is constant discipline. Let us go into training and stay in training."[46]

Mott also asserted that an uncompromising intolerance of personal sin must be maintained. Obedience to Christ demanded purity. He believed that "every habit, every indulgence, every association, every attitude of mind or spirit, every motive that we discover in actual experience or in the experience of holy men which does not lead to God" needs to be surrendered.[47] More positively, the Christian should develop a private prayer life, and participate in public prayer and the use of holy communion, and seek out the Holy Spirit. When temptation comes it should be seen as a reminder of the presence of Christ. The Christian should also attempt to associate with spiritual Christians, and seek to serve those in need.

In this approach there was nothing mysterious about becoming a Spirit-filled Christian. Mott asserted that "Christ may be made a reality to a man by the deliberate and indiscourageable resolution to make Him a reality." In effect Mott was saying that God responded to the human act of will. To those for whom the higher life seemed forever out of reach, Mott responded, "My brother, you are groping not for something that is trying to elude you."[48]

This appeal to a strong resolute character, based on a psychology of the will, is essential to understanding Mott and shows the affinity between the theology of the "higher life" and Victorian notions of manly character. While at college Mott read John Foster's *Decision of Character*, which argued that successful people – great generals, political leaders, religious leaders, etc. – had decisive minds, were usually physically fit, had the passion to turn ideas into actions, were possessed of great courage, and had a "conclusive manner of thinking," or in other words they weighed the facts and came to a definitive conclusion.[49] After the "meeting of the ten nations" at the Mount Hermon conference, Mott said that he spent the night doing "conclusive thinking" before he decided to become one of the student volunteers. That Foster's book had continuing importance for Mott cannot be doubted. He often recommended it to students and in 1907 had the book reprinted and wrote an introduction lauding its importance. Foster's model of decisive, courageous, passionate, and manly leadership was never far from Mott's mind, and it would seem from his speeches and writings that in his thinking it was also a virtual prerequisite to the "higher life" and successful Christian service.

The means to the "higher life" may have been rooted in character and therefore subject to human exigencies, but the end to which holiness Christians strove was to reach outside the mortal coil to obtain spiritual power. Nevertheless, power in the nineteenth-century was preeminently seen as a male domain, and when Mott appealed to the desire for power his analogies were recognizably male-oriented:

> The present is pre-eminently an age of power. The military and naval power of the nations is vastly greater than in the past both in point of defensive and also of destructive ability. The power of organization is far more highly developed than ever before, whether in industry, commerce, politics, social movements, or religious enterprises. The accumulations and achievements of wealth are immeasurably beyond those of earlier times. Power over the forces of nature is so much in advance of the past that the triumphs of our day would have been regarded as almost miraculous two generations or even one generation ago. But Jesus Christ is the same, yesterday, to-day, yea and for ever – as in the past, so to-day the source of all superhuman power.[50]

Mott's not so subtle appeal in this passage was to the perceived male desire to be powerful. Men in the military, industry or politics were recognizably engaged in the male prerogative to exercise power, be it over men, machinery or nature. While religious leaders were traditionally depicted as weak – the poor in spirit, the meek, and the peacemakers – Mott chose to present them as exercisers of divine power. Others might appear to be powerful, but "apart from Jesus Christ a man is comparatively weak," Mott believed.[51]

Other SVM leaders also emphasized holiness movement ideas. Robert Wilder in particular was a devotee of the Morning Watch. "Anyone who knew Robert Wilder intimately," his daughter Ruth Wilder Braisted wrote, "knew that the secret of his life was that daily hour he spent in prayer and

Bible study – the Morning Watch that he kept with his Maker. . . . And it was in this hour that he found spiritual direction and strength for each day."[52] Wilder himself once described a busy day in which he nearly forsook the Morning Watch, but someone appeared at his door to reminded him to begin his usual devotional hour. Wilder responded that this day must be an exception because of the press of affairs. The door then shut and the person vanished. Wilder did not recognize the man but thought he might be another missionary. He went to the door to find out, and what followed was one of the great religious experiences of his life.

> As I reached the door I found the retreating form was that of the Lord. I laid hold of him and brought him back, and when the door was locked and we were alone, he placed the pierced hand on my brow and gently smoothing out the furrows he said "Thou art troubled and cumbered about much serving, but one thing is needful." Words cannot describe the tender rebuke and exhortation which flowed from his lips, things unutterable known only to him and to me. Oh, how my heart burned as he opened to me the Scriptures and how the load was lifted as he took it upon his own shoulders. It was an hour in the heavenlies.[53]

This is probably the only instance of an actual epiphany to be found in the entire literature of the Student Movement. Wilder recorded the experience in his diary and does not seem to have written or spoken of it anywhere else. While the event itself should be seen as exceptional and possibly only an imaginative exposition of his inner feelings, it does point to the profound spirituality of many in the Student Movement and of the possible individual responses to the influence of the holiness movement.

A regular speaker at the Northfield conferences and at the SVM conventions, Robert Speer was another SVM leader devoted to the "higher life." Speer had been converted to the missionary cause in March 1887, during Wilder's and Forman's first speaking tour. He was the SVM's second traveling secretary, who in the 1889-90 school year recruited 1,100 volunteers.[54] "In my student generation," George Sherwood Eddy remembered, "there were two young giants who towered head and shoulders above the rest of us – John Mott and Robert Speer."[55] Speer was also a model of the virile Christianity promoted by the Student Movement. As a linesman on the Princeton football team for four years, Speer helped to invent the technique of "boxing the tackle." Once when repeatedly provoked by an opposing player, Speer recollected, "I squared off and let him have it flush on the jaw in the sight of all the players and spectators. I was immediately ordered off the field but I went off clothed with a sense of righteous indignation."[56]

Like Wilder, Speer was educated at Princeton Theological Seminary and embraced a warm-hearted and practical piety. More biblically and theologically literate than Mott, Speer's addresses were more traditionally sermonic. As Eddy recalled, "Speer was the prophet and Mott the statesman" of the SVM.[57] Speer attended the July 1894 Keswick Convention, whose theme was "the promotion of practical holiness," and he spoke glowingly of its Christian spirit and teachings in an address the following year at the Northfield conference.[58]

Speer's speeches often touched on holiness themes, but his address "Faith in God," delivered at the 1896 Northfield Conference, contained most of the holiness themes of which he was fond. He asserted the need for "an unconditional and unwithholding surrender;" and far from seeing the higher life as a retreat from the world, he averred that it involved the "most intense aggressiveness and service."[59] Regardless of subject matter, his sermons often arrived at the theme of spiritual power for service. "Faith in God" refers to Gideon, the Old Testament warrior-leader whom he com-mended for his "strength," "virility" and "power." Referring then to Christ's call to become as little children, Speer turns on its head what is ostensibly a lesson in humility:

> Who but a little child would be ambitious enough to claim the moon as a plaything on the nursery floor? Who but a little child would have the strength to carry it over all the well-nigh insuperable obstacles which stood in the way of the acquisition of that greatest of all human attainments, the power of human speech? When Christ picked out the child-spirit as the standard of spirit, as the condition of entrance into his kingdom, he named the spirit of most intense, assertive power....A life of true faith is a life of power."[60]

The three most visible leaders of the SVM – Mott, Wilder and Speer – were avid aficionados of the holiness movement, either in its Keswick or Methodist traditions. Other SVM leaders followed their lead, and the abundance of holiness movement addresses at the Northfield conferences insured that the *enduement of power* (as they phrased it) from the Holy Spirit was a dominant theme of the movement. Thus even in the most ostensibly intangible and impractical areas of Christian life, the SVM managed to project a masculine image with a practical down-to-earth methodology.

*   *   *

The SVM's emphasis on a masculine and business-oriented Christianity was both an ideology and an ethos. Its leaders presented an image of the movement and of Christian service that appealed to a new lay-oriented college-educated class, which was weary of denominational squabbles, theological cant, and anything that smacked of defeatism or complacency. It was a new generation, unchastened by experience, ripe for a challenge worthy of its best efforts. Not content with old dogmas or a merely intellectual faith, the leaders sought empowerment from on high. Undeterred by great obstacles, they inaugurated a new crusade whose audaciousness knew no geographical boundaries.

Ironically, however, while the student volunteers saw themselves as forward-looking, they were in some respects quite reactionary. While posing as the religious version of modern businessmen, their emphasis on character formation and the importance of the will harkened back to the earlier entrepreneurial-based, producer-oriented culture of the nineteenth century. All of this would soon seem archaic in the new consumer-oriented culture of the twentieth century, run by technocrats and corporate managers, which they also claimed to be.

Moreover, their emphasis on a masculinized Christianity, while clearly motivated by an honest desire to refashion religion to make it more attractive to men, could also be interpreted as one part of a larger effort by churchmen to assume control of denominational organizations run by women. For example, the rapid growth of women's missionary societies between 1880 and 1900 was clearly threatening to the male-dominated mission boards, and an attempt to recruit more male missionaries by making religion, and specifically missions, more attractive to men, is not difficult to interpret as an attempt to regain control by men.[61] The widespread disbanding of women's boards and their integration into men's groups, largely in the 1920s, clearly points in this direction and was so understood by women at the time.[62] To its credit, however, the SVM was never a part of the organized effort to disenfranchise women in the churches, and in fact women's visibility and strength in the SVM consistently increased over the years. Still, the SVM, as an institution of late Victorian culture, exemplified and embodied the ambiguities of its time. Living in an era of great transitions, its leaders had the luxury, or the misfortune, of pointing in more than one direction at once.

Chapter Three

Women in the Missions Movement

> The Gospel is the most tremendous engine of democracy
> ever forged. It is destined to break in pieces all castes,
> privileges, and oppressions. Perhaps the last caste to be
> destroyed will be that of sex.
>
> Helen Barrett Montgomery[1]

If the SVM emphasized the importance of what were held to be
traditionally masculine characteristics – practicality, business-like
efficiency, energetic leadership, bold vision, heroism, virility – it might be
wondered how women could find the movement a congenial atmosphere.
That they did, and in great numbers, is evident from the volunteer
statistics. By 1905 women became the majority of the SVM's members
who annually sailed as missionaries, and by 1908 the majority of its new
members. Men continued to dominate the leadership of the movement, but
women became its mainstay.

From its beginnings, women were always a substantial part of the
SVM's success in recruitment. One of the factors that accounts for the
triumph of the Wilder-Forman recruitment tour in 1886-87 was the growth
of the college Young Woman's Christian Association (YWCA), whose
members were a natural recruitment field for the SVM. Many of the

colleges Wilder and Forman visited that year were either exclusively women's colleges or else they were co-educational institutions. In either case it was the collegiate YWCAs that were their major entre to potential women volunteers. In the end, of the 2,200 volunteers recruited at that time, about 500 were women. Of the 6,200 volunteers reported at the 1891 SVM convention, 1,860 or exactly 30 percent were women.[2] From these beginnings, the collegiate YWCA would always be an important base of support for the SVM.

Yet the SVM was not as successful as the larger missionary community in attracting women. Already by 1900 women constituted 60 percent of the total American missionary force, a proportion it would maintain throughout this period. Yet of the 4,878 students who became SVM members between 1893 and 1900, only 2,006, or 41 percent were women. Of the 12,417 who volunteered between 1901 and 1910, only 5,649 were women, representing 45 percent. The proportion of women volunteers picked up quickly in the next decade, especially during the war years. By 1920 there were 8,964 women volunteers, or 55 percent, out of the total for the decade of 16,431.

The statistics compiled for the volunteers who actually sailed show that a consistently larger portion of female volunteers eventually became missionaries than their male counterparts, about 5 percent in any given year. Of the 8,742 SVM missionaries who sailed between 1886 and 1920 the aggregate numbers of men and women were almost equal, with the number of women exceeding the men by only 104, there being 4,423 women and 4,319 men. Female SVM volunteer missionaries only constituted about 47 percent of the movement's sailed membership during its first two decades, but by 1905, at least half of the SVM volunteers sent abroad were women. The percentage of women continued to grow until in the post-World War I era the sex mix of the SVM missionaries was consistent with the ratio between men and women in the rest of the missionary community.

The disparity between male and female recruits in the SVM during its first two decades reflects the separate history and distinctive missions ideology of women during that time. The intercollegiate YWCA, so important to the SVM's success among college women, was not simply a mirror reflection of the YMCA. Although it shared much in common with its male counterpart, the YWCA must be understood on its own terms and seen in the light of women's special place in Victorian culture. Also, the role and impetus for missionaries was different for women and men, and this too played a part in the SVM's recruitment of female missionaries.

The YWCA

Like the YMCA, the YWCA began in London.[3] The British YWCA had two root organizations, both beginning in 1855. One began as a women's prayer group that later took on a social dimension, looking after the needs of the new class of female industrial workers that had appeared in large numbers over the previous generation. The other began in response to the need for nurses during the Crimean War. The home of one of its patrons became a boarding house for the nurses sent out to hospitals under the leadership of Florence Nightingale. In 1877 these two operations were merged. The new organization expanded to Europe and in 1892 formed the World's Young Woman's Christian Association, which included associations in Great Britain, America, Norway and Sweden.

The American YWCA traces its origins to the Ladies Christian Association of New York City, which emerged from a women's prayer circle in 1858 as a result of the great revival of 1857-58. Like its British counterpart, the middle- and upper-class women of the New York YWCA formed their organization to meet what they perceived to be the social and religious needs of the burgeoning new class of urban female laborers. Similar to the YMCA, the New York association was concerned about the spiritual welfare of young people newly arrived in the city, but, unlike the YMCA, it was also concerned about the perceived vulnerability of young women in the urban environment, especially to prostitution. Consequently, the New York association established boarding rooms, a reading room, Bible classes, religious activities and an employment agency for young women newly arrived to the city. It especially targeted female workers in the expanding printing and clothing trades, where young women were frequently hired.

The Civil War experience of women in the famous Sanitary Commission, in the dozens of relief societies that eventually merged into the Ladies' Christian Commission, and in the individual experiences of thousands of women who due to the exigencies of war assumed responsibilities traditionally held by men, led to a burst of female activism after the war. Women's missionary writer Helen Barrett Montgomery wrote that for women the Civil War was "a baptism of power."[4] Not only was this the period in which the women's suffrage movement gained new momentum, but it was also the time in which women began organizing their own mission societies. As women began to move more boldly into the public sphere, the Christian women of Boston in 1866, inspired by the YMCA, established the first American organization to use the name Young Women's Christian Association.

The Boston association had motivations similar to the New York organization, and its activities quickly became a model for others to follow. The Boston YWCA set out to provide assistance to young people who had recently arrived in the city and were attempting to be self-supporting. It provided young urban women with inexpensive lodging and meals, recreation, a reading room, employment services, health care, Bible classes and a training school for cloth making. The training aspects of the services expanded in the 1870s to include training for domestic service, such as sewing, dressmaking, millinery, cooking and dietetics. The demand for female office workers that began during the Civil War gave impetus for the YWCA to include training for office work, which included bookkeeping, penmanship, and later typewriting, when typewriters became common in the 1870s. And eventually there were classes in telegraphy and stenography. In a less practical bent, classes were also offered in singing, astronomy, botany, and history. Physical education was included in the 1870s, beginning with simple calisthenics and later expanding to include more vigorous activities with the construction of a gymnasium in 1882. Physical improvement was thought necessary because so many of the women coming into the YWCA were undernourished and so physically weak that it was thought they could not stand the strain of a full day's work in an office or factory. A young women's Traveler's Aid organization was established to help rural women and later also to help immigrant women negotiate the dangerous urban environment, where it was believed they were endangered by white slavers.

YWCA organizations quickly spread during the late 1860s and 1870s to 15 other cities on the East coast and in the Midwest, which together with the establishments in New York and Boston formed what were considered the pioneer associations. Beginning in 1871 biennial conferences were held, but the creation of a national organization was still a long ways off.

The student YWCA traces its origins to the Young Ladies' Christian Association of Illinois State Normal University, established in 1873.[5] Five other student YWCA's were established on campuses in the Midwest by 1880. In addition to these, there were covert coeducational associations at this time, such as those at Lawrence College, Wisconsin and the University of Michigan, using member's initials on their official rosters to hide their sex. The YMCA records at Lawrence College for 1882-83 list A. Wilson as president and C. Althouse as corresponding secretary, but unbeknownst to the national organization "A" stood for Annie and "C" for Carrie.[6]

After the YMCA convention in Louisville in 1877 launched the Intercollegiate YMCA, Luther Wishard dutifully traveled to hundreds of schools attempting to organize YMCAs, but he encountered a problem in the coeducational schools of the Midwest. The YMCA, which included women as auxiliary members in these years, was moving in the direction of becoming an exclusively male organization, but this was largely ignored by the Midwestern schools, which tended to be coeducational. Wishard's own experience in Indiana conformed to the coeducational pattern, and, having little experience in the East, which did practice male exclusivity, when Wishard arrived at coeducational schools as the intercollegiate secretary, he simply organized coeducational associations.

When the presence of women delegates to the state conventions came to the attention of the International Committee, it revealed for the first time to the national leadership the existence of coeducational college associations. Wishard estimated that by 1882 there were already 60 to 75 mixed associations. Wishard was immediately recalled to the New York office, where the Chairman of the International Committee, Cephas Brainerd, a long time proponent of male exclusivity, carefully explained to him the YMCA's exclusive mission to males and the impossibility of coeducational associations. Wishard quickly admitted his mistake and agreed to correct the problem that he had created.

Between February 1883 and the summer of 1886, Wishard succeeded in persuading women that it would be to their advantage to have a separate organization. He pointed out that men had the leadership roles in the YMCA, and that exclusively female college associations would be more effective in reaching other women.[7] In the end, after much travel and persuasion, Wishard's efforts worked. By 1886 there were between 80 and 90 college associations specifically organized as YWCAs, and nearly all of the coeducational organizations had separated.[8]

Despite the vibrancy of the YWCA movement, there was still little in the way of a national organization. The biennial conventions that had been held since 1871 had produced the shell of what would become a national association, the International Board, but it had no budget or staff, and its only major function was to organize the conventions. It was the college YWCAs that took the lead in pressing for a national organization. The student associations first grouped themselves into state organizations and then planned to present to the 1885 International Convention a proposal for a permanent national organization that would promote the creation of more associations and hire a permanent traveling secretary for the college associations. For reasons that were murky at the time and can now only be surmised, the proposal was never made. Mary Sims, a historian of the YWCA, believes that the adult leaders of the college associations scuttled the proposal because they did not want the theologically conservative college associations merged with the more liberal city associations.[9]

Unaware of any political machinations on the part of their own leaders, the disappointed students held their own national convention at Camp

Collis at Lake Geneva, Wisconsin, in August of 1886 – meeting at the same time as the Mount Hermon conference. Consisting of nine Midwestern state organizations meeting as a constitutional convention, the women at Lake Geneva created what was eventually called the American Committee of the YWCA. Now there were in effect two national organizations, for both the American Committee and the International Board developed and expanded over the years, each including both city and college associations. What prevented unification was a dispute over the basis of membership. The American Committee insisted that all association members also be members of evangelical Protestant churches, while the International Board wanted a more broad-based membership. The two organizations finally merged in 1906, after they agreed to accept the American Committee's basis of membership and to grandfather in those under the International Board who did not meet the new standard.

The students, however, achieved their immediate goal when, following its formation, the American Committee quickly established a student department and appointed a traveling college secretary, Nettie Dunn of Hillsdale College, Michigan. The American Committee also actively promoted intercollegiate activity. In 1891, for example, it established the Summer Bible and Training School, first held at Petoskey Bay on the eastern shore of Lake Michigan and moved the next year to Camp Collie, Lake Geneva. Other conferences followed, the first occurring when Moody agreed to hold a women's summer conference for the International Committee at Northfield beginning in 1893. Conferences and attendance slowly multiplied. At the first student conference there were only 61 delegates. Twenty-five years later there were 10 student conferences with an enrollment of more than 6,000.[10]

When the SVM was organized at the end of 1888, the Intercollegiate YWCA was well poised to make a significant contribution to the movement. It would be the talent pool from which the SVM would largely draw its female volunteers. From the beginning the SVM leaders made a great effort to include the YWCA. Not only had Wilder, as the chief promoter of the movement, visited female institutions and recruited volunteers among the YWCAs, but the YWCA always had at least one member on the SVM's executive committee, and there was always at least one female traveling secretary active for some part of the academic year, who would naturally be drawn from one of the college associations. Furthermore, the YWCA could draw on a women's missionary movement, with a fully developed ideology, whose success since the Civil War paralleled its own.

The Role of Women in Missions

Because the SVM recruited among college students, the disparity between men and women volunteers before 1908 may be accounted for, in large measure, by the fact that it was still men who made up the large majority of college students during this period. The number of female college students, however, gradually increased until it peaked in the 1920s. In 1870 only 21 percent of American college students were women, but by 1920 they had increased to 47 percent, a trend that would then decline until the 1960s. Also the number of colleges that were open to women was increasing. Many academies and seminaries and then colleges were opened specifically for women in the nineteenth century. Excluding women's colleges and technical colleges, by 1870 one-third of American colleges were coeducational, and by the turn of the century coeducation was the norm.[11] By 1901 there were 600 institutions of higher education open to women in the United States, and by 1916 there were 721.[12] The Intercollegiate YWCA kept pace with the rapidly increasing number of women college students, but was still far outdistanced by the college YMCAs. In 1901 there were 19,115 YWCA college members, as opposed to at least 131,624 YMCA college members. By 1916 there were 65,129 women members, while male membership had increased to at least 199,913.[13]

These figures indicate that while the YMCA was more popular for men during these years than the YWCA was for women, the women in these organizations were disproportionately drawn to the SVM. In 1901 women constituted about 13 percent of all association members, but more than a third of all those who became student volunteers that year. In 1916 women constituted about 25 percent of all association members, but more than half of those who became SVM members.

The lower proportion of women in the student associations suggests that women who attended college in these years were more secular-minded than the general population of women in the country. That the women who were drawn to the associations were also disproportionately attracted to the SVM strongly suggests that missions for them offered a more viable career path than the available domestic options. For men, on the other hand, becoming a missionary was only one of many available options that could be pursued.

This pattern was exacerbated by the arrival of the First World War. As the United States worried about its military preparedness long before entering the war, college students increasingly found themselves redirected into the burgeoning defense industry. The number of new male SVM members peaked in 1914 at 990, and then it steadily declined during the war years, reaching its nadir in 1918 when only 510 men volunteered. Women volunteers also peaked during the war years in 1914, when 909 became SVM members. But female volunteers did not drop off as dramatically as male volunteers. There were 814 new women SVM members in 1916, 812 in 1917 and 903 in 1918. In 1917, when America finally entered the war, college men were drafted or volunteered by the thousands. As the college population declined, women kept the number of student volunteers steady by their high enrollment. As they saw men meeting the call for sacrifice from their nation, they responded too as Red Cross workers, YWCA workers, and student volunteers for the mission fields. Following the war, the SVM maintained its momentum in recruitment, and women continued to lead the way. In 1919 753 men and 1,036 women volunteered. In 1920, a con-vention year, 1,066 men and an astounding 1,521 women volunteered. The ratio between men and women volunteers had now completely reversed from what it was at the beginning of the movement.

The affinity of women for the SVM was even more remarkable when one considers that throughout the late Victorian period women interested in missions did not have to look to male-dominated missionary organizations, such as the SVM, to pursue their vocational goals. There were plenty of women's organizations through which they could explore and nurture their missionary vocation. With the first female mission societies established in the 1860s and early 1870s, by 1880 there were already 20 female societies and by 1900 there were 41. Also, women no longer had to be married to go to the mission fields. In the first half of the nineteenth century, mission boards had been reluctant to send out single women, but by 1910 the number of married and unmarried women missionaries were about equal.[14] Women, therefore, who were interested in missions, could operate entirely independently of men. They could apply directly to female organizations without the mediation of any male-dominated recruitment agency or denominational board.

Given the availability of women's missionary organizations, the reason for the large number of women in the SVM, and how they should find that the approach of the SVM would resonate with their own purposes, is an interesting historical question. In part the answer lies in that the pragmatic leadership of the SVM, despite its largely male orientation, simply could not ignore the large number of women becoming missionaries. As early as 1830 women constituted 49 percent of all American missionaries. By 1880 they reached 57 percent, and by 1929 they were at 67 percent.[15] Women in fact were well known to be more responsive than men to a missionary calling, so that the leaders of the SVM, if they were to maximize their effectiveness as missionary recruiters, had to find ways to appeal to women by adapting their message to them. They did this by using women speakers and by balancing in their rhetoric old and emerging notions of Victorian womanhood.

The nineteenth-century rationale for female missionaries was rooted in the ideology of domesticity.[16] Following the Civil War, evangelical women who promoted female missionaries distanced themselves from the women's rights movement and rejected the notion of gender equality. The impetus for their movement did not derive from women's activism in the abolition or women's rights movements, but rather from their participation in the benevolent societies formed during the Civil War to look after the needs of the soldiers, such as the Sanitary Commission. They embraced the ideas of Catharine Beecher, who urged that the traditional "domestic sphere" of female activity be expanded to include appropriate areas of public need.

Whatever Beecher may have believed about herself, she accepted the prevailing view of middle-class culture that men and women were in general not equal, but that women were superior to men in the areas of moral and religious sensitivity and in their capacity for nurture. This position relegated the role of "Christian womanhood" to working in the home to ensure a religious environment that could have a transforming impact on the family. Beecher argued that Christian womanhood, applied to appropriate places in the public sphere such as teaching and nursing, could transform the world. Thus during the Civil War women acted as nurses and care-givers for wounded soldiers.

Following the war, women's missionary societies were established to send women to foreign countries to perform these same functions. Women were not placed on an equality with men in missionary work, but rather their efforts were seen as supplemental to the main missionary work of evangelization. However, in the rigidly patriarchal countries of much of the East, male missionaries could not reach many women, for they often lived secluded lives such as those women in the zenanas of India and the harems of Afghanistan. Thus there was a need for women evangelists. Also the example of a missionary's clean, well-ordered household run by a woman, would have a salutatory effect on the women living in crowded grass huts or mud-brick houses. Because female evangelism and role-modeling was not work that male missionaries could do, the justification for women's missions was aptly summed up in what was perhaps the watchword of women missionaries, "women's work for women."

Women's households as socially acceptable spheres of activity may now have been theoretically expanded to include the entire world, but women were still largely relegated to the traditional female duties of running the missionary household, nursing, and teaching. The ideology of domesticity began to break down in the 1890s, just as the SVM was learning to appeal to women. The new thrust was increasingly toward total equality in career opportunities, a position that gained much wider acceptance on the mission field than it did domestically. In the long run, this position undermined the rationale for the special need for female missionaries and the societies that supported them, because it denied that there were gender-specific tasks to perform. In the short run it helped to expand the job descriptions available to women interested in becoming missionaries and offer a far greater sphere of opportunity than was then available in the United States. Thus a missionary career continued to be a very appealing option to ambitious women at least until the 1920s when greater opportunities became available domestically.

In the 1890s the SVM leaders, despite their conservative evangelical religion, appealed to women in the new mode of equality, and yet their appeals were often hedged by more conventional ideas. In 1893 an annual young women's conference was added to the two men's conferences held at Northfield in the summer. All of these conferences had missionary addresses, but the theme of the 1894 women's conference was specifically missions. The missionary and other speeches addressed to young women at the conference were extensively recorded in the journal *Northfield Echoes*, whose account gives a good indication of the prevailing approach of the moment toward women.

The records indicate that the notion of women's work for women was not abandoned. The unreachability of many women by male missionaries made this approach necessary for years to come. Bishop James M. Thoburn of India noted that in his evangelistic meetings in India held in public places it was unusual if more than one woman were present, and in tent meetings more than four or five women would be remarkable. "Hence the great mass of women must be reached by their own sex," he explained. "Here is where the responsibility of women in the mission field lies. The women will never hear the gospel unless they hear it from their own sex."[17] But despite the traditional theme of women's work, Thoburn offered women a greatly broadened sphere of opportunity. "In this country there is a great deal of discussion about the rights and privileges of Christian women in the church. When you go out to India, no one ever thinks about such things, and a woman may assume privileges that will startle people here." In fact, he continued, "There is hardly anything you could not do."[18] In his list of possibilities he included evangelism, medicine, music, teaching, and writing.

Although the assumption of gender specific roles was not abandoned, the essential equality of men and women was asserted at Northfield and suggested in general an expanding place for women in the work of missions. At this same 1894 conference Mrs. A.J. Gordon, the wife of the

Boston minister who had such an impact on Wilder and who spoke often at SVM conferences, gave an address entitled "Women as Evangelists," which was still controversial in some evangelical circles a century later. She argued that the Day of Pentecost, on which the Holy Spirit descended on the disciples of Jesus in the upper room and thereby inaugurated the Christian Church, began a new dispensation. Salvation was now not only universal, as the Apostle Peter interpreted the fulfillment of the prophesy of Joel on that day, but men and women were placed on a level of equality (Acts: 2:17). "Sons and daughters were to prophesy," she reported, and "spiritual gifts and qualifications were to be bestowed and exercised equally by servants and handmaidens."[19] Gordon then cited a number of New Testament women as examples "to show that the weight of Scripture testimony and example is in favor of women doing the work and exercising the gifts of evangelists."[20] But despite the clear thrust toward equality that her address made, it still contained a traditional trope for female domesticity. She noted the example of the four daughters of Philip the Evangelist in *The Acts of the Apostles*. His daughters were prophets, but they stayed at home to take care of the housekeeping.

> These "daughters" seem to be notable examples of what women may be to-day; faithful home makers, keeping the machinery of their households wound up so that it will run without continuous watching; and then consecrating the spiritual experience of their mature years to leading others into the same truth which has saved and sanctified them.[21]

Far from being merely a sop to conventionality, Gordon may in fact be commending her own example to her auditors. The mature wife of a successful evangelist-pastor, she attempted to maintain a well-run home and also to make forays into the male-dominated field of evangelism. Her address therefore points in two directions: the total equality of women in religious work, and the continuation of the subordinate position of women in their primarily domestic sphere of activity. Between these two options, Gordon asserted a female equality that was to be worked out within the traditional Victorian gender-role conventions. The ambiguity of this position, which was accepted by most missionary women at this time, allowed for an expanding role for women while not directly challenging the ideology of "separate spheres."

The tension between the themes of equality and "separate spheres" was further played out in the Student Movement's emphasis on character. By associating character with masculine traits, it might be wondered if Victorians conceived of women having character at all. However, despite character being a largely gendered term, Victorians when pressed could speak of female character. This can be seen most clearly in the Student Movement's depictions of Christ. Notwithstanding their emphasis on the manliness of Christ, these writers and speakers did not present an overly masculinized Savior. If they were at all tempted to do this, perhaps they refrained when they remembered that much of their audience would be women.

The Jesus depicted by the Student Movement biographers of Christ was a conflation of the traditional feminine virtues of religious, moral and maternal sensitivities with the values of middle-class manliness. The masculine Jesus was an indomitable leader of men in the spirit of the aggressive military hero or successful entrepreneur. The feminine Jesus, on the other hand, was presented as a high-minded speaker of the truth, who loved children, sympathized with the plight of women in an insensitive patriarchal society, and with the poor and sick. Harry Emerson Fosdick in *The Manhood of the Master*, for example, pointed up "his overflowing tenderness, his warmly affectionate nature." Fosdick's Jesus loved family, home and friends, and children responded to Him. Yet this was also the Jesus who was the practical leader of a great cause, who could be filled with "righteous indignation," and who struck fear into the hearts of the Jewish leaders. Jesus, Fosdick reminded his readers, promised "to cast fire upon the earth," (Lk. 12:49) and came "not to send peace, but a sword" (Mt. 10:34). What struck Fosdick was the balance in of Jesus' character. Although men and women "represent two spheres of character," he concluded, "we take it for granted that both should find their ideal in Christ."[22]

In addition to its conflicted but forward-looking notions of gender, the YWCA promoted an ideology of "usefulness" that was the counterpart to the YMCA's emphasis on a business-like practicality. A staple of nineteenth-century revival rhetoric, "usefulness" was at the center of an ideal Christian woman's character. The president of the Canadian Association at the 1894 Northfield conference contrasted what he perceived to be the contemporary ideal of womanhood found in the common culture with the ideal asserted by the YWCA: "It seems to be the proper thing in these days for the lady to do the useless work and for the servants to do the useful work. The [Bible] classes are formed in the Association that usefulness may be promoted."[23]

The usefulness that the leaders of the YWCA had in mind was the creation of a Christian culture. The primary means to achieve this end, and the spirit that was supposed to permeate all of their social work, was evangelism. The YWCA was a middle-class organization whose focus of activity by the 1890s was on the immigrant working girl in the urban environment. The YWCA city work may be seen as the Christian counterpart to the work of Jane Addams at Hull-House. But where Addams's work tended to emphasize cultural refinement as a means of social betterment, the YWCA emphasized vocational, physical, and explicitly Christian education.

The women involved in the Intercollegiate YWCA were encouraged to take up the inner city work, which was often referred to as home mission work. The college missionary bands of these associations shared in their ideology of usefulness and social betterment. Foreign missions, far from being an extravagant offshoot of the core ideology, were simply seen as an extension of the domestic urban work to foreign lands. Those who wished to be foreign missionaries were therefore encouraged to join in the home work so that they would be better prepared when they went abroad.

Just as the female missionary bands were not cut off from the wider world of the YWCA, neither were they segregated from the mainstream of the SVM. The college missionary bands were encouraged to read the same missionary literature that was provided for their male counterparts. Similarly, the female leadership committees of the missionary department of the YWCA were told to be as exacting in their efforts as the men. "To accomplish tangible results," one YWCA leader informed the Northfield women, "it is evident the work of this committee must be made a business, and cannot be done in a haphazard way."[24] Female college students, although they could not be seminarians, were told to prepare themselves rigorously for the work. Pauline Root, a missionary medical doctor, told the students that the educational requirements of men and women missionaries ought to be equal: "It would not be a bad scheme for any girl who was going to a mission field to know Hebrew, and to continue to read her Greek testament. She needs – as does a man – to be prepared to meet a thinking people and to be ready to give a clear reason for all her beliefs."[25]

In short, the SVM was successful in recruiting female missionaries for a variety of reasons. Despite the movement's conservative evangelical roots and the legacy of the ideology of domesticity that inaugurated the women's missions movement after the Civil War, the SVM successfully employed the language of equality without threatening traditional Victorian conventions about womanhood. Moreover, it successfully exploited the college woman's desire to find a sphere of opportunity that equaled her ambition. Finally, the SVM's emphasis on a vigorous masculine practicality did not have to be jettisoned; it had only to be nuanced to fit the preexisting ideology of "usefulness" that YWCA women already embraced.

A Social Gospel for Women

Whatever the specific tasks missionary women assumed, one of their primary roles was to be in elevating Eastern women to a belief in the fundamental equality of all people under God, within of course the limits of middle-class ideology. It was carried on both by the example Western women set in foreign cultures and by the education they gave Eastern women in the finer points of domesticity. Root addressed this issue at the 1894 conference for women in these words:

> One thing upon which I have insisted is that poor converts shall be educated. It is part of the work which some of you might do, you might go into these villages with their miserable little mud huts, perhaps only one room to a house, no sanitary conditions whatever, everything dirty and filthy, and educate those people who are not even allowed to wear clothing above the waist by the high caste people, who in time of famine would not be given one drop of water from a Brahmin's well to keep them from dying of thirst. A middle class woman would not dare to wear silk in the streets; but the Brahmins in the city cannot interfere in the least with our educated girls, who are on the contrary highly esteemed by Hindoos, Mohammedans, and Christians.[26]

The special need for a social mission to women in non-Christian countries was a commonplace belief by this time. James S. Dennis's *Christian Missions and Social Progress* was especially poignant regarding the condition of Eastern women. And this material was reproduced in the SVM's version of Dennis's work, the mission study booklet *Social Evils of the Non-Christian World* (1897). Victorian Americans placed great emphasis on what Dennis explained as "the conception of an elevated, honored, and sacred womanhood," and therefore it was particularly shocking that non-Christian societies not only failed to honor women with a special status, but were actually guilty of degrading them. For Dennis this was "the most conspicuous and unmistakable insignia of false religious systems."[27]

One of the great strengths of Dennis's book was in his cataloging of the social evils of the non-Christian world regarding women. Marriage in most non-Christian countries, he reported, was little esteemed and adultery and other abuses were common. In Islamic countries the Koran sanctioned four wives and allowed concubines and slaves. Women in general in Japan were little respected, and husbands could openly keep concubines in the home with the wife's knowledge. In Siam not only was polygamy common but so was polyandry. India combined all the worst aspects of the non-Christian world's treatment of women, allowing prostitution, concubinage, adultery, easy divorce, temple prostitution (deva-dasi, or "slaves of the gods") – not to mention the problem of child brides, child widows, and the zenana system.[28] In the case of a husband's death, women in India still feared sati (widow-burning), and in China the only two honorable options were suicide or permanent widowhood. In nearly all non-Christian countries, Dennis observed, women were kept in ignorance, segregated from society, subject to autocratic husbands, and victimized by all manner of social evils.

Not only wives, Dennis explained, but also female offspring were ill-treated. Female infanticide was widespread all over the non-Christian world, but especially in China, India and the Pacific Islands. Dennis cited a contemporary Indian census (probably 1890) that found there were only 92 women for every 100 men, with some area proportions as low as 70 to 100. Women were also central to these culture's indulgence in "personal sins." China filled its brothels with young girls who were often blind. Japan's houses of ill-repute were generally taken for granted by the population, although the unfortunate "inmates are virtually the galley-slaves of lust, having often been sold by fathers or brothers to the cruel service."[29]

The glaring weakness of Dennis's book was its failure to consult indigenous sources. But relying solely on Western sources to describe and analyze Eastern cultures was typical of the missionary literature of this time and received little comment.[30] Three years after the publication of Dennis's book, women at the Ecumenical Missionary Conference in New York in 1900 created the Central Committee for the United Study of Foreign Missions, an organization that annually produced mission study books for women that generally confirmed the picture of women in the East as Dennis had described it.

Largely organized by Abbie B. Child, Secretary of the Woman's Board of Missions and a member of the SVM's advisory committee since its inception, the Central Committee produced mission study books for women from 1900 to 1938, when the committee's work was assumed by the Missionary Education Movement. When Child died in 1902, the management of the committee devolved to Lucy Waterbury Peabody, who served for 28 years. On the tenth anniversary of the mission series, Helen Barrett Montgomery, a one-time missionary to India, wrote *Western Women in Eastern Lands*, the first history of American women in missions and one that presented a clear Social Gospel rationale for missions. It was very successful, selling 50,000 copies in the first six weeks and helping to make Montgomery the foremost spokesperson for women's missions in the United States.

Montgomery argued in her history that the original impulse for women to be involved in foreign missions was to challenge the "degradation of women in heathen lands." Explaining the conventional wisdom of that time and her own, she asserted that women themselves needed to undertake the task, because men could not reach the women secluded in zenanas and imprisoned by culture. Following this logic, female missions enthusiasts formed the first women's missionary society in 1860-61, the Woman's Union Missionary Society, whose jubilee was extensively celebrated in 1910-11 and was promoted by Montgomery's book.

Montgomery likened the advance of women's rights in America to the liberation of women in non-Christian lands. She believed that what made reform possible in America was its Christian religion. Conversely, what made the position of women in other lands so intractable was that "the wrongs of Hindu, Chinese, and Moslem women are buttressed behind the sanctions of religion, and are indorsed by the founders of their faith..."[32] Picking up where Dennis left off, Montgomery outlined the condition of women in China, Japan, Korea, among "savage tribes," Moslem countries, and India. Everywhere she saw women degraded, abused, and kept in ignorance. No where did she see a process of evolution toward a higher status for women apart from Western and specifically Christian influence. She concluded that "if religion itself debases womanhood, the only hope is in a new and purer faith."[33]

In sketching the achievements of women missionaries, she noted especially the establishment of schools, hospitals and other social agencies designed to better the condition of women. Before social workers in 1884 had established Toynbee Hall in London or other similar settlement houses in the United States, she observed, missionaries had long been practicing this particular variant of the Social Gospel: "Girls' clubs and boys clubs, close neighborliness between the privileged and the less privileged, industrial training, story-telling, lessons in domestic science, all had their beginnings in the foreign mission field a generation before they were adopted in the home lands."[34]

Looking back on the half century of women's work, Montgomery compared the women missionaries to Harriet Tubman leading slaves to freedom. Adumbrating on the advances already made, she observed that "there are evidences that age-long habits of subserviency are loosening, that women are shaking off the lion's paw of cruel custom."[35] She pointed to the edict against foot-binding by the Empress in China following the Boxer Rebellion, the spread of education in Siam, the lessening of concubinage in Japan, and the movement against the harem and the veil in

Egypt. In her view, although there was much left to do, much had been accomplished by the work and influence of women missionaries. At the 1920 SVM convention, recounting again the degradation of women in non-Christian lands, Montgomery plaintively asked the potential volunteers, "What are you going to do for these other sisters of ours who need schools and hospitals and friends...[?][36]

Women in the SVM

The themes of women's degradation and "women's work for women" were given a regular hearing at the SVM conventions, summer conferences, and in Student Movement journals. Although women could not be ordained, they were told that they could serve abroad as teachers, doctors, nurses, writers, social workers, and YWCA secretaries.[37] Even if women went abroad as missionary wives, rather than as independent missionaries, they were assured that they were still essential to the cause of Christianizing the East. In an article for *The Student Volunteer Movement Bulletin,* Lucy Peabody maintained that "Only women can demonstrate the model home." But beyond homemaking, she envisioned missionary women as model mothers, whose missionary impulse was in part a maternal concern for abused, neglected or underprivileged children. "One might fancy," Peabody suggested to her female student audience, "a statue representing woman's foreign missionary work: a colossal figure of a woman, strong and beautiful, to whose open arms come flocking the children of the world."[38]

Consistent with this image of women as homemakers and child-care providers, women were rarely featured speakers at the SVM conventions. The usual explanation given for this was that women's voices in the days before loudspeakers could not be heard in large convention halls. General convention addresses, however, were directed at both men and women, and the specific theme of women in missions was usually handled in smaller conferences within the conventions. The first convention in 1891, which only included about 600 delegates and had no smaller sessions, simply included a session in the general program devoted to "Woman's Work for Woman," presided over by Nettie Dunn. The 1898 convention held a similar session, a "Conference of Woman's Work." Thereafter women's issues and appeals, directed specifically at potential female volunteers, were usually dealt with in conferences devoted to individual countries. For example, in a series of addresses on China, one address would be devoted to the "needs" of Chinese women.

Women convention speakers were not always relegated to speaking on women's issues. Geraldine Guinness spoke to the general convention audiences in 1894 and 1902 on holiness themes as well as on "Women's Work for, by and among Women." Guinness had been an English missionary to China since 1888, eventually marrying Dr. F. Howard Taylor, the son of the founder of the China Inland Mission, J. Hudson Taylor. In 1901 she and her husband traveled to about 150 American and Canadian educational institutions in a major promotional tour for the SVM.[39] She became an important mission writer, producing early in her career such popular works among missions enthusiasts as *In the Far East* (1889) and *The Story of the China Inland Mission* (1894).[40] Mott introduced her to the 1894 SVM convention by saying, "There is one whose words on the printed page have brought more inspiration and blessing into the lives of American students than any one living to-day among the young volunteers that are now at work in the field."[41] Guinness, who went on to write a number of books on China missions, also wrote the biography of the famous SVM martyr, *Borden of Yale*.[42]

While no woman had the stature of a Mott, Speer, Eddy or Wilder in the SVM, several women were prominent in the movement at the second echelon. Abbie Child and Lucy Waterbury Peabody served among the other distinguished missionary leaders on the Advisory Committee of the SVM. In addition to Guinness, several women were noted for their speaking ability, such as Dr. Pauline Root and Una M. Saunders. After 1898 the YWCA always had two members on the SVM executive committee, and Bertha Conde, in addition to writing many pamphlets and books and working for the YWCA, served on the executive committee through the first two decades of the new century.

Perhaps the best remembered of the late Victorian era women missionary leaders in the Student Movement is Ruth Rouse. Baptized at the age of 18 in Charles Spurgeon's Metropolitan Tabernacle in London, Rouse attended Girton College, Cambridge, where in 1892 she was given an SVM declaration card by Wilder, which she signed about two years later. In 1894 she met Mott and Speer at the summer conference at Keswick. In 1895 she worked as the editor of the *Student Volunteer*, and in the following year served as a traveling secretary for several organizations for women within the Student Movement. She then moved to the United States, where at the request of Mott she worked as a traveling secretary for the SVM in 1897-99 and again in 1904-05. She served briefly in India as a missionary with the YWCA from 1899 to 1901 before she returned for health reasons. In 1903 she began to work for the WSCF, and in 1905 she officially became with Mott one of that organization's two traveling secretaries, a position she held until the end of 1924. During these years she visited as many as 65 countries, speaking as an evangelist and organizer for the WSCF among women. She wrote a number of pamphlets in the missionary cause, spoke at many of the major missionary conferences, and wrote dozens of articles for Student Movement journals. Because of her wide influence and range of interests she was considered by some to be a "female John R. Mott." In later years she became the historian of the WSCF and the ecumenical movement.[43]

*   *   *

Women missionaries in the Gilded Age and Progressive Era saw themselves as revolutionaries, liberators, and up-lifters of their sisters around the world. As the benefactors of the nineteenth century American women's movement, whose origins they traced to Christianity, they understood themselves to be in possession of a powerful religious truth that could literally "set the captives free." Confident in their own convictions, and further assured of eventual success because of their possession of the social and medical tools necessary to change the lives of women in other cultures, they set out to liberate their sisters in bondage. They would tear down the prison walls of tradition and expose the errors of non-Christian religions that allowed women to be the victims of unregenerate male dominance.

Ironically, as Jane Hunter has pointed out, turn-of-the-century missionaries pursued their revolutionary goals without being self-consciously feminist or by directly challenging Victorian concepts of womanhood.[44] Yet in large measure it was because of the incompleteness of the women's reform movement in America that many women pursued the option of becoming foreign missionaries. Explicit in many of the SVM recruitment addresses to women was the argument that as missionaries they would be able to pursue career goals that would be denied them in America. In seeking to liberate their Eastern sisters, Western women were also seeking to liberate themselves. At a time in which women's reform ideology was uneasily suspended between "separate spheres" and full equality, women missionaries were using a conservative ideology for radical ends. Rejecting the "professional" woman's appeal for gender equality and open-ended career possibilities, they nevertheless became missionary professionals whose career goals abroad could be as unlimited as the most ambitious woman's in the homeland.

The dramatic increase in the number of women SVM members after 1908 coincided not only with the increase of women in colleges and in the

Intercollegiate YWCAs, but also with the rise of the Social Gospel within the Student Movement. It is doubtless more than coincidental that women missionary volunteers, who had a long tradition of viewing missions as social action, should find membership in the SVM congenial at the very moment when the SVM was accentuating the idea of missions as a Christianizing as well as an evangelizing endeavor.

Chapter Four

"THE EVANGELIZATION OF THE WORLD IN THIS GENERATION"

> What we need to discover in the social realm is the moral
> equivalent of war; something heroic that will speak to men
> as universally as war does, and yet will be as compatible
> with their spiritual selves as war has proved itself to be
> incompatible.
>
> ---William James[1]

The early Christians felt a sense of urgency in their missionary endeavors because they believed in an imminent peroseia and the inauguration of the millennium. However, few nineteenth-century Christians shared the belief that Jesus was soon to return, and those concerned with missionary work were divided on the issue. The Great Commission of Jesus Christ ("All power is given unto me in heaven and in earth. Go ye therefore, and teach all nations ... [Mt. 28, 18-19]) was clear in its directions, but for many it lacked a sense of urgency because it gave no time limit for the endeavor.

For others the Great Commission was problematical even as a summons to great human exertion to spread the gospel. They interpreted it to mean that the success of evangelizing the world depended entirely on Christ alone and not on human efforts at all. People who believed this tended to point to the many obstacles hindering the Christianization of the world. Consequently, the great task of mission enthusiasts in the nineteenth century was twofold. First, they had to create a sense of urgency about missions that would not be based on immediate expectations of a second advent. Second, they had to show that world evangelization in the immediate future was a real possibility, and that human effort blessed by divine empowerment was equal to the task.

These objectives were largely met by the famous watchword of the SVM, "The Evangelization of the World in This Generation." The watchword was more than simply a catchy slogan; it was a credo, a statement of belief, a guiding principle, an inspiring war cry. In eight words it summed up the meaning and purpose of the SVM. Yet it was also a highly ambiguous statement that required extensive explanation and engendered a protracted debate.

The Theology Behind the Watchword

The controversy over missions in the church in the mid-nineteenth century centered on the antinomy between divine sovereignty and human responsibility. While stressing the first half of the Divine/human equation, an editorial in the January 1878 issue of *The Foreign Missionary*, emphasized the human difficulty of missionary work and the inviolateness of the Divine prerogative. Of the missionaries it said, "Duty is theirs; results are with Him." The success of missions was to be attributed to the mediatorial work of Christ in heaven, and when His priestly offering would be complete in heaven, then "He shall see of the travail of His soul and is satisfied" (Isaiah 53:11). To those who would stress the urgency of the missionary task the editorial averred, "No man has a right to limit the intentions of the Almighty, or gauge the times and the seasons for the accomplishment of His own plans, and yet this is constantly done in regard to missions." It magnified the immensity of the task: "It is no child's play to change the religion of a nation; to overthrow the systems that have been welded for successive ages into the very being of the people." In addition to the sheer human immensity of the problem there was the spiritual counterforce to consider: "It is no easy task to thwart the machinations of the Evil One, and to conquer the god of this world, whose sway is so terrible and whose hold upon it borders on Omnipotence itself."

Evangelism, the editorial concluded, was a slow task. It took 250 years to convert the Roman Empire, and the evangelization of the world would probably be the work of generations or centuries and perhaps millenniums.[2]

At the time of *The Foreign Missionary* article, the ever pugnacious Royal Gould Wilder issued the first edition of his new periodical, *The Missionary Review*. Like William Lloyd Garrison's opening edition of the *Liberator* a half century earlier, Wilder's opening articles threw down the gauntlet to the moral complacency that he believed marked his generation. The initial aim of the publication, he wrote in the first article, was "to develop an interest in foreign missions which shall speedily double the present amount of giving, praying, going and working in this cause." He estimated the current number of American missionaries in the world to be about 450. With a number so small, he argued that "those who complacently fancy we are really evangelizing the world by the present scale of effort, or that we are even making any sensible approximation towards it, only show how readily human hearts can beguile and deceive themselves." He believed that the Presbyterian Church, his denomination, would have to increase its annual giving to $25 million (up from less than $1 million), and increase the number of its missionaries to 6,000. This effort would have to be maintained for a generation, and other denominations would have to increase their efforts in like proportion for there to be hope of evangelizing the world and "ere Christ shall see of the travail of His soul and be satisfied." It was for this purpose that God created the church, Wilder asserted, and "only as she engages in it with a purpose to accomplish it, and with agencies and efforts adapted to accomplish it, is she fulfilling her mission."[3]

In the periodical's second article, "Who will go For Us?", Wilder lamented the great disparity between the number of evangelical ministers working among the U.S. population, which he estimated to be about 1 in 700, and the less than one to a million available for service in the heathen lands. To the young men about to enter the ministry he asked, "And does He bid you work only in hospitals, where the inmates are already supplied with nurses and medicine, have every needed care and comfort, and are already cured, or stubbornly refuse the offered medicine, while the battle-field, near by, is strewn with the wounded and dying by millions?" Ministers do not need a special calling to the mission field, he argued. If they are called to preach, then they ought to go where the need is greatest. "There is not one element or teaching of the Gospel to justify the present surplus of ministers in Christendom, while millions of the heathen are perishing, not knowing the name of Jesus."[4]

Wilder believed that if a sufficient number of missionaries were sent into foreign lands they would be able to accomplish the evangelization of the world in one generation. But heretofore his argument lacked the urgency to compel Protestant leaders to work toward this end. In another article in this same edition Wilder rounded out the argument that the founders of the later SVM would condense into the watchword of the movement. Wilder attacked the mission board of the Presbyterian Church for not grasping the magnitude of the task before it. Yes, the missionaries had achieved much success in foreign lands, but their efforts were not able to keep up with the natural increase of the population. Consequently "the mighty throng of the heathen, rushing into eternity with no knowledge of the crucified Christ, [is] constantly increasing." While the writer in *The Foreign Missionary* was content to have the world evangelized over generations and centuries, Wilder believed that the logic of the Great Commission compelled a maximum effort to save this current generation. Quoting from a Presbyterian leader, Wilder asserted "that to evangelize the world means to evangelize the present generation." In an argument made clear by subsequent elaboration, Wilder believed that what Christ meant by "the world" was each generation that existed before His return and not simply a geographical entity to be evangelized over time. The Great Commission therefore placed a duty on Christians to evangelize their own generation, and relieved them of responsibility for past or future generations. "And hence," Wilder concluded, "must not the church enlist measures and agencies adequate to accomplish this work in a single generation?"[5]

The ideas behind the watchword of the SVM were inchoate in this first edition of *The Missionary Review*. Mott, however, attributed the formulation of the watchword to Arthur Pierson, although its exact origin was never definitively determined. It seems to have first come to people's attention at the Mount Hermon Conference of 1886. Robert Wilder noted that the watchword or its equivalent was frequently heard in the addresses of the Conference, and that the sense of urgency implied by these words played no small part in convincing men to volunteer for foreign missions both at the time of the conference and in subsequent years.

Later, when the watchword came under attack in the latter part of the 1890s, it was asserted that in part the urgency felt by the early student volunteers was from their association of the watchword with the bringing about of the second coming of Christ. A mission enthusiast from Germany, Dr. Gustave Warneck of the university at Hale, believed that the impetus for the watchword rested on the words of Jesus in Matt. 24:24: "This gospel of the kingdom shall be preached in all the world for a witness unto all nations; and then the end shall come." Certainly Pierson,

Moody, and Ashmore as premillennialists may have embraced the watchword in response to their sense of urgency over Christ's coming, but for many who did not believe in the immediacy of Christ's return, the watchword itself sounded the note of urgency. It acted as a substitute for premillennialism as a spur to action.[6] Above all, this was the great power of the watchword, and its sly genius.

The Crisis

But the watchword was not mere cleverness and legerdemain, for to a large extent its power derived from the radically changed world that the students of the 1880s faced, which their fathers had not. The great missionary upsurge that occurred at the end of the nineteenth century was not simply the natural linear development from the early missionary efforts of the century. There was a new impulse for missions in the three decades or so preceding the Mount Hermon Conference. Pierson for one believed that recent events in the world had created a new and compelling impetus for world evangelization, which demanded an all-out effort with the goal of completing the task within a single generation. Fired by this conviction, Pierson produced the most influential promotional missions book of the period, *The Crisis of Missions*, which he completed in 1886 following the Mount Hermon Conference. In it Pierson made the case for world evangelization in terms that would be echoed in the addresses and literature of the SVM for a generation.[7]

Pierson observed that in the world before 1850 the barriers to the evangelization of all peoples on earth were well-nigh insurmountable. China, India, Africa, the Moslem countries, and the Roman Catholic countries were all largely if not completely closed to Protestant missionaries. Travel to these places was still difficult and dangerous, and native languages were still generally unknown to Westerners. Women in many of these regions, especially India and the Moslem countries, were insulated and isolated in their societies to such an extent that the traditionally male missionaries had no hope of reaching them with the gospel.

In the second half of the century, largely as a result of the Western countries' desire to expand commerce, the countries of the then-developing world were opened up generally by treaty and intimidation. The British East India Company received a new charter in 1812 that provided for the toleration of missionaries. This allowed to missionaries a degree of freedom hitherto unknown, but when the governance of India by "John Company" was discontinued and replaced by a crown government following the Sepoy Rebellion in 1857, the evangelization of India by

Western missionaries entered a new age. Missionaries for the first time found the country truly open to their efforts.

During this same period, doors were also opening in East Asia. The first Protestant missionary arrived in China in 1807, but the Treaty of Tientsin in 1858 opened that vast country to both commerce and the gospel in a new and dramatic way. Commodore Perry's arrival in the bay of Yeddo in 1853 with waving flags on 17 bristling ships of war was enough to open the Empire of Japan to American commerce and guarantee the protection of missionaries. Similarly Korea was open to American commerce and Protestant missionaries by treaty in 1882, and, in the latter years of the century, Burma, the Karens, and Siam were also opened.

Other parts of the world were also becoming available to Western missionaries. In the Muslim world the Koran proscribed capital punishment for any apostates, yet the Sultan of the Ottoman Empire in 1856, following the Treaty of Paris that ended the Crimean War, abolished the death penalty for Christian converts. In the 1878 Treaty of Berlin, which divided up much of the Ottoman empire between Britain and Austria and also created Serbia and Romania as independent states, Christians and Jews were guaranteed civil and religious liberty. This went a long way in making the area of the old Ottoman empire relatively safe for missionaries for the first time.

Pierson noted that as late as the 1870s maps of the great interior of Africa were marked "unexplored." Livingstone's and then Stanley's explorations into the "Dark Continent" took a large step in changing this condition, so that by the end of the 1870s the first missionaries were entering even that forbidding land.

Pierson was also greatly encouraged by what he saw happening in Roman Catholic countries. In Europe Catholic countries seem to have been in relative decline since the eighteenth century. Spain, Austria and France no longer held sway, determining the balance of power on the continent. Protestant England, with its far flung empire, was the commercial giant of the world. By 1870, following the Italian Revolution, the Pope lost his temporal power and became a veritable prisoner in the Vatican. Some Protestants saw apocalyptic significance in this event. The "twelve hundred and sixty" days in *The Revelation to John* given over to the dominion of the antichrist seemed finally to have come to an end, Pierson crowed.

In Latin America the Catholic church was receiving similar blows. In 1873 the Mexican government abolished the established religion and dealt a fierce economic blow to a church that had previously owned one-half of all the real estate in the country and had an annual income of around $20 million. In 1846 Chileans began a religious revolution that secularized much of the civil procedures and affected a separation of church and state. And for good measure the next year they expelled the papal nuncio. Under the enlightened leadership of Dom Pedro in the 1870s and 80s, Brazil abolished slavery, established freedom of religion, and extended legal protection to Protestant missionaries over the protests of the Catholic clergy. "It is plain," Pierson believed, "that these priest-ridden masses are weary of their thraldom," and that now anything seemed possible, perhaps the conversion of the great masses of the Catholic nations to evangelical religion and even the long-sought reform of the Roman church itself.

It might be thought that all these "open doors" would be a cause for rejoicing to an old mission enthusiast like Pierson, and of course they were. But for him they also constituted "the crisis of missions." The Protestant churches, he said, faced a "grand opportunity and great responsibility; the hour when the chance of glorious success and the risk of awful failure confront each other; the turning-point of history and destiny." The crisis consisted of a number of dangers. The doors so providentially opened might not stay open for long. The non-Christian nations of the world were in flux, but they would soon settle down again. "A nation ready to be moulded is liable to be marred; the pliant sapling may be easily deformed, or the plastic clay shaped for dishonor."[8] Therefore, he concluded, the Church must rush in with the evangel while people were still open to receiving it.

Already it seemed to Pierson "that Satan's active agents are entering these open doors, preoccupying these open fields." The evils he had in mind were Western style rationalism, materialism, agnosticism and atheism. As old faiths were toppled and superstitions rejected, the "house of heathenism" was being swept clean of its evil spirits. However, being left empty, there was the danger that "seven other spirits more wicked than the first [would] enter in and dwell there; and the last state is worse than the first."[9]

In this crises, the church that exhibited "sluggishness, selfishness, and ... stinginess" inhibited the fulfillment of the Great Commission in its hour of greatest need. Such a church, Pierson believed, was guilty of "an apathy that verges on apostasy."[10] Some of these churches, Pierson concluded, were paralyzed by a new liberal theology that posited a religious relativism that denied the unique claims of the gospel and rejected the idea that the unconverted were damned. But the notions of a "second probation" after death and a "final restoration," he believed, were unbiblical. The relativist notion that religions developed in an evolutionary process, and that Christianity was currently at the top but by no means in complete possession of all religious light, was in fact "the leaven of a new theology" that the church should reject as heresy.

The great need of the church was to energize and organize itself so that it could meet the great challenge before it. He urged every church to fund its own missionary, preferably someone of their own number, so that they would be personally committed to the effort. He called for an expeditious training process for missionaries to speed their arrival on the mission field. The four years of college and three years of seminary, studying Hebrew, Greek, and Latin, was not necessarily important for every missionary to have. Lay volunteers under proper supervision could constitute an irresistible army. It was time too for the denominations to stop duplicating their efforts on one field and leaving another unattended. Pierson called for a world missionary council to map out the fields and divide up the work. Above all, Pierson called for thoughtful, practical measures that would meet the crisis. If only "sound, sensible business principle[s]" were applied, Pierson believed, then "no practical hinderance would be found sufficient even to delay the prosecution of the work solemnly committed by Christ to His church." Surveying all Christendom, Pierson concluded that if 10 million committed evangelicals could be found to supply the missionaries and their funding, then "even with this tenth part of Christendom the world may be evangelized before the twentieth century dawns."[11]

Pierson's book was not highly original. The intellectual groundwork had been laid out over the previous decade in the missionary journals of the time, and even this work was a culmination of the previous century of activity and thought. Pierson's contribution lay in synthesizing and shaping the argument for a massive new effort on behalf of missions. He succeeded not only in marshaling the major arguments that the SVM would draw on for a generation, but in setting the agenda for the second stage in modern missions history: the effort to evangelize the world in a single generation.

The Volunteer Appeal

The first generation of the SVM until the beginning of World War I succeeded in elaborating and refining Pierson's arguments, but not developing them or allowing them to evolve into new areas. The best place to find the early pronouncements of the SVM missions ideology are in its pamphlet collection. At the second Northfield Student Conference in 1887, where 100 students arrived excited about missions, the leaders succeeded in producing a pamphlet entitled "An Appeal to the Churches." It was the first of a series of pamphlets that would issue from the SVM urging the need for an increased missionary effort. Generally short, 10 to

20 pages, and written in turgid prose, the pamphlets elaborated the Pierson arguments and explained the need for the SVM.

In 1890 11 numbered pamphlets appeared. Mott wrote the first one, giving the history of the SVM. Grace Wilder wrote issue No. 2, entitled "Shall I Go", giving the by now standard argument that the burden of proof rested with those who chose to stay. Robert Wilder explained the pledge of the SVM, Speer explained the workings of the college band, and W.W. Smith explained the work of the volunteers in the domestic churches.

Once the volunteers began to go to the mission field, they were often called to write pamphlets explaining the need for more missionaries in their respective countries. Hence there were a series of Macedonian calls issued by missionaries themselves: "An Appeal from China," "An Appeal from India," and "An Appeal from Japan." The appeal from Japan concluded with these urgent words: "Brothers and sisters, `come over and help us,' and *come now* [his emphasis]."[12] Yet the appeals were not always so benign. "An Appeal to the Churches" used heavy-handed guilt-inducing tactics: "Every tick of the watch sounds the death-knell of a heathen soul. Every breath we draw, four souls perish, never having heard of Christ."

George Sherwood Eddy in his 1893 pamphlet, "The Supreme Decision," appealed to students to make their career decisions based on Jesus' words in the Sermon on the Mount: "Seek ye first the kingdom of God."[13] If a Christian, he argued, had truly surrendered his life to Christ then seeking the kingdom of God ought to be the highest priority in life, and "the touchstone of your life in the choice of a profession." Then he listed some of the possible professions that might attract his college readers. For example, he argued that if one chose to enter the legal profession one could certainly act as a Christian lawyer and thereby advance the kingdom of God. But in doing this, he asked, was advancing the kingdom the highest motive or was it only secondary? Furthermore, the spiritual opportunities offered by the legal profession versus the ministry were not in proportion. Unless a student could conclude that being a lawyer offered a greater opportunity to advance the kingdom than the ministry, then the student could not faithfully say that the kingdom was the highest priority in his decision. Eddy concluded that, all things being equal, there were more than enough lawyers in the country, but the same could not be said of missionaries in the world. Therefore the conscientious student ought, like Charles G. Finney before him, to abandon the law to plead not "for men's temporal rights, but ... for men's eternal interests."[14]

Eddy presented similar arguments concerning the vocations of medicine, teaching, business, and even the ministry itself, and concluded, "the field is one. But it is because the field is one, that we plead for the neglected portion of that field with its even larger opportunity, yet far smaller supply of workers."[15]

To give graphic illustration to his argument, Eddy appended two charts showing either small white dots on a black surface, or small black dots on a white surface, which purportedly illustrated the disparity of domestic and foreign workers in the field. Charts such as these dramatically illustrated what should still have seemed quite obvious: that there were many Christian ministers and doctors in the West and few in the non-Christian East. Given the Bible's injunctions to proclaim the faith to all the world, this disparity was presented as a lack of faithfulness on the part of Western Christians and thereby became a spur for greater missionary effort.

With an interesting twist on a well-known Bible image, Eddy brought home his argument in yet another way, seeking to shame his complacent countrymen:

> Did He [Jesus] not teach that the preference was in favor of the lost sheep? He taught to leave the ninety and nine in the fold and to go out in the wilderness and find the one; but we leave the ninety and nine in the wilderness and crowd to the fold to feed the one."[16]

Eddy's pamphlet, originally published in 1893, was still in use two decades later. Others reiterated the ideas so current in the 1890s well into the Progressive Era. For example Samuel M. Zwemer wrote a pamphlet in 1911 entitled "Are More Foreign Missionaries Needed?", which repackaged the case made by Eddy for a new generation.

The Watchword Controversy

If the arguments to appeal for missionaries were enduring, so was the watchword of the movement, although it proved to be much more controversial. The watchword was accepted by the British version of the SVM, the Student Volunteer Missionary Union (SVMU) in 1896 at the Liverpool Convention. A discussion of the relative merits of the watchword was held by the executive committee of the SVMU, with Wilder defending the watchword and Frank Lenwood opposing it. Lenwood believed that the watchword, although in many ways helpful also caused difficulties. Its ambiguity left it open to many interpretations, and for many people it implied a prophecy rather than an ideal for the church to pursue. It invited a "religious mathematics," by which he meant the tendency of SVM speakers to argue simplistically that if a certain proportion of missionaries to non-Christians were achieved, then the world could be evangelized. His most telling comment was that the goal of evangelization was too narrow, and that what the Great Commission called for was not the mere proclamation of the gospel but the Christianization of the world.[17]

In the following year Dr. Gustave Warneck, the influential editor of *Allgemeine Missions Zeitschfift* (German Missions Journal), also attacked the watchword. Like Lenwood, he disliked the watchword because the mere heralding of the gospel by itinerating preachers, which the watchword implied, was too narrow a definition of what Christ preached and Paul practiced in the New Testament. Also, he opposed what he perceived to be the motivation behind the watchword, which was to bring about the second advent, arguing that men cannot "push forward the hands of the clock in advance of the true time."[18] In a letter to the Ecumenical Conference on Foreign Missions held in New York in 1900, Warneck continued the attack. "Mission history," he argued, "should teach us not to specify a time within which the evangelization of the world is to be completed. It is not for us to determine the times or the seasons, but to do in this our time what we can." Moreover, the church should avoid "catchwords", which are "romantic will o' the wisps." The watchword implied an undue haste that was inconsistent with the slow hard work needed to win souls:

> The Mission Command bids us go into all the world, not "fly".... The Kingdom of Heaven is like a field, in which the crop is healthily growing at a normal rate, not like a hothouse. Impatient pressing forward has led to the waste of much precious toil, & more than one old mission field has been unwarrantably neglected in the haste to begin work in a new field.[19]

In view of the mounting criticisms, Mott began collecting testimonials about the efficacy of the watchword, and eventually published a book that was at once an explanation and an apology for the watchword, as well as the most definitive statement of the purpose and motivation of the SVM ever written. *The Evangelization of the World in This Generation*, published in 1901, defined the watchword to mean not necessarily the achievement of conversions, but rather giving "all men an adequate opportunity to know Jesus Christ as their Savior and to become His real disciples." This definition precluded the simple heralding of the gospel as adequate to evangelization. Responding to Warneck by name, Mott eschewed the "hasty or superficial preaching of the Gospel," explaining that the volunteers fully recognized that evangelization necessitated "frequent repetition of the facts", "patient instruction," and surmounting the barriers of "language, age, grade of intelligence, heredity and environment." In addition to traditional preaching and personal persuasion, effective evangelization would include educational, literary, and medical missions work. "In a non-Christian land everything which manifests the spirit of Christ is in an important sense evangelistic."[20] The watchword in Mott's view did not mean the conversion of the world, for true Christianization of nations often takes centuries, but it did mean presenting the gospel in such a way that it would be understood, so that it would be knowledgeably accepted or rejected. Thus evangelism for Mott was only the first step in Christianization.

Moreover, the watchword was not theologically exclusive. Volunteers did not have to be premillennialist, Mott asserted, in order to embrace the Watchword. It "does not involve the entertaining or supporting of any special theory of eschatology." In fact "Men entertaining widely different opinions as to the second advent of Christ accept alike this view of world-wide evangelization."[21] The watchword was not a prophecy, neither did it set a time limit in which the task must be completed. It was a goal, and a statement of what would be humanly possible if a determined effort was made.

The watchword in Mott's opinion had been very effective in galvanizing the volunteers to action, giving to individuals a life's mission and to the organization a common purpose. Mott concluded his book with mounting hyperboles about the usefulness of the watchword.

> As a rallying cry it has been of great value, affording a strong ground of appeal to men to become volunteers. It has attracted the attention of the Church, lifted its faith and moved it to greater sacrifice and prayerfulness. It has kept before the volunteers as well as other Christians the universality and urgency of their purpose....it lends greater intensity to one's missionary zeal and activity. It prevents unnecessary delay. It leads to the study of what is involved in the evangelization of the world in a generation. It calls out enterprise, self-sacrifice and heroism, and stimulates hopefulness and faith. It brings to the individual the inspiration which results from union with many others having the same ideal and purpose.[22]

Despite the brilliant success of the SVM by the end of the first decade of the new century, and the inspirational role that the watchword had undeniably played in that success, old questions and arguments were again raised concerning the wisdom of its continued use. The arguments against it were raised again by Lenwood in an article in *The Student Movement* in 1909. Lenwood opposed the watchword for a number of reasons. He did not like its ambiguity, which led many to conclude that it was a human attempt to complete the conditions necessary for the second advent. Also the words "this generation" were ambiguous because the age boundaries of the term were not clear, and because the various ages of the volunteers implied, as Warneck phrased it, a "flying boundary." He opposed the watchword for its practical impossibility, and because undertaking the job on a world-wide scale in a single generation implied superficiality and poor workmanship.

Furthermore, he objected to the emphasis on evangelization rather than Christianization. The mere proclamation of the gospel was not a completion of the Great Commission, which also commanded teaching, baptizing and making disciples of the nations. In fact by emphasizing evangelization over Christianization, was it not possible that limited resources would be taken from important efforts to Christianize which may not be soon restored, so that the coming of the Kingdom would actually be delayed? Surely, "world-evangelization against a time limit," Lenwood admonished, "was not the best way to glorify God."

Moreover, Lenwood argued that Western Christians were yet unworthy to undertake to Christianize the world. "Suppose that the Church among the Kaffirs were in a position to evangelize the whole world, we should all be filled with the deepest misgivings, for we should feel the wide presentation of a crude form of Christianity to be a calamity of the most far-reaching kind." He did not want Britain's contemporary understanding of Christianity to be stamped on the world and determine its future religious history. "The Churches of far-off lands must bring the glory and the honor of the nations unto Him before we shall know enough of the Gospel's meaning for such a stupendous task." If a watchword was desired, let it be taken from the Bible. Lenwood suggested "Prepare ye the way of the Lord, make His paths straight", or "Thy Kingdom Come."[23]

Lenwood and others who opposed the Watchword did not so much defeat their opponents as wear them out. In the second decade of the twentieth century the SVMU simply stopped using the watchword. In 1922, when the SVMU decided to drop the watchword officially, Wilder, then president of the American SVM, asked to be allowed to come to Britain to defend the watchword before a final vote was taken. Tissington Tatlow, the head of the British movement, declined his offer, explaining that the watchword had not been a viable concern for more than a decade and therefore was not worth his effort to defend it. The watchword in America suffered a similar fate. Never officially dropped, it continued to be used in official statements issued by the organization up to the 1920s and last appeared as a banner over the quadrennial convention platforms at the 1924 convention.

Mott's Arguments for Missions

John Mott, as the Chairman of the Executive Committee of the SVM for a generation, as the chairman of every SVM convention through 1920, as the leading missionary statesman of the first quarter of the twentieth century, and as the writer of 19 books and an additional six-volume collection of addresses and papers, was a tireless promoter of missions. In his countless speaking engagements in the United States, and in his numerous world tours, Mott was also probably the outstanding apologist for missions and communicator of the missionary ideology in his time. Reviewing his addresses during the period of his leadership of the SVM, they appear remarkably consistent. And in the light of the larger body of missionary literature from the period, it is clear that Mott's words reflect not only his own ideas, but also the general thinking of the organization he led.

Mott believed, not surprisingly, that the central task of the church through the ages was missions. There is no reason to apologize for missions, he proclaimed in one address, for it is found in the Bible, the Apostles' Creed, the Lord's Prayer, in the concept of the Fatherhood of God and the brotherhood of man, and in the life of Christ who died for the whole world.[23] Referring to the centrality of missions for Christians, Mott asserted that "It must be pressed upon them that an active missionary spirit is inseparable from a real Christian life; and that a man may well question whether he is living the Christian life (i.e. having Christ live in him) if he is indifferent to the needs of half of the human race."[25]

Mott also believed that missions had a "reflex" effect on the domestic church. If Christians did not attempt to evangelize abroad, then they were guilty of hypocrisy. Quoting Archbishop Whately, Mott said, "If my faith be false I ought to change it, whereas if it be true I am bound to propagate it." In addition to hypocrisy, Mott feared "spiritual atrophy" if Americans failed to support missions. "Continuance in the sin of neglect," Mott solemnly averred, "arrests the life and stunts the growth." It also results in spiritual powerlessness, for "the commands with reference to the Holy Spirit are associated with bearing witness," and failure to bear witness abroad would result first in spiritual weakness, then worldliness, and finally desolation.[26]

Mott believed that one way to exhort young people into undertaking Christian missions was to present the great difficulty of the task before them. Mott did not shrink from pointing to the possibility of martyrdom on the missionary field. "Christ's appeal, when on earth, was to the heroic. Such an appeal always brought a heroic response, and always will. He never hid His scars to win a disciple."[27] Mott believed that the more difficult he made the task seem, the more it would appeal to the self-sacrificing idealism of his young audiences.

Mott anticipated the counter argument that the domestic need for evangelism, as well as education, medical care, and other material needs, was very great, and therefore Americans ought first to take care of their own problems before they attempted to meet the world's needs. Mott agreed that American needs were great, but countered that the needs of the world were also great, and, most important, the proportion of laborers was greater in the United States than in other lands. He estimated that in the United States there was one Christian worker for every 48 people, while in other lands the proportions might vary from one for every 100,000 as in Asia Minor, or one to undetermined millions as in China.[28]

Mott's hope and confidence may not have been ultimately based on numbers, organization, money, ability, plans, and enthusiastic conferences, but he saw the abundance of these as providential indications of ultimate success, and, therefore, strained through the filter of his faith, his talks were filled with this practical side of the missionary effort. He was clearly enamored of modern trends. He spoke with pride in 1910 that there were "now over 300 classes for the *scientific study* of foreign missions."[29] Aware of the Progressive Era's increasing reliance on and confidence in the expert, Mott spoke of missionaries as "experts", who are "face to face with the facts. They know the need. They have staked their lives upon the enterprise. They are a remarkable body of men. They are absolutely trustworthy."[30]

Like Pierson before him, Mott rhapsodized about modern advances in travel due to the railroad and steam ship. He marveled over the cable and telegraph systems that were quickly circling the globe, as well as news agencies, the Universal Postal Union, which together "have united ... the separated continents into one great nation." Most important, these advances "by increasing our knowledge of the heathen and their accessibility, thereby have increased our obligation."[32]

Mott valued many other advances and modern conveniences, which aided the missionary cause and proportionally increased Christian responsibility. Mott valued the printing press, because it allowed for rapid dissemination of Gospel information, and he appreciated the superiority of Western medicine, because it opened the hearts of the "heathen" to the gospel. Mott had a pragmatic opinion of Western colonialism, because the protection of Western governments eased mission work. He was also unsentimental about the financial power of American evangelical Christians, which Mott estimated to be $13 billion in total assets. If American Protestants had given only half of 1 percent of their wealth, he calculated, "their contribution to foreign missions would have been over $65,000,000, instead of less than $4,000,000."[32] If American and European Christians would be good stewards of their wealth, he concluded, then indeed the world could be evangelized in a single generation.

In his book *The Evangelization of the World in this Generation,* Mott conceded that world evangelization within his generation was not probable, but that was not the point. For Mott the point was that it was possible. There was no country in the world, he believed, where if vigorous efforts were made missionaries could not be sent. The open doors to missionaries around the world were for Mott a providential occurrence. He feared, however, that the open doors available to missionaries would not stay open indefinitely. Therefore, in Piersonesque language, he spoke of the "urgency" of the moment, of a missionary "crisis", and of a providential opportunity that the current generation alone was called to meet.[33] "There are strategic times as well as strategic places, and surely this is one of them. The present is not only our greatest opportunity, but so far as you and I are concerned it is our only opportunity. It will not come back if we miss it."[34] On another occasion he asked his audience, "When have so many nations been absolutely plastic, yet soon to set like plaster on the wall? Shall they set in pagan or Christian molds?"[35]

Often Mott's appeal was cast in military terms: "The summons is for nothing less than a great advance. A small advance will not do."[36] His addresses were filled with military metaphors: "forward movement," "advance," "strategic points," "battlefields of the Christian Church," "difficulties are the drill-ground of character." He called for a new "crusade" and a "world-wide war" on behalf of Christ. "The time has come to take the whole world into our plan. ... We must lay siege to the great citadels and fortresses as well as work along the lines of least resistance."[37] In addition to quoting Napoleon, he also often quoted Moltke, whom he described as "the great German military genius," who said "First ponder, then dare."[38] He quoted William James that the great need of American society was to discover and embrace the moral equivalent of war. James argued for something like what became the Peace Corps, but Mott believed that only world missions offered a challenge big enough and great enough "to call out the best energies of the minds and hearts of the American and British people, something that will preserve a pure faith and a triumphant spirit, and really preserve our religion. Without it I see no hope."[39]

Although Mott claimed to respect other religions and some of the good effects they could sometimes have, he was never a religious relativist. On his world tours he saw "the injustices, the cruelties, the abominations, the shame, and the degradation in the pathway of the working and influence of those religions."[40] Mott believed that only Christianity could provide the undergirding for civilization in the developing countries.

Mott also believed that missions was the special calling of Britain, Canada and America.[41] God, he said, had given to these nations the financial means, workforce, and technical ability to carry out the task to a successful conclusion. With these great means available, Mott concluded that the words of Christ were particularly apt for Anglo-Saxons: "Unto whomsoever much has been given, of him shall much be required." In addition to the material resources available, Mott argued that "our much includes the vision which God has been pleased to give to the Christians of the Anglo-Saxon race, as to no other race; and along with that he has given us the spirit of determination and of self-denial to help realize the vision."[42]

Mott could also speak disparagingly of the oriental nations as "those lower civilizations."[43] And, although he did not emphasize the point, he did believe that missionary work and the spread of civilization were linked, and that missionary work preceded the latter. "All true civilization," he asserted, "is found in the pathway of the missionary host."[44] For those who believed more in Western civilization than in Christianity, Mott's convictions were probably taken as a commonplace and compelling argument for missions. But Mott was aware that, while Christianity smoothed the path of civilization, the relationship was not always reciprocal, for there was often a stark contrast between Western Christendom and Christianity. "We must Christianize the impact of Christendom on the non-Christian world," Mott preached, complaining that "so many of the men who have represented the Christian lands of the West in political, commercial, and military pursuits and errands in the East, have so seriously misrepresented the faith and character of their home countries." One way to counter this trend, he suggested, was to continue to support the YMCA in foreign lands, for through this means young men abroad would come under an influence that would help to "safeguard their character, and at the same time enable them to exert a positive and aggressive influence on behalf of Christianity."[45]

Mott believed that one role of the missionary was to mediate between the West and East. Missionaries were not only in a position to present to "discerning Oriental minds in a concrete and winning way the best side, the ideal side, of our Western life – our Christian life," but also to interpret the East to the West through their literature and in person when they were on furlough. "Without a doubt," Mott boasted, "they constitute the greatest force for the promotion of friendship, good-will, and brotherhood between races."[46]

Although Mott lived at a time that in retrospect was the climax of the era of colonialism and often spoke its haughty ethnocentric language, he was remarkably prescient in his vision of what would later be known as "world Christianity." In a 1908 address he spoke of the "imperial character of our undertaking" and of "empire-building in terms of the world," yet he did not mean by this a colonial approach to missions. "Our policy will become more one of co-operation; less and less that of foreign control. Our spirit will become increasingly one of sympathy and service rather than one of domination." In this address, two years before the Edinburgh Conference of 1910, Mott lamented the "waste" in missionary effort, resulting from a duplication of effort between the various denominations. "God is unmistakably summoning us to a larger unity," he declared. "I firmly believe a carrying out of a comprehensive plan of co-operation in the missionary work of the various Christian communions would be the equivalent of doubling the missionary forces."[47]

*   *   *

In its arguments for world evangelization and for individuals to become missionaries, the SVM assumed the claims to uniqueness of the Christian faith, which included a Bible literally interpreted and the correctness of the Protestant evangelical faith against all the other Christian alternatives. This SVM ideology also assumed the inherent superiority of Western culture, and therefore the West's ability to uplift the "heathen" nations with the technology, education, and democratic ideals that were the fruits of two millennia of Christian culture. Finally it assumed the unique role and opportunity established by providence for the Anglo-Saxon race to evangelize the world. In short, the success of the SVM as a recruiter of missionaries rested squarely on its ability to exploit various assumptions of the Victorian world view.

The leaders of the SVM were not unaware that the foundations of this world view were being chiseled away by modern scientific ideas and methods. Higher criticism of the Bible, Darwinian science, cultural relativism, liberal theology were all clearly seen as the enemies of evangelical religion. The college students from whom they recruited their missionary force could not be insulated from these trends, and in fact were most susceptible to them. Although the SVM achieved great success in the milieu of late Victorian culture, its ability to adjust to a Christian audience that was slowly dividing into Fundamentalist and Modernist camps was not unlimited. And if the SVM's underlying assumptions were increasingly problematic in the late Victorian world, could it hope to flourish in a post-Victorian culture, when the ideas that gave it life were no longer taken for granted by the general population?

Chapter Five

CREATING A WORLD MOVEMENT

...the conflict which is to decide the destiny of the West, will be a conflict of institutions for the education of her sons, for purposes of superstition, or evangelical light; of despotism, or liberty.

--- Lyman Beecher[1]

As Americans moved west in the nineteenth century, they brought with them the institutions of their society that fostered culture: government, churches, and one-room school houses. Colleges were also established. In the first half of the century most of these colleges were founded by churches and run by clergymen. Lyman Beecher, who in 1832 was the first President of Lane Theological Seminary in Cincinnati, argued in *A Plea for the West* (1835) that institutions of higher education were crucial to creating a Christian culture in the West. It was a commonplace in the propaganda for home missions that Christian colleges would set the tone for the emerging civilization by providing its godly leaders. In the second half of the century the many secular state colleges established in the West were often seen as a possible threat to Christian civilization, and therefore converting the student bodies of these colleges to Christianity became a primary object of the YMCA and the YWCA.

While Americas in the nineteenth century, such as Beecher, were busy building Christian colleges or attempting to Christianize secular colleges, Christian missionaries were employing the same Christianizing and civilizing strategy by establishing numerous colleges in the mission fields. By the 1890s when college associations were well established in the United States, YMCA leaders began to dream of establishing associations in the colleges that by then existed around the world. If the intercollegiate idea could catch on in the colleges of Europe and in the non-Western nations, then they could become, in Mott's phrase, the "strategic points in the World's conquest" for Christianity. Student volunteer movements could be launched in all of these colleges, providing the missionary numbers necessary to achieve the goal of world evangelization in a single generation. This dream gained institutional form in 1895 with the establishment of the World's Student Christian Federation (WSCF).

Trail Blazing

Luther Wishard was in many ways a rather unimpressive man. Over weight and nearly blind, possessing neither a handsome visage nor a commanding presence, he was not a great speaker or a natural leader. Nevertheless, Wishard was instrumental, if not indispensable, in launching the Christian intercollegiate movement as a world organization.[2]   Wishard's vision of a world-wide Intercollegiate YMCA began to take shape in February 1878, when still in his first year as the secretary of the intercollegiate movement. Hearing of a college group of Christians in Japan who wanted to associate with Christians in Amherst planted the seed in Wishard's mind of a world-wide student Christian organization. Although Wishard originally conceived of an exclusively American movement to non-Christian lands, he was prompted to include European universities in his plans when about two years into his secretaryship he received a letter from a Swiss YMCA asking about the American movement and making apparent its plans to establish its own college associations. Although in the first decade of his college work Wishard would be focused on the immediate goal of strengthening and extending the American intercollegiate movement, the greater goal of extending that movement world-wide was never far from his mind.

At a state convention in Milwaukee, Wisconsin, in 1880 Wishard met Frank K. Sanders, the son of missionaries in Ceylon. At the time Sanders was an undergraduate at Ripon College, and Wishard was able to inspire in Sanders the desire to establish a college association at Ripon, a goal that he later achieved. In 1882 Sanders wrote to Wishard that he was returning to Ceylon to teach for four years at Jaffna College. Wishard and Sanders kept up a correspondence, chiefly discussing the possibilities of establishing an association at Jaffna. On March 15, 1884 Sanders wrote to Wishard that he had established the first college association outside of North America at Jaffna College. Several more associations followed, one at a Normal Training School in Tillipally, Ceylon, and two in India, at Ahmednagger and Pasumalai. The credit for these associations must go to Sanders, but from 1880 Wishard had given regular encouragement and inspiration through his correspondence. Conversely, Sander's success further encouraged Wishard as to the feasibility of an international movement.[3]

While studying for the ministry at Andover Seminary, Harlan P. Beach also met the ubiquitous Wishard. Beach was interested both in college associations and in missionary work. When he left for China in 1883, he promised Wishard that he would seek to establish a college association there. When the time seemed ripe to fulfill his promise, Beach contacted Wishard to ask how to proceed. The result was that in 1885 the first student YMCA in China was established at the Tungchou Academy and Seminary.[4]

During his first European tour in the summer and fall of 1881, Wishard spoke of the American intercollegiate movement to a variety of European Christian forums in England, Germany and Scotland. In 1884 James B. Reynolds, who had just graduated from Yale and was going to Germany for further study, was pressed by Wishard to look for an opportunity to start a German college association. Reynolds, who had been active in the Yale association, took up the challenge, and in the college year of 1884-85 he established the first college YMCA in Europe at the University of Berlin.[5]

In 1885 Wishard turned his attention to the possibility of extending the college movement to Great Britain. His invitation to J.E.K. Studd to tour American colleges in the 1885-86 school year had the double purpose of exciting American college students about missions and also exciting Studd about the possibilities of establishing American-style college associations in Great Britain. Studd was impressed with what he saw, but he declined to be the pioneer of a British student movement. He considered the obstacles too great in

Britain, and he was committed to his studies at the London Polytechnic Institute. Undaunted, Wishard did not give up on spreading the student movement to Britain, and his relationship with Studd would prove invaluable later.

By 1885-86 with the burgeoning growth of the collegiate YMCA and YWCA in the United States, the promising recent initiation of the Inter-seminary Alliance and the Medical Missionary conferences, and now the development of college associations in India, Ceylon, China and Europe, Wishard could give serious thought to an extended world tour to assess the possibilities of establishing college associations around the world. The Mount Hermon student conference of 1886, already noted for being the birth place of the SVM, also provided Wishard with another opportunity to pursue his world vision.

As a step in the direction of establishing links with other student movements, Wishard formed a committee near the conclusion of the Mount Hermon conference to issue a letter to all the mission colleges to extend greetings from the students of America. The letter recounted the events leading up to the advent of the Mount Hermon One Hundred, and then stated the students' eagerness "to establish permanent lines of communication between you and ourselves, by which you can keep us constantly informed as to the needs of your work, and its claims upon all of our students." Those interested were directed to contact the College Secretary of the International Committee, L. D. Wishard.

Following the 1886 Mount Hermon Conference, Wishard received a letter from Sanders, who announced that in returning home from the subcontinent via the near East he had succeeded in establishing college associations in the "Synon Province College, Eirmi, Central Turkey and Aintab."[6] He also received letters from Beach in China and another missionary in Japan, announcing that associations had been established in Tungchou and in the Methodist College in Tokyo.

In 1887-88 Wishard took a more direct hand in sending missionaries to Japan and India. Learning that the government colleges in Japan wanted American English teachers, Wishard saw a missionary opportunity. Working inter-denominationally, he helped to establish the Foreign Education Commission, which would provide funds for the passage to Japan of missionaries to teach English. At the 1887 Northfield Conference, Wishard enlisted John T. Swift, and eventually at least five others, who traveled to Japan in 1888 where they proved helpful when Wishard arrived during his world tour two years later. Wishard also worked to secure the Rev. Dr. Jacob

Chamberlain of India to speak at the 1887 Northfield Conference, where he appealed for American secretaries for Indian City Associations that were needed. When a formal appeal came from the Madras missionaries for YMCA city association secretaries, Wishard secured David McConaughy, secretary of the Philadelphia Association, who in Madras also proved very helpful during Wishard's tour.[7]

Having failed to convince Studd to pursue a British student moment, Wishard invited Henry Drummond, a noted Scottish professor of natural science and a student evangelist, to the 1887 Northfield conference in the hopes that he would be persuaded to launch an American-style student movement in Britain.[8] Drummond's place in the broader student movement is important both for its own sake and for the light it sheds on the Anglo-American relationship.

As the natural outgrowth of his religious and scientific interests, Drummond published *Natural Law in the Spiritual World*, an attempt to reconcile modern science with evangelical Christianity. A large part of Drummond's appeal to students was his conflation of traditional evangelical piety with liberal views on the doctrine of the inspiration of the Scriptures. Drummond embraced the Higher Criticism of the Bible, believing that God spoke provisionally and in non-scientific terms to the primitive Hebrew people. Thus he saw development in the Bible. He also saw human elements in the authorship of the Bible. At the Northfield conference, he rejected the claim of a previous year's speaker, probably James H. Brooks, that a Christian needed "to crucify his intellect." Rather, he appealed to the Northfield students not only to be tolerant of others, but to accept that "other men can see bits of truth as well as ourselves."[9] When Drummond returned to Northfield in 1893, the conservative speakers urged Moody to confront him about his liberal positions. Moody declined. None of the early leaders of the student movement – Moody, Wishard, Ober, Mott or others – would allow the great aim of evangelism to be side-tracked by theological matters. For them Drummond was an evangelical Christian, who embraced the holiness movement, and was a successful evangelist of students – nothing else mattered.[10]

Following the Northfield conference, Ober arranged for Drummond to tour American colleges on the East coast and to speak at a Chautauqua meeting. Wishard hoped that Drummond would inspire the American students, which he did. "He fully met our expectations, yes highly surpassed them, in the impression he made upon the students," Wishard concluded. Then he added, "but greatly to our disappointment we found him utterly disinclined to carry anything home with him in the way of organized methods."[11] Drummond indicated his disdain for organization, techniques and methods during his address at Northfield on the student work in Scotland. First, the success of his evangelism was not widely advertised, because, as Drummond explained, "we felt it to be such a sacred thing that we were afraid of losing the blessing that was coming upon us. We find that reports of religious work tend to cheapen and destroy the power and delicacy of the work."[12] When questioned by Moody as to the staffing of his organization, Drummond equivocated: "Nobody knows who runs this work. We have no college association." He eschewed a formal organization because he believed that it might create barriers for some students to join. Wishard offered another reason: "Drummond was an individualist; he was not constituted to comprehend and appreciate, much less employ, methods and details of organization."[13] Here again the British and Americans differed. But this is not to say that because they differed there was no mutual appreciation and respect. Mott summed up the importance of Wishard's efforts years later: "Professor Drummond and Mr. Studd furthered mutual understanding between British and American students and helped greatly to prepare the way for some permanent bond between them."[14]

Without either Studd or Drummond to launch an American-style student movement in Britain, Wishard determined to go to the British universities himself and invite students in Moody's name to return with him to Northfield for the summer conference of 1888. He planned to devote himself "to fully saturating them with the spirit and methods of the American Movement and then send them back to their respective Universities to do as students for their fellows what they after all could do better even than Studd, the alumnus, or Drummond, the pro-fessor."[15] After this idea suddenly "seized, gripped, [and] possessed" Wishard one morning in early March, he wasted no time implementing it, and arrived in Liverpool on April 2, 1888.

Brandishing the name of Moody, and making the most of his British connections, Wishard presented his plans to the British students. Through the agency of Studd he spoke at Cambridge and Oxford, and through Drummond he spoke at Edinburgh and Glasgow. Soon he was receiving invitations to speak at city associations. Then, through several admirers of Moody in London, Wishard raised a funding supplement to provide for 11 students to attend Northfield. The students of Utrecht in Holland heard of Wishard's mission and commissioned a student of their own to attend the American summer conference, and Wishard was easily able to secure ten British students to fill the 11 spots available.

Following his British tour, Wishard traveled on to Germany to attempt to secure other delegates, but seeing that the German student movement was not as well developed as even the British movement, and also wanting to attend the World's Conference of the YMCA in Stockholm in August, Wishard decided to forego the Northfield conference that summer. He secured Reynolds to escort the 11 students to Northfield so that he could spend the summer in Europe exploring the possibilities of establishing European student Christian movements.

Wishard made several important inroads into continental Christianity that summer. Working in Germany with Christian Phildius and Count Packler of the Berlin City Association to promote a German student movement, Wishard secured Fritz Mockert to pioneer what became the German Student Christian Alliance.[16] At the World's Conference of the YMCA, he met with the Scandinavian students to discuss the American student movement. He also met the new General Secretary of the Stockholm City Association, Karl Fries, and convinced him of the importance of the student movement. Fries later became the first president of the WSCF.

Returning to New York in early September, Wishard spent only three months in the United States before leaving from San Francisco for his long-planned world tour. Prior to departing, however, he was able to launch one more European student movement. While in Germany he had received a request from a Scottish woman Miss Jane Howard, who was working with college students in Paris and wanted Wishard to come for a few days to help with a work that was not going well. Pressed for time, Wishard declined, but he recommended a full-time association secretary to create a Parisian student movement. Once back in the United States Wishard secured financing, and was able to appoint James B. Reynolds to the position. Using Paris as a base, Reynolds worked with students throughout Europe for three years, thus laying the groundwork for a unified European student movement that led directly to the formation of the WSCF.

Reynolds toured every European country except Spain and Portugal, visiting 44 universities. Everywhere he went he told students of the American student movement and encouraged the development of national movements in Europe. Often working behind the scenes, he helped to bring about student conferences in Germany, Scandinavia and Scotland. Also he selected a steady stream of European students to attend the annual Northfield conference. "These delegations on their return," Mott later commented, "did much to quicken the interest of their comrades in the Christian student movement."[17] Writing of his European experiences in *The Intercollegian* between 1889 and 1891, Reynolds also helped not only to inform but to interest American students in the activities of their European counterparts.

Reflecting on his experience among European students in an address before the Universities' Congress, at the World's Columbian Exposition, 1893, Reynolds suggested that the predominant characteristic of Americans in contrast to Europeans was their practical activity: "In America, if a man makes a discovery, he immediately embodies it in a machine, or he organizes a society and launches a propaganda to sustain it. In Europe, he merely writes a book, and trusts to the diffusion of knowledge to make it known." Reynolds conceded that the European approach tends to produce more "serious thought," and "greater conscientiousness and deeper spirituality," but that this "is much less certain to achieve a `forward movement.' " Reynolds concluded his address by urging that American and European Christians needed to continue to work at more open communications, and develop a willingness to benefit from each other's virtues.[18]

To this later sentiment Wishard, had he been present, would surely have given a hearty yea and amen. By the end of 1888, with Mott prepared to take his place as the student secretary of the Intercollegiate YMCA, Wishard was ready to act on his feeling. He procured financing from private sources, securing at least one pledge of $1000 a year from John Wanamaker, then the Postmaster General and also a long-time financial supporter of Moody.[19] Later Wishard boasted that Wanamaker read the biennial correspondence he issued during his tour to President Harrison in the White House.[20] But for the moment, visions of self-importance aside, Wishard prepared to travel around the world, merely doing the initial work of trail blazing like his hero Livingstone and hoping that others would soon follow.

Association students were kept regularly informed of Wishard's four-year tour as his steady flow of letters, about 60 in all, were published variously in *The Watchman, The Young Men's Era,* and *The Intercollegian.* Leaving San Francisco in December 1888, Wishard traveled to Japan, India, Celon, China, the Middle East, Turkey, and Europe.

Wishard described for his readers some of the high points of his tour as well as those events that were merely interesting. He related that the work went so well in Tokyo that it was difficult to find buildings large enough to hold the audiences who wanted to attend. At Nagasaki "over 50 students pledged themselves to enter immediately upon earnest investigation of Christianity." At Okogama packed meetings were being held in a hall holding more than 1,600. On the first night Buddhist priests attempted to disrupt the meeting, but the students themselves ensured order by threatening to eject disturbers.[21]

Writing in the *Intercollegian* after his stay in Foochow, China, Wishard asserted that this experience demonstrated that association techniques used in America could also be effective among Chinese students.[22] This may have been one of the ideas Wishard was testing on his round-the-world tour. Writing in his memoirs two decades later, he sounded more assured of this approach than he may have been at the time: "I found when I entered into the student life of Asia enough of difficulties to intimidate the bravest, so I adopted the policy at the very beginning of dealing with situations there just as I would do at home. I often avoided obstacles just because I did not sufficiently realize their existence to seriously reckon with them."[23] Commenting on the Tungchow Association, Wishard pronounced it "the most thoroughly organized student's Association in all Asia." The association was very successful in its use of American techniques, which Wishard listed: Bible study, devotional meetings, "personal work" in evangelizing, addresses enlivened by the use of a magic lantern, regular religious meetings, and monthly foreign missions meetings (the association was then supporting a student in a Zulu mission in Natal.)[24] Apparently, then, without much fear of cultural distinctions fine or great, Wishard was ready to leave an American stamp on college students all over the world. For Wishard, the lesson of China was that what worked on Main Street could work on any street.

During the first three years of his trip, which included Japan, India and China, Wishard believed that he had achieved good results. In the year that remained of his trip, however, Wishard experienced largely frustration. For the most part it involved a traversal of generally barren mission fields in the Middle East and Asia Minor, in which Wishard often spent days at a time traveling on horseback moving from one isolated mission station to another.

Summing up his four-year world tour, Wishard counted 139 city associations and 43 student associations in the 20 mission countries he had visited in Asia. He added two student associations in European Turkey and one in Bulgaria. His four-year odyssey to survey the possibilities of establishing student associations around the world was a remarkable achievement and led inevitably to the establishment of the WSCF three years later.

Wishard promulgated the lessons he learned from his tour in a book entitled *A New Programme of Missions: A Movement to make the Colleges of all lands centers of Evangelization* (1895).[25] He recounted how the missionary department of the Intercollegiate YMCA had in effect expanded into the SVM, and how the student movement in the United States now included 500 institutions with about 30,000 members. He recounted how the movement had expanded to Europe, and he discussed the 216 missions he had visited in Asia and Eastern Europe, arguing that foreign college students had the aggressiveness, spirituality and financial ability to make a successful world movement. The college associations formed, he explained, would not be in competition with the churches, but rather forces for unity, and college students, he argued, as the "educated class" of the East, were its most logical leaders.

Wishard's proposal was for the West to produce 30,000 missionaries and distribute them to Christian colleges around the world, a half-dozen for every 200,000 people in the non-Christian world. The mission colleges would be strategically placed stations, and their goal would be to become missionary producing institutions that could evangelize their own lands. Because, as in the United States, the college associations would be working in union with city associations, Wishard believed that they would be compelled to "practical, aggressive methods of Christian work which characterize the Sunday School, the YMCA, and other Christian enterprises directed by business men." Wishard's sweeping plan for world evangelization would rely on indigenous missionaries, trained and energized by Western institutions, to provide the necessary numbers to make a success of the "present crusade of evangelization, which it is hoped may be the last."[26]

Creating the WSCF

The American leaders of the Student Movement in the last two decades of the nineteenth century increasingly strove to make their movement international. Decades before indigenous churches began to struggle for a larger share in the leadership of the Christian religion in their own nations, Wishard had already envisioned their indispensability to world evangelization and taken the first steps to make his dream a reality. Also, in the first half of the 1890s the

European seeds that Americans had been planting for a decade were at last showing fruit. During these years, Britain, Scandinavia and Germany all developed organized student movements, which by 1895 were ready to be organized into a single federation.

The seven universities of the four Scandinavian countries were apparently chagrined into pursuing greater unity when in the summer of 1889 they received the simple message of the Japanese students of Kyto, "Make Jesus King." When at Wishard's urging the Kyto students had sent their message to the Northfield conference, Richard Morse, the General Secretary of the YMCA, relayed the message to Karl Fries in Christiania. When Fries read the letter to the Scandinavian Missionary Conference, the general reaction was expressed by K. M. Eckhoff of Norway: "If students can gather round Jesus Christ as their King over there in the Far East, why not also here in the north?"[27] In 1890 the first Scandinavian Christian student conference was held, and later all four nations organized national student movements.

British students received a more direct impetus for organization. The British student Christian movement, despite Moody's visits, Wishard's machinations, the "Cambridge Seven's" example, and Drummond's evangelism, had thus far failed to congeal into an organization. This changed with the arrival in Britain of Robert Wilder. In May 1891 Wilder graduated from Union Theological Seminary. He then accepted an appointment from the Presbyterian Board of Foreign Missions to be a non-denominational missionary to students in India. On his way to India, however, he decided to tour Europe and specifically Great Britain to advance the cause of missions among students. Addressing the Keswick conference in July 1891, Wilder made what was generally agreed to be a tremendous impression on British students. He simply retold the story of the Student Volunteer Movement and matter-of-factly presented the needs of the mission field and the command of Christ to go. In response, he received a variety of speaking invitations from the British universities, which he deferred taking up until January 1892 due to illness.

Beginning in Edinburgh at Drummond's Oddfellow's meeting, Wilder toured the British universities – Glasgow, Aberdeen, Cambridge, Oxford, London – telling the story of the SVM and urging on the British the need to launch their own student missionary movement. The lack of any intercollegiate organization was a great hinderance, but Wilder succeeded in persuading the British to hold a convention of British universities in Edinburgh, April 1892, with representatives from all the institutions to which he had spoken plus those from Ireland. With Wilder himself presiding, the convention formed the Student Volunteer Missionary Union of Great Britain and Ireland. Wilder then traveled to the Scandinavian countries, where he addressed students and attended the second conference of Scandinavian students, urging them to form a single SVM, which they finally did in 1897.

While Wishard, Wilder, Reynolds, Fries and others played important roles in the growing movement toward a world organization of student Christians, it was left to John R. Mott to finally knit the separate threads into a single fabric. Early in 1894, Mott wrote years later, he "was seized with the conviction that the time had at last arrived when a world-wide union of Christian students might be achieved."[28]

In the first half of the 1890s as the growth of the collegiate YMCA and the SVM gained increasing international attention, Mott also gained the notice of the Protestant Christian world as the leader of these movements. While on a European speaking tour in 1894, he received invitations to attend student conferences in the summer of 1895 from organizations in Great Britain, Germany, Scandinavia and Switzerland. Latter on, he was also invited to lend his assistance to an evangelistic campaign among Indian students planned for the winter of 1895-96. In addition he was invited to visit Japanese students in 1896. These six invitations led him to decide that the time was right to make an extended two year world tour of the student Christian world for the purpose of creating a federation of college associations.

Later that fall Mott and Wishard agreed that the time had arrived to organize a world federation. They received approval from the supervisory committee of the North American Student Movement and the Foreign Department of the International Committee of the YMCA. Through correspondence with the British, Mott had secured an agreement to establish a union between the American and British student movements. Meeting at the Keswick summer conference in 1895, the British and Americans agreed to delay the formal creation of a federation until they could attempt to bring in the German and Scandinavian student movements as charter members.

Mott, Wishard, and a delegate from England, J. Rutter Williamson, then travelled together to the German Conference at Grosse-Allmarode. In Germany, due largely to the efforts of Fritz Mockert, an annual national student conference had been held since 1889, and student associations were slowly gaining in strength. By the summer of 1895 the German student movement was large enough to form the German Student Christian Alliance. And despite the initial opposition of Packler, due to his suspicions of anything Anglo-American, and his unwillingness to entrust power to a student delegation, the Germans also agreed to seek to form a world federation. Mott, Wishard, Williamson, and now the German representative Johannes Siemsen, then proceeded to the Scandinavian student conference at Vadstena, Sweden.

The Scandinavian Student Conference at Vadstena, August 13-18, was held in the castle of Vadstena, which had not been occupied for 300 years. Windows, furniture, and special lighting were all arranged to make the castle habitable, and in the end all agreed that a more scenic and romantic location for the launching of the new organization could not have been found. The surroundings suggested an historical allusion to Mott: "Never since the Wartburg sheltered the great German reformer when he was translating the Bible for the common people, has a medieval castle served a purpose fraught with a blessing to all mankind."[29]

Mott presented the plan of world-wide federation to the entire conference. And with the delegates approval, Karl Fries of Sweden and K.M. Eckhoff of Norway met with the American, British and German representatives. Luther Wishard was designated to represent the Student Christian Movement in Mission Lands. Thus the four major intercollegiate movements of Europe and America, and those of the mission lands, were all represented at Valstena.

Meeting in what Mott described as "four long sessions," the delegates drafted a tentative constitution that would serve until the first federation convention could be held in 1897. Mott proposed that the organization be a true federation of student organizations, rather than simply a union of intercollegiate YMCAs around the world, which was Wishard's original vision. "It would be better to encourage the Christian students in each country to develop national Christian student movements of their own," Mott explained, "adapted in name, organization and activities to their particular genius and character, and then to link these together in some simple yet effective federation."[30] Three tests for admission were agreed to: "(a) The movement should comprise a group of universities. (b) Its objects should be in harmony with the objects of the Federation. (c) It should afford evidences of stability, including a permanent supervisory committee."[31] The objects of the federation would be to unite student Christians from around the world, to gather information about students from all countries, to promote evangelism and Christian nurture on college campuses, and to make college campuses the "strategic points in the world's conquest."

The pride of small student movements was assuaged, and the fear of Anglo-Saxon dominance offset, by giving every national or international organization in the WSCF one vote on a general committee. To ensure that small organizations would not be overrun, the committee elected Karl Fries to be the Chairman of the committee, a position he held until 1920. The committee then elected Johannes Siemsen Vice-Chairman, John Mott General Secretary, J. Rutter Williamson Corresponding Secretary, and Luther Wishard Treasurer.

Mott then set off on a world tour that took 20 months and repeated Wishard's tour but in reverse order. Following Wishard's strategy to accomplish the evangelization of the world, Mott believed that colleges throughout the world could be the bases from which the world would be won for Christ – hence the title of the book that detailed the events of his world tour, *Strategic Points in the World's Conquest* (1897). If colleges were to be the training centers for world evangelization, the first step in any given college would be to organize a student YMCA and then promote within that association a Student Volunteer Movement for Home Missions, which would be made up of people dedicated to full time Christian service within their own country. Armed with this strategy, Mott set out to conquer the world for his Lord.

The first lap of Mott's tour was largely exploratory. Traveling through the traditionally Catholic countries of Italy, France, Austria and Hungry, he noted a few glimmers of hope for Protestant missions, but in general he concluded that Protestantism would have to fight a long uphill battle to win over these nations. Moving next to Constantinople, he personally witnessed atrocities against the Armenians, who he described as being "shot down like dogs" by the "barbarous Ottoman Government."[32] Finally, working his way through Syria, Palestine and the Nile Valley, Mott enjoyed some evangelistic successes at the YMCA in Nazareth, the Syrian Protestant College at Beirut, and the Training College at Asyut. His most fruitful work, however, lay ahead in Ceylon, India, Australasia, China and Japan.

Though Mott was a widely acclaimed student evangelist, perhaps his greatest talent in fostering the Student Movement lay in the practical areas of facilitating the creation of student organizations and in promoting the methods of the American Associations. Arriving in Ceylon, where he spent the better part of December 1895, Mott worked with Robert Wilder and others to hold a conference at Jaffna College for the eight Christian educational institutions of the island. Mott then moved on to India, where he spent about 11 weeks and visited about 30 educational institutions. With rising student interest and the active encouragement of Mott, the Indian National Council of the Young Men's Christian Association assembled and created a college department. The result was the unification of the 12 Indian and the 10 Ceylon college associations into one organization to be called the Intercollegiate Young Men's Christian Association of India and Ceylon. At the conclusion of the Indian conferences a final meeting was held by the Indian leaders in Madras to determine how to organize those who had volunteered for full Christian service during the conferences. The result was the creation of the Student Volunteer Movement for India and Ceylon. Among the 10 present were some old American hands: Wilder, Forman and Mott. They appointed Sherwood Eddy to be the first traveling secretary – Eddy at that time was working as the YMCA secretary for India of the American International Committee. There were then three SVM organizations in the world: one in North America, one in Britain and now one in India and Ceylon.

Mott spent the next four months touring the colleges of Australasia (Australia, New Zealand, Tasmania, and the islands of the South Pacific). This tour was added en route at the instigation of members of the Student Volunteer Missionary Union of Great Britain, which also agreed to pay the additional expenses. In touring the colleges Mott found only five student Christian organizations. He convinced them to reorganize themselves as student YMCAs. He also organized Associations in 20 other educational institutions, getting them all to agree to use the American techniques of Bible study, personal work, and missionary study, among others. Holding a convention in Melbourne, the student groups formed the Australasian Student Christian Union and organized a SVM as a part of the new union.

Mott next traveled to China, where news of the success of his Indian conferences preceded him and resulted in a united call from Chinese missionaries for Mott to conduct similar conferences for them. D. Willard Lyon, the YMCA secretary in China from the American International Committee, organized four- to six-day conferences from August through October in Chefoo, Peking, Shanghai and Foochow, and two-day conferences in Tientsin and Hankow. He had found five student associations in China when he arrived, and after visiting nearly all of the colleges in the nation, he organized 22 more associations. At a concluding convention in Shanghai, the Chinese students voted to unite their associations into the College Young Men's Christian Association of China with Lyon as the General Secretary of the new organization. Mott mentioned that China by this time had nearly 200 student volunteer missionaries mostly from America and Canada, but with a few from Britain. As the conferences proceeded, the Anglo-American volunteers organized a SVM for China, with the details finalized and then unanimously accepted at the Convention.

Proceeding on to Japan, where he spent 12 weeks, Mott found only eight student associations. After a successful tour of the country organized by John Swift, secretary in Japan of the American International Committee, Mott boasted that he successfully reorganized three student associations, added 20 more, and facilitated 215 conversions. At the culminating convention held in Tokyo, with only two-thirds of the associations attending due to the resumption of classes, student delegates formed the Student Young Men's Christian Association Union of Japan and were admitted to the WSCF. Mott did not attempt to create a SVM, as he judged the student movement was not yet ready for it in Japan.

Summarizing his tour, Mott reported that he had visited 22 countries, 144 educational institutions, organized 70 new student YMCAs, organized five national intercollegiate organizations, saw the beginning of 11 Christian publications, inducted 12 countries as corresponding members of the WSCF, saw 2,200 commit to keeping the morning watch, and witnessed 505 people accept Jesus Christ as their savior. Finally, he saw 300 students commit to become student volunteers for home missions. Relative to the task of world evangelization, these figures may seem paltry. For Mott and his generation, however, his efforts to create a world-wide student organization were tremendously successful, and laid the groundwork for the future accomplishment of their lofty goals.

In addition to the nine intercollegiate organizations that now made up the WSCF, two other organization were later added, and two others were later organized from existing national participants. The most important of them was in South Africa. Organizing the intercollegiate movement in South Africa was largely the work of Wishard and Donald Fraser, a British SVM leader. Andrew Murray, a famous South African preacher and holiness writer, was quickly converted to the new movement and acted as sponsor for Wishard and Fraser, personally organizing much of the tour by writing letters of introduction and giving instructions to Christian leaders in all of the colleges in the colonies. The tour concluded with a student convention in Stellenbosch in July 1896, with nearly 500 representatives from 30 colleges. The result was the creation of the Student's Christian

Association of South Africa, which joined the WSCF at its Williamstown conference in July 1897. Also, at this convention, a previously formed student missionary organization became the Missionary Committee of the Student's Christian Association, the South African SVM.[33]

The Significance of the WSCF

By the beginning of the new century Student Volunteer Movements stretched around the globe, and although this is not the place for a extended history of the SVMs associated with the WSCF, some of the broad outlines of this American missionary expansion can be given. Every other year the WSCF issued a questionnaire to its member organizations in an attempt to obtain useful statistics of the world student movement. A tabulation of the figures given in the *Reports of Student Christian Movements*, issued between 1897 and 1923, indicate that by 1920 the various Student Volunteer Movements of the WSCF had recruited at least 11,079 missionaries. Of this total America and Canada are responsible for 8,140 and Britain for 2,322, so that Anglo-American missionaries account for 94.5% of the SVM missionaries in the world. Next in numbers sent are the Australasians with 181, the South Africans with 161, and continental European with 275 missionaries sent.[34]

Not included in these missionary figures are the home missionaries recruited in mission lands. This is in part due to the wording of the questionnaires. The WSCF invariably asked for an accounting of the number of missionary volunteers, but indigenous professional Christian workers rarely saw themselves as missionaries. However, often in response to the question regarding the SVM in their lands, the respondent would lament the absence of an active SVM. This is still not to say that volunteers were not recruited. The reports occasionally give tantalizingly vague information or hints about recruitment for home missions. Writing about China in the 1899-1900 report, D. Willard Lyon noted monthly missionary meetings, a missionary committee doing evangelistic work, and 260 volunteers. The 1914-15 report on China noted 39 Volunteer Bands in 10 schools and a Student Volunteer Movement for the Ministry (begun in 1910) with two full-time secretaries. The 1922-23 report stated that since 1910 the home missionaries recruited by the SVM for the Ministry included 160 then working in various churches, and many more in other forms of Christian service or still in school.[35]

From India the reports constantly bemoaned the failure to create a strong SVM, yet the reports also noted student evangelistic work, including "open air preaching, the conduct (sic) of Sunday schools and the circulation of Christian literature."[36] In 1905 Lydia Mary Cooke reported the formation of the Women's Home Missionary Society of India, directed at Eurasian and English women in India. The 1910-11 report noted no national organization, but did note five local Volunteer Unions with at least 33 volunteers and 26 volunteers then in service. Also the schools continued to promote evangelistic work, such as teaching in the Sunday schools and street preaching. The 1922-23 report noted "Home Missionary" societies in the churches and that, "generally speaking, missionary societies look to the Movement for their workers" and that "a number" of volunteers had recently been recruited.

While it can not be shown statistically that college associations produced "home missionaries," this is what the anecdotal evidence indicates. Also, the fact that the non-Western nations did generally produce indigenous churches suggests that recruitment, though not formally pursued through an organized SVM for Home Missions, did occur informally.

Creating the WSCF cannot be attributed merely to Wishard's trail blazing, Wilder's inspiration, or Mott's organization. Throughout the second half of the nineteenth century Protestant missionaries, American and European, had been founding colleges in non-Christian lands in order to introduce Western knowledge to Africa and Asia and to create an indigenous, educated Christian elite on these continents. The missionaries who founded these organizations had always hoped that they would produce the indigenous leaders who would both supply the leadership of the church and also be the principle means of affecting long-term social changes. America's Student Movement leaders, through the creation of the WSCF, simply helped to bring that goal into sharper focus for students and mission educators alike.

Yet, while it must be admitted that the Student Movement leaders were largely building on what had gone before, they also brought something qualitatively new to missions. The Progressive belief in large efficient organizational structures is clearly seen in the creation of the WSCF. The SVM may have lauded the heroic early pioneers of missions, but their romanticism was largely confined to their imaginations. The WSCF was a religious parallel to the huge corporate structures that emerged in America after the Civil War, and which Americans learned to master through scientific management in the Progressive era. With the creation of the WSCF the romantic age of missions had now passed and a new generation of managers and experts had taken over.

Although Wishard's and Mott's vision of a world-wide Student Movement that would promote home missions did not achieve its goal of realizing the watchword, it did demonstrate the possibility of ecumenical cooperation on the mission field, and it gave a large number of mission leaders practical experience in a far-flung ecumenical organization. Moreover, missionary leaders by the late nineteenth century were growing aware that interdenominational cooperation in mission lands, by avoiding duplication of effort or unnecessary competition, would further the cause of world evangelization. Consequently, missionaries hailed the creation of the WSCF as a great achievement.

Fifteen years after the formation of the WSCF, the ecumenical idea among missionaries had developed sufficiently to receive an official endorsement and launch its own nascent world-wide organization. Two great Protestant missionary conferences were held in 1888 and 1900, and a third conference, which was held in Edinburgh, Scotland, in June 1910, would be the watershed in the history of twentieth-century ecumenism. Preparations for the Edinburgh Conference were pursued by a 19-member international committee over two years. The influence of the Student Movement on the conference was notable both for the SVM and WSCF leaders that took a major part in its preparation (especially Mott, Fries, Oldham, and Tatlow), and for the optimism and ecumenical spirit that it had helped to foster over an entire generation.

Mott chaired the convention, running the proceedings with a skillfulness that dazzled the international gathering of 1,200 missionary and church leaders. With the twin themes of the missionary goal of world evangelization and the need for denominational cooperation to achieve that goal, the Edinburgh Conference opened a new chapter in ecumenism by creating the Continuation Committee, which would attempt to put into effect the sanguine words heard at the conference. The 35-member international Continuation Committee elected Mott its chairman, who then devoted much of the rest of his life to ecumenism. Mott's work bore fruition in 1921 with the establishment of the International Missionary Council, and this organization together with others developed in the 1930s led directly to the establishment of the World Council of Churches in 1948. Aside from its success in missions recruitment, the impetus given to ecumenism through the organizational genius of Mott in the creation of the WSCF, albeit serendipitously, was the Student Movement's greatest achievement.

*   *   *

After his South African tour in 1896, Wishard steamed to Europe via the Indian Ocean and the Suez Canal, and then visited Italy, Paris, and finally London, where he saw the dying Henry Drummond. Drummond's career had come to an end in 1894 when he began to manifest a nervous disorder that slowly left him immobilized and in pain. Wishard laid his hand on the hand of the friend with whom he differed so greatly in matters of theology and method and said, "Drummond, you have taught me some of the greatest lessons of my life."[38] They parted with gleaming eyes. Eight years later, under doctor's orders and to avoid a nervous breakdown, Wishard himself retired from the strenuous Christian work that had defined his life and went into business in 1902 at the age of 48.

On the eve of the twentieth century, the Student Movement and evangelical Protestants in general mourned their greatest loss of all with the passing of Dwight Moody. Carried by students from Mount Hermon, Moody was laid to rest on Round Top, a hill topped with a ring of trees in the rear of Moody's home in Northfield. Moody and many others had preached and held discussions on this hill, and it is where many students during the summer conferences had knelt in prayer and come away resolved to become student volunteers. Mott eulogized his idol at a New York memorial service on January 8, 1900. "In the death of Dwight L. Moody," he said, "the Christian Student Movement loses one of its greatest friends and promoters. Among no other class of men has his influence been greater, more helpful, or more continuous than among students."[3]

With the death of Drummond in 1897, the death of Moody in 1899, and the retirement of Wishard in 1902, one generation of student movement leaders had now passed from the scene. But a new gen-eration, already in place, with an organization that stretched around the world, was well-prepared to lead the movement through the uncertain crosscurrents and hidden shoals of the twentieth century.

Chapter Six

EDUCATION FOR A MORAL CRUSADE

If we are to have able missionary leadership at home, intelligent adoption of the missionary calling as a lifework, financial support in proportion to the need, prayer with the spirit and with the understanding also, if we are to have the broadest and most virile types of Christian character in the membership of the Church, there must be a thorough promotion of missionary intelligence.

---John R. Mott[1]

Americans in the first decade of the twentieth century were in an optimistic and expansive mood. The depression years of the 1890s were behind them, and prosperity had returned to agriculture as well as industry. Having handily won the Spanish-American war, America was widely accepted as a world power. During these same years the increasing size of America's missionary enterprise reflected not only the nation's sense of having come of age as a world power, and therefore having greater international responsibilities, but also its confidence in the superiority of Western civilization. Theological liberals and conservatives, Social Gospelers, and premillennialists, all joined in a Protestant consensus that espoused the need and the rightness of spreading Western civilization and religion around the world. With a vainglory untempered by wide experience in the world, Americans offered non-Christian lands not only the gospel, but also hospitals, schools, social reforms, modern technology, and an ideology of progress.[2]

The Educational Department of the SVM published during these years a library of missionary literature that presents an unforgettable picture of the social and religious "needs" of Africa, Asia and Latin America and opens a window into the souls of Western missionaries. The Protestant Anglo-American world view revealed in this literature is that of the white middle-class entrepreneur. Seen in this light, as John and Jean Comaroff have suggested of British missionaries, the unstated purpose of missions was to forge a universal Western middle-class hegemony, emphasizing the values of hard work, self-improvement, timeliness, gender-based division of labor, democracy, and of course Protestant Christianity.[3] According to the Comaroffs, this explains why missionaries were concerned about the apparently tangential issues of sanitation, clothing, housing, and architectural styles. For the missionaries, whether they consciously rationalized their actions or not, control of the physical environment was one way of gaining control of the culture. The code word used to signify the amalgam of ideas and assumptions that made up the middle-class world view, a word that summed up not only what the middle class aspired to themselves but also what they wanted for non-Christian peoples, was, of course, character.

This interpretation of American missions is supported by examining the way in which Americans gained control of their own environment. Some missionaries to Native Americans, in an effort to civilize as well as Christianize them, had insisted as early as the seventeenth century on Western style clothing, farming and town life. Beginning in the 1830s middle-class Americans, according to at least one school of historical interpretation, attempted to exercise social control over themselves and the laboring class by passing temperance laws, Sabbatarian laws, and sponsoring urban evangelization.[4] Josiah Strong urged Americans in *Our Country* (1885) to gain control of the wild West through funding domestic missions that would establish Protestant churches and schools, and work for the passage of Protestant-inspired laws. These institutions and laws would be directed against Catholics, Mormons, socialists, and others who did not fit into Strong's vision of a Protestant Anglo-Saxon world hegemony. The YMCA and the YWCA attempted not only to evangelize but also to Americanize the immigrants that it worked with in America's new urban centers, and this type of social work was considered by the SVM to be good training for those who aspired to be missionaries.

In all of these activities missionaries or evangelists were the agents of middle-class attempts at taming other groups who generally appeared dangerous to the social order. This is not to say that the middle class used religion in a cynical or hypocritical way. Rather, the Christian religion was honestly believed and sincerely applied as an antidote to the social chaos that they believed threatened all societies. Similarly, the SVM missionary literature, which appealed to a Christian and humanitarian idealism, also suggested in its moral absolutism that non-Christian cultures were evil, morally repugnant, and largely unregenerate social systems that would require heroic efforts to save. Moreover, they presented Christian missions as a paternalistic endeavor, grounded in the belief in a hierarchy of races, which was often benignly expressed as "the white man's burden." This racist ideology and the provincialism that pervaded the movement were not unique to the SVM, but reflect long-standing aspects of American and specifically Victorian culture.[5]

The Educational Department

The first several years of missionary recruitment following the 1886 Mount Hermon conference produced thousands of student volunteers, but by 1890 it was clear that many of these had fallen away. The SVM leaders reasoned that the cause was a failure to maintain or channel the initial enthusiasm that induced students to sign the volunteer pledge. The leaders concluded that education in the emerging discipline of missions would probably hold the students as well as promote an interest in missions in others. Their subsequent creation of an educational department also reflected the Progressive spirit of the SVM, for increasingly missionaries were expected to be "experts" in their field.

At first Campbell White, himself a student volunteer, was recruited to tour the colleges to promote mission studies. In 1893, when the first edition of the SVM journal *The Student Volunteer* appeared, outlines for mission study classes were included. The first year focused on China and the second on India. Students were also informed of the best books to procure and encouraged to create missionary libraries.[6]

In 1894 D. Willard Lyon accepted the position as the first Educational Secretary of the SVM before becoming a missionary to China. Although only at the job for one year, he organized the educational department along the lines that it would continue to follow into the next century. Under Lyon's competent leadership, the purpose of the educational department, to establish a series of classes for college students that would be an adjunct to the Bible classes directly promoted by the collegiate YMCA, was greatly advanced. The Report of the Executive Committee for 1894-95 boasted that in its first year there were 120 missions classes with an average attendance of over 1,200 students.[7]

Harlan Page Beach, a former China missionary, was the second Educational Secretary for the SVM, serving from 1896 to 1906. Beach built on Lyon's firm foundation, creating the beginnings of a broad library of missionary literature that succeeded not only in promoting the study of missions in its own time, but also in providing an enduring record of how turn-of-the-century American evangelicals viewed the peoples of distant lands. In fact the world view contained in the collection of books issued by the educational department is one of the most interesting and revealing legacies of the entire Student Volunteer Movement.

Beach organized a four-year curriculum for college and seminary students, wrote several of the text books for the classes, selected and promoted the writing of other text books, and trained the teachers for the classes at the summer workshops held at Mount Hermon.[8] At the end of the 1897 academic year there were 267 classes with 2,361 students attending.[9] By 1905, the year before Beach retired from the SVM, there were 1,049 classes in a total of 668 separate institutions with an enrollment of 12,629.[10] Beach also promoted the creation of missionary libraries in each campus Association. During its first four years, the educational department sold $20,000 in missionary literature.[11]

In 1897 Beach began writing four-year curriculums for his mission classes. Each year was divided into three terms, and the course over the full four years covered mission theory, biography, biblical background, history, specific mission fields, types of services available, comparative religion, and other areas. In short, conscientious students would be introduced to everything they needed to know, according to the standards of the day, to make an informed decision about pursuing a missionary career. Also, the SVM through these courses could keep the students' attention focused on missions and thereby help to ensure their continuing enthusiasm.

That students precisely followed Beach's "Proposed Four Years' Cycle of Missions Studies" is doubtful. Given the variety of books available, the recorded annual sales and the record of classes held, it seems that students read what interested them and did not feel bound by Beach's recommendations. Nevertheless, regardless of the sequence in which they were read or the failure of students to read every book in a cycle, it seems clear that the books produced by the SVM were in fact widely read by the students within the movement and are therefore a good register of the missionary thinking of the period.[12]

That the volunteers read the books designated in the four-year cycles of the educational department was also confirmed indirectly by Mott. In the Report of the Executive Committee for 1919/20, Mott listed 14 books that enjoyed the largest circulation of those listed in the SVM collection during the first two decades of the new century.[13] This list, together with the books listed in the cycles, provides a good sense of what students were reading in this period. The books range from treatments of specific countries to a Social Gospel approach to the entire non-Christian world, and from treatments of specific missionary vocations to a general introduction to what all missionaries could expect to meet in the field. The brief discussion of some of the more prominent books that follows is an attempt to capture the missionary world view of the early twentieth century.

Model Missionaries

Beach liked to initiate students recently attracted to missions into the SVM's missions study cycle with a set of missionary biographies. Accounts of the lives of missionaries, as they were given by the SVM, were recapitulations of middle-class, Protestant ideology, usually written in stirring fashion and designed to appeal to a youthful audience. Beach's *Knights of the Labarum* was such a set, a collection of four biographies, comprising the lives of Adoniram Judson, Alexander Duff, John MacKenzie and Alexander Mackay.[14]

The title was taken from the famous story of the emperor Constantine, who after he saw the miraculous vision on the Minovrian Bridge in 312 A.D. adopted a Christian standard, the Labarum, which the early Christian emperors continued to use. The knights of the Labarum was a troop of 50 guards given the honor of protecting the sacred standard. Beach's evocation of romantic military imagery for missionaries was calculated to appeal especially to young readers touched by the wanderlust, with a zest for the heroic, and a desire to accomplish great things in the world. It was also a reflection of the standard of manly Christian character to which the SVM often appealed.

The biographies were written to underscore simple Christian truths and to anticipate the problems that students might encounter. All four of the missionaries were presented as excellent students who became interested in missions while in college and had to overcome parental objections before leaving for the mission field. Each was tempted to pursue other work, especially the doctor MacKenzie, and the engineer Mackay. In addition to the chance that secular callings might sway a potential missionary into other pursuits, there was the chance that once on the mission field the missionary might find secular activities more fulfilling.

As an exemplar of the true evangelical missionary spirit, Judson, the missionary to Burma, kept his mission priorities straight.

> Judson did not believe that he was first a promoter of civilization, then an educator and finally a herald of the gospel. The last function was pre-eminently his, and to accomplish his work he made large use of eye-gate and ear-gate [i.e. he preached the gospel].[15]

Beach's biographies were designed to answer a number of the questions that students might likely have asked. Did some students feel that to become a missionary might be to throw away their lives? Beach directed the students to look at Judson's accomplishments. At his death, more than 7,000 of his converts gathered to pay their respects. Judson left behind him 63 churches, 163 missionaries and their native assistants, a Bible translated into the Burmese language, as well as a grammar and dictionary to assist future missionaries. Most important, Judson left behind the legacy of his own example in the "greatest work in the world."[16]

Did students feel that they could not be effective preachers and evangelists? If they were inclined to scholarship, perhaps then they could follow the example of Duff, who by the age of 28 had established an English-speaking college in India: "What larger work can any young man of twenty-eight hope to accomplish?" Beach asked.[17] If inclined to engineering and concerned with social justice, they could follow Mackay's example in Uganda, and begin to introduce modern technological and democratic ideas to peoples still entirely under the sway of witch doctors and slave traders. If students were interested in medicine, they could follow the example of MacKenzie, who became a medical missionary to China and helped to introduce modern medicine to that country. Missions, then, offered students a variety of professional options and a virtually unlimited field of opportunity.

While *Knights of the Labarum* recounted for the benefit of uninitiated students the twice-told tales of some of the most famous and successful missionaries of the nineteenth century, less well-known missionaries appeared in *Modern Apostles of Missionary Byways*, a collection of six biographical sketches by as many authors, four of which were reprints from other publications.[18] Four of the six missionaries were apparent failures, their lives fraught with difficulties that they met with the muscular Christian's accustomed heroism and patience, but without the crowning achievement of converts. For example, Captain Allen Gardiner (1794-1851) of the Royal Navy attempted pioneering missionary work in the Southern African kingdom of Zululand (later Natal), but had to flee after three years due to war between the colonists and natives. Looking around for further pioneering work to do, he spent two years in Chile, and then New Guinea, and finally ended up on Picton Island (the Falklands), where having to flee unfriendly savages, he died of starvation on a beach awaiting supplies that never came.

The overall impression a student was likely to get from *Modern Apostles of Missionary Byways* was that the life of a missionary would not always be joyous or ostensibly successful. The work of pioneering missionaries required great tenacity, devotion to duty, and physical courage. But more than this, it required an inextinguishable hope gained from a certainty of ultimate success. Each of these pioneering missionaries had a vision of the ever-expanding Kingdom of God that emboldened them to lay foundations for an edifice that they never saw in their lifetimes, an edifice that by implication could be constructed by a second generation of missionaries, the student volunteers themselves. Still, in the guise of a call to the heroic, the SVM demonstrated in this book an admirable honesty in regard to the failure, suffering and early death that awaited many volunteers.

Once the volunteers had assimilated missionary ideology through reading biographies, perhaps they might wonder what the modern missionary's life might be like and what they could expect to find once in the field. Arthur J. Brown's *The Foreign Missionary* (1907) was designed to meet this need.[19] It was a prolix discourse intended to present the life, issues and problems likely to be encountered by missionaries and to offer helpful advice. His book was so well regarded that it was revised in 1932 and again in 1950 and so remained in print until 1960.[20]

Brown, the Secretary of the Board of Foreign Missions of the Presbyterian Church in the U.S.A., in the 1907 edition of his book described modern ocean voyages and suggested the first reactions a young missionary was likely to have to the new surroundings of a missions land. He pointed up the difficulty and importance of learning the language, the variety of work available to the missionary, and the rationale for missionaries' salaries being the same regardless of time on the field. To ease the difficulties sure to be encountered in the tropics, where most missionaries would go, he recommended that a missionary be outfitted with a pith helmet, white umbrella, "coloured glasses," and a white duck suit. He also offered medical advise, recommending vaccinations, mosquito-nets, the use of a syringe to avoid constipation, moderate use of quinine, and the need for a small medicine case.

But more important than novel experiences and missionary accoutrements was the picture of the model missionary that Brown painted while attempting to describe the proper missionary motivation and the type of persons for whom the mission boards were looking. The missionary motivation he presented was the argument from Scripture to present the word of salvation to those who had not heard it. All other considerations were secondary. But the philanthropic impulse, the desire to bring civilization to less developed people, the quest for the discovery of new knowledge and for exploration were not unworthy or discouraged; but they were of only secondary consideration to the primary task of achieving the Great Commission. Furthermore, the aim of the missionary was to create self-reliant native churches, not permanent dependencies.   Therefore Brown spent much time discussing the natural resentment of "natives" against Western missionaries reluctant to cede power to indigenous churches. That Brown felt it necessary to make these distinctions suggests that secular pursuits and empire-building were in fact strong motivations to missionaries that needed to be checked early on.

The qualifications to be a missionary were strict, according to Brown. "The government commissions all who graduate at West Point and Annapolis," he explained, "but the boards take only the picked men of the colleges and universities. No other profession guards its doors more carefully."[21] This of course was patently ridiculous. The volunteers were obviously college graduates, but the only consistent reason after graduation that the SVM recognized for its volunteers being rejected was physical health. In order to calm cultural fears that missions, as other religious endeavors, were unmanly, Brown shamelessly exaggerated the difficulty of becoming a missionary.

Brown also asserted all the usual bromides about manly Christian character. The mission boards of the denominations, he asserted, looked for candidates who appeared to have the toughness necessary for the job. "If any one imagines that weaklings or milksops can be appointed," he warned, "he might apply for appointment and see." Extending his rhetoric to include both genders, Brown cautioned that the boards wanted devout but also practical people: "The boards do not send the pale enthusiast or the romantic young lady to the foreign field, but the sturdy, practical, energetic man of affairs, the women of poise and sense and character." Missionaries cannot afford to be impractical people on the mission field, because their job requires leadership and organizational skills. In Brown's view'

> The typical missionary is more like a high-grade Christian business man of the homeland than a professional cleric. He is preeminently a man of affairs.[22]

Moreover the missionary, in Brown's estimation, must possess the martial virtues of courage, tenacity and devotion to duty in order to bear up under the burden of an isolated and lonely life far from home and civilization, with the certainty of disease, discomfort and the possibility of hateful mobs, cruelty and death. The boards are looking for "The man of patient persistence in well-doing, who does not easily lose heart, who courageously and inflexibly sticks to his work however discouraging it may be, the man who, like General Grant, 'proposes to fight it out on this line if it takes all summer,' is the type that is wanted for missionary service."[23]

In the missionary biographies and in Brown's picture of the generic missionary, the ideology of missions is very apparent. Steeped in Western middle-class values of self-improvement, progress, and manly Christian character, the SVM literature echoed the addresses of its leaders and undoubtedly helped to bolster the image of missionaries and perhaps the self-image of those considering missions as a profession.

Mission Lands

In addition to books that dealt with more generalized mission topics, some of the most popular books that the SVM produced were concerned with specific countries and continents. Most of these books provided brief but accurate geographical, political, social, cultural, historical and religious sketches. However, once they left the concrete and attempted analysis, they often revealed more about themselves than the countries they attempted to interpret.

Douglas M. Thornton's *Africa Waiting: or the Problem of Africa's Evangelization* is a good example of a brief presentation of a mission land in the SVM literature.[24] Originally a British Student Volunteer Movement Union book published in 1897, it was reprinted by the American SVM in 1906. It was the sole comprehensive missionary handbook then in existence on Africa. Only 143 pages, Thornton's book gave a brief lesson on African geography, languages, history, races and religions. It told of the great African missionaries and explorers, such as Johann Ludwig Krapf, David Livingstone, and Alexander Mackay. It also expounded on the horror of the on-going slave trade and liquor traffic. It directed potential missionaries to the North, which had twice the population of the South but half the missionary force. Finally, it provided a variety of helpful appendices on healthy living in Africa, Protestant missions in Africa, and mission statistics from 1896. Although the picture of Africa presented by Thornton is too cursory to be of much help to anyone actually going to Africa, it would have been very helpful for anyone seeking general information upon which to make a decision about where to be a missionary.

The reader of missionary literature, in addition to learning about faraway lands, would also encounter Victorian views on social issues. The SVM's view of the importance of race is revealed in a number of its books. Beach's attitudes about race rose occasionally in his writings, but never more fully than in *The Cross in the Land of the Trident* (1895).[25] Completely in step with his time, Beach interpreted the world largely in racial terms. Every race could be judged by Western standards of material, social and political progress, with its success or failure attributed largely to the relative strength of its character.

Comparing Indians to Westerners, he concluded that the former were in general smaller and less developed physically: "As a workman, therefore, he is worth only one-sixth as much as an American." Yet, "While less muscular than the European, the Hindu is more graceful in his movement, and on the whole even better looking." The high death rate and general susceptibility to disease cannot be accounted for entirely by diet and climate: "Early marriages and the inter-marriage for centuries of more or less consanguineous parties doubtless have much to do with their feebleness."[26]

Race and environment were linked in Beach's thinking, for he believed that the soil, the "Prize of the East," led to "a continuous influx of new race elements, and in consequence the Hindu shared some of the advantages of the intermixture of varied bloods. If caste and other causes had not prevented a larger amalgamation of races, he would, however, have been a stronger man than he is." He concludes that

> Whether the result of environment or not, it is true that compared with the Anglo-Saxon, the Hindu has been overcome by nature rather than made himself nature's conqueror. Hence we have a weaker race than the western Aryans have come to be.[27]

In the lexicon of missionary literature weakness and strength with respect to race can refer to physical prowess or intellectual capacity, but generally they refer to character traits, especially to the will. And often when the physical body and intelligence are referred to, they are seen as a reflection of character traits. What Beach is saying in this passage, then, is that the Hindu, unlike the Western Aryan, lacked the strength of will to conquer the natural environment. The positive aspect of this racial theory is that it assumes that weakness of character could be largely overcome by accepting the missionaries' religious and cultural agenda. The negative aspect is that, despite great potential for progress, it is far from clear that non-Western races would ever obtain an equality with the West due to innate physical and intellectual inferiority resulting from the long period of evolutionary development that had already transpired.

Beach's first book, *Dawn on the Hills of T'ang* (1898), introduced the student to China and at the same time showed Beach's belief that Providence and Western-style progress were one and the same. He updated the book in 1907 with an account of the Boxer Rebellion. At pains to explain that the missionaries were not the cause of the rebellion, he gave an account of the Western reforms and the coup d'etat by the reactionary Empress Dowager and the various Western provocations that led up to the rebellion. The preservation of the missionaries in Peking for 55 days, Beach wrote, "can only be accounted for by a distinct supernatural Power working in their behalf."[28]

Beach concluded that after the rebellion progress was again being made, Western ways were now more readily accepted, and missionaries therefore had now an even greater opportunity because missionary-educated Chinese would be very valuable in the new China. In this view Providence is on the side of China's Western style reformers and of course on the side of the missionaries, who were providing the educated elite as well as the progressive ideas that were leading to a new Westernized China. But, lest it be forgotten while emphasizing the importance of progress, Beach reminded his readers that, as with every other country, "China's greatest need is character."[29]

Despite tremendous progress in industrialization and democracy, Japan was no exception to the condescension generally shown to non-Western countries in missionary literature. Otis Cary's *Japan and its Regeneration* (1899) included a section on the "Mental Characteristics" of the Japanese, whom he described as "keenly intelligent," but then spoiled his remark with the patronizing comment that "Most of the men and a considerable proportion of the women are able to read books written in a simple style." In general he agreed with the common perception of Westerners that the Japanese were imitative rather than inventive, but he added that their imitations often included small improvements. Also, he generally affirmed the observation that the Japanese were "great in little things, and little in great things," pointing out their skill in "painting flowers, small birds, insects, and tiny bits of scenery," but their inability to successfully paint "pictures of men, large animals, and broad landscapes." The Japanese, he concluded, were weak in the arts and literature, and had produced no great orators.[30]

Despite Otis's obvious effort to be even handed by pointing out as much good as he could about Japanese culture and society, he never ceased to judge everything he encountered by Western standards. Even in his brief description of Japanese history, he likened the factionalism of its politics to that found in Sir Walter Scott's historical novels of Scotland, with the various Japanese warlords being compared to the MacDonalds, Campbells and Douglases.[31] The pedagogical effectiveness of this approach for provincial American college students is obvious, but the inability to understand Japan by its own lights, which his comparisons suggest, also has its drawbacks. Seeing Japanese culture and politics not as unique, but rather as at a more primitive stage of development in the light of the Western model, allowed missionaries to see their goal as not simply introducing Christianity to another people, but rather as introducing civilization to a backward or benighted people.

Otis himself recognized the limitations of this view when surveying Japanese history in the decades immediately following Perry's opening in 1853. At first, Otis explained, the Japanese agreed with the Western missionaries and equated Christianity with Western civilization, but when in around 1888 the inevitable anti-foreign reaction came, many saw that Christianity to be successful needed to take on a Japanese form.[32] Perhaps missionaries were beginning to fear that Japanese "character" might lead to civilization and progress without Christianity. It is ironic, then, that Otis, who perceived the problem in equating civilization and Christianity, was unable to free himself from this Western perspective.

More immediately suggestive of the national mood at the turn of the century was Arthur J. Brown's *The New Era in the Philippines* (1903). The latter part of the nineteenth century was of course an age of imperialism, and the United States, despite its own colonial past, soon found itself caught up in the imperialist zeitgeist. Having acquired the Philippines, Puerto Rico and Guam in the Spanish-American War, Americans suddenly found themselves with their own share of "the white man's burden" to shoulder. Brown, having made an extensive tour of the islands following the American subjugation, was an excellent choice to prepare a book on the Philippines for potential American missionaries.[33]

Brown felt it necessary to make an extensive defense of the American decision to acquire the Philippines. He averred that America did not intend to acquire the islands, but that once Dewey controlled Manila America's decision was inevitable. After all, what else could the country do? The Philippines could not in good conscience be returned to the brutality of Spanish rule, he reasoned. They could not be turned over to another imperial power, for this would only result in a worse rule. And they could not be left alone, because that would result in certain despotism. Thus America, feeling its "obligations toward the community" and its "responsibilities before God and man," could no longer enjoy the isolation of a "hermit country."[34] Quoting from the former Secretary of State John

W. Foster, Brown cast the American commitment to empire in the light of a divine mission:

> ...there is a sentiment among the Christian people that an overruling Providence has in this matter called our nation to the great work of giving to those varied races good government, the reign of justice, education, and all the blessings which follow in the train of enlightened Christian civilization.[35]

Having affirmed here the uniting of Western-style progress, providence, and a divinely ordained American paternalism, Brown proceeded to define the island population in racial terms. He identified three main groups inhabiting the islands, none the equal of an American, and the lowest of which, the Negro, he described as "an ignorant, degraded race" and as "nomadic savages on the lowest plane of barbarism."[36] Yet he did not see this as a permanent situation. As it took the unaided Anglo-Saxons centuries to develop the character to sustain self-government, Brown argued, so the Malays would need several decades of tutelage under American laws, politics, educational institutions, and the Protestant religion before they too could come of age. Arguably one could interpret this to mean that the Filipino would one day be the equal of the American, but Brown no where makes this clear.

Brown had few good words for the Roman Catholic Church in the Philippines. The church was the foundation for Spanish political rule and held about 420,000 acres of the best agricultural land as well as much valuable urban property. Citing the Taft Commission report, he also concluded that there was widespread personal corruption among the clergy. While in no way being sympathetic towards Roman Catholicism, Brown did make a distinction between the old Spanish bishops, whom he described as "unscrupulous," and the new American bishops, whom he saw as honest reformers. Reflecting the anti-Spanish racism of the period, Brown described a meeting he had with a Spanish Bishop and the missionary interpreter with him:

> I wish I had an artist's power to sketch the profiles of the two men. They typified the whole wide-world difference between American Protestantism and Spanish Romanism – the missionary with his high forehead, frank blue eyes, clear cut features whose every line and expression betokened temperate living and high thinking: and the Bishop – well there was a noticeable difference.[37]

Brown's attitude toward his religious competitors, the Roman Catholic Church, was not universally held by Protestants in this period. When the 1910 Edinburgh Conference decided not to include Latin America as a mission field, many objected. Robert E. Speer's *South American Problems* (1912), was in effect a minority report, which at its heart was his attempt to answer the question, "Are Protestant Churches in South America justifiable?"[38] He concluded that Protestant missions were justified in South America for the same reason that the Catholic Church justified them to Nestorian, Armenian, and Coptic churches: To attend to their social need and to counter the "travesty of Christianity" that their churches presented.

Speer also reviewed the history and current social/political situation of Latin America. The region had to deal with what Speer regarded as the legacy of Spanish cruelty and cupidity, and on-going political instability. The continent had severe problems of alcoholism, sanitation, disease, and a high mortality rate. What economic progress had been made was due largely to the American and European immigration, rather than to indigenous efforts. Education had largely been neglected, so that illiteracy ranged as high as 85 percent (in Brazil) and as low as 50 percent (in Argentina).[39] The moral standards of the continent were suggested by the one-fourth to one-half of the Latin American people who were illegitimate.

The cause of Latin America's backwardness, Speer argued, could not be laid to climate or geography, because these were largely advantageous. The root cause was in the people themselves. Despite their many good qualities, "the tone, the vigor, the moral bottom, the hard veracity, the indomitable purpose, the energy, the directness, the integrity of the Teutonic people are lacking in them." To sum up, "The deepest need in South America is the moral need. The continent wants character."[40] Speer's conflation of a moral cause with a racial cause for Latin America's apparent backwardness is typical of much of the thinking of this period. In Speer's mind, race and culture were connected, and they evolved together in time. Therefore in Speer's view it was not self-contradictory to depict a people as backward because as a race they lacked attributes that we at the end of the twentieth century normally attribute to cultural values. Race and culture were simply not as clearly distinguished then as they are today.

In all of these missionary studies the cultures and accomplishments of non-Western nations and peoples can be understood in largely racial terms. Societies were viewed as occupying some stage in a Social-Darwinist evolutionary scale with the Anglo-Saxon nations at the top and peoples living in tribal communities, whether in Africa, the Philippines or elsewhere, as occupying the bottom rung. In this view, God had ordained the Anglo-Saxon people to be the bearers of Christianity and Western style progress to the "backward" nations. Although denied in theory, the dual role of the missionaries in practice, as bearers of Christianity and Western civilization, was so intermixed as to be virtually indistinguishable.

Comparative Studies

In addition to writing of specific countries or mission lands, SVM literature also included comparative studies of religion and society, as well as studies that attempted a broad analysis of Islam. Combating the growing belief in cultural and religious relativism, these books not only represented Christianity and Western culture as superior to the animistic beliefs and folk practices of traditional cultures, but also did not shrink from presenting a comparison of Western religion and civilization to those of the cultured ancient civilizations of the East, with the latter receiving scathing denunciation. In attempting to relate religion and culture to what they interpreted as the social consequences of those beliefs, missionary writers consistently judged non-Western societies by the moral and social standards of the West. For them the West was presented with a clear philosophical choice, cultural and religious relativism or the absolute standards of the Christian religion.

Samuel M. Zwemer's *Islam, A Challenge to Faith* (1907) would be of some help to the missionary student of Islam, for it gave Islam's history, a brief overview of its religious tenets, and a brief history of the missionary effort among Moslems.[41] The picture it presented of the Islamic faith, however, was that of a religious monstrosity. Citing the fruits of a century of study by European and American critical scholars, Zwemer concluded that "Islam is a composite religion. It is not an invention, but a concoction..." He included a chart showing Islam's plagiarisms from Sabeanism, Arabian Idolatry, Zoroastrianism, Buddhism, Judaism and Christianity.[42] Even the pilgrimage to Mecca, the Kaaba and black stone, Zwemer complained, were borrowed directly from the pre-Islamic pagan stone-worship of Arabia.

Equally scandalous to Zwemer was the character of the founder of Islam, the Prophet Mohammed. According to Zwemer's interpretation, Mohammed broke the laws even of pagan Arabs by marrying a captive woman before the prescribed three months, by robbing caravans on pilgrimage to Mecca, and by committing incest by marrying the wife of his adopted son. But he also broke the laws of the Old and New Testaments, which he said he approved, by teaching that oaths could be broken, perjury committed, and killing justified, if all were done in the cause of Islam. And his private married life and his "love-adventures," "which are the fireside literature of educated Moslems in all lands where Mohammed is the ideal of character and standard of morality," are too brutal and coarse for decent eyes.[43]

The importance of character to SVM leaders is underscored once again by this depiction of Mohammed. The Prophet was crucial to Zwemer's analysis of Islamic countries because Zwemer pictured him as the ideal character type for Moslems. For Zwemer the founder of Islam was the diabolical opposite of Christ. This perversion of character at the center of Islam might stand as an object lesson to student volunteers of what could happen when character formation took a wrong turn, thus explaining much that was wrong in the Moslem world and elsewhere. The ethics of Islam, for example, were a reflection of its founder's character, according to Zwemer. Consequently, the Koran allows polygamy, divorce, wife-beating, slavery and murder in the course of a holy war.

Like Zwemer, S.H. Kellogg in *A Handbook of Comparative Religion* (1899) opposed the increasingly accepted relativism of the comparative religion school of thought.[44] Kellogg drew a sharp distinction between the Christian charity of accepting the various Christian denominations as legitimate expressions of the true faith, and extending this idea by analogy to all the great world religions. The comparative religion school viewed all religions as being at various stages of an evolutionary development, and that all provide the means for humanity to approach God. In this view, some Christians were able to see even in what was regarded as primitive idolatry an expression of the love of God. This attitude if generally accepted would of course undermine the urgency of Christian missions even if it did place Christianity at the top of the religious hierarchy.

The bulk of the book was a careful comparison of the salient points of Christian doctrine to that of the world's other great religions. Needless to say, non-Christian religions fared rather badly. Although Islam embraces monotheism, it exaggerates Christian doctrine by presenting a capricious god, who arbitrarily elects some to heaven and some to hell, who establishes things as sin that are only incidentally immoral, and who himself commits "gross crimes." Hinduism offers no personal god, and instead presents a multitude of gods whose behavior is morally reprehensible. In addition, rather than presenting a concept of good and evil that might morally elevate its adherents, Hinduism offers only the morally neutral concept of karma. The other religions fare as badly. Buddhism has no god, and its heaven is a depersonalizing nirvana. Confucianism is not a theistic religion. Shintoism and Chinese Taoism offer no transcendent spirit world, but rather present a pantheistic universe with spirits that are one with the world, who appeared in the course of its evolution.

Kellogg did not claim that in contrast the Christian West was perfect, but only that "the state of society and the atmosphere of public opinion in America or Great Britain" (the leading Protestant countries) was substantially different from that found in India, China, and other non-Christian countries. In Kellogg's view, the West had its faults, but it had completely done away with such notorious crimes as slavery and polygamy, and "in a word, is there a spot on the whole earth outside of Christian lands, where a decent man would of choice bring up his children?"[45] The persuasiveness of this appeal was predicated on the assumptions that cultural relativism is morally insupportable and that cultural and social conditions are in large measure a result of long term religious influences. Both of these views were widely shared by Victorians.

Embracing the same assumptions, James S. Dennis wrote *Christian Missions and Social Progress*, a very influential book of the period that surveyed the "social evils" of the non-Western world. Originally a series of seven lectures, Dennis's book presented Christianity as the only antidote to the social poisons he found in the societies of non-Christian lands. The SVM extracted the second lecture and prepared it as a mission study booklet, *Social Evils of the Non-Christian World* (1897), which catalogued the evils of the East and Africa "in order to make plain the imperative need of a moral crusade" and the necessary role that Christianity alone could play in achieving the moral reconstruction of the world.[46]

Surveying the non-Christian lands, Dennis detailed a dreary panorama of alcohol abuse, opium addiction, gambling, slavery, cannibalism, human sacrifice, brutal despots, minimal literacy rates, dense ignorance, medical quackery, and abuse of the poor, sick, aged and deceased. Cruel, insensitive or degrading customs abounded in non-Christian lands. In many countries scanty attire offended the Victorian sensibilities of the missionaries. In Japan, for example, there was the persistent problem of nudity and "promiscuous bathing."[47] Other barbaric costumes included tattooing, "abominable dances," orgies, foot-binding, and self-torture. In many countries burial rites failed to give sufficient dignity to the deceased. In China babies were often left unburied and exposed to be eaten by dogs. The Parsis of India placed their dead in a "Tower of Silence," an enclosure open to the sky where vultures preyed upon the decomposing bodies. There were also the more generalized problems of vast poverty, unsanitary conditions, and frequent famines.

Despite these reports, many missionaries and mission apologists found much to admire or at least respect in the ancient civilizations of the East. The SVM recruits were regularly warned to come well-armed with Western knowledge and be prepared for years of study in the foreign culture, because its people were rightly proud of their intellectual tradition and would defend it fiercely and with intelligence. Dennis, however, made no concession to cultural relativists. The non-Christian lands, he explained, know little or nothing of modern science, industrial technology, political economy, being "deeply wrapped in the slumber of ignorance." Most of their doctors were guilty of quackery, their remedies frequently being incantations to the gods or demons and their medicines consisting of a witch's brew of spiders, snake's eggs, bones of animals, dog's flesh, monkey feet, and boiled toads. Knowing nothing of modern medicine, their remedies if not useless were dangerous and often cruel. Dennis described the doctors variously as "witch-doctors, magicians, diviners, medicine men, and devil-doctors." If missionaries did nothing else but introduce modern medicine to replace the quacks, it would "still be a noble mission."[48]

The dismal picture that Dennis painted of the degradation of life in non-Christian lands gives the modern reader a sense of the powerful attraction that missions had for idealistic young people of that era. For them the allure of missions came from a sense that the world beyond Christendom was truly benighted, being bereft of moral values and religious truth. Therefore it desperately needed a "moral crusade" that Christianity alone could accomplish.

This is the rhetorical meaning behind Dennis's reduction of culture to morality. By judging cultures morally, they could only be seen in terms of moral absolutes to be embraced or rejected. With Victorian interpretations of Christianity and cultural assumptions as the absolute standard against which all other cultures would be judged, the potential missionary could not fail to see that Western Christians could uplift non-Christian nations and set them on the evolutionary track toward the telos of Victorian absolutes. And there was little that Dennis did not believe that Christian missionaries could accomplish for the moral, social and cultural betterment of non-Christian nations.

Looking to the Future

The Edinburgh Missionary Conference of 1910, which took place 100 years after the formation of the first modern American missionary board, the American Board of Commissioners for Foreign Missions (ABCFM), is generally credited as the birth place of the modern ecumenical movement. But while there was an air of triumph at the conference, it was also an opportunity to take stock of the missionary enterprise, and at least some of what was said was critical of the marriage of Western civilization and the Christian religion.

Mott, as Chairman of Commission I, "Carrying the Gospel to All the World," benefited from a vast quantity of information that came to him in response to questionnaires sent to missionaries all over the world. Eventually this material was presented in the published report of the committee, but prior to that Mott created from it his own book, *The Decisive Hour of Christian Missions* (1910).[49] The book also included the leading ideas of the Edinburgh Conference, and therefore it was seen as the concise statement of the spirit and intentions of the conference. Originally planned as an SVM textbook, it was widely reprinted and translated into German, French, Danish and Swedish.

The great importance of the Edinburgh Conference was the effort in denominational cooperation that was launched there. Mott argued that missionary work had up to that point been largely explanatory and experimental. Such work, he believed, was generally completed, and the task then facing the churches was two-fold. First, the churches needed to gird themselves up to send a missionary army of sufficient size to finish the job. Second, they needed a strategic plan to follow. The Edinburgh Conference, Mott believed, was only the beginning of a cooperative effort that would create this plan. For example, they next needed to identify and focus on "strategic races, nations, and regions," and they needed to divide up the mission fields so as to avoid duplication of effort.[50] In short Edinburgh was a clarion call for Christian unity that was rooted in the missionary agenda and general pre-war optimism of the Western world.

Consistent with this optimism, Mott believed he perceived in mission lands a great openness to Western Civilization, a rising concern for human rights and equality, an increased awareness of the inadequacy of non-Christian religions, and encouraging evidence for the growth of Christianity. But also, ominously, he believed he detected a rising nationalism in non-Western nations. Therefore the time for effective missions, Mott feared, might be short. The nations, he concluded, were in a period of transition and therefore malleable, but this would not last. Soon "the present plastic condition of the nations will have given place to a condition of rigidity, and the influences which might be so effective if brought to bear now, will then be exerted in vain."[51] Though Arthur Pierson had written similar things a generation before, the difference is that Mott now believed the time of rigidity was at hand.

Although a staunch supporter of the superiority of Western civilization, Mott was not blind to its faults or its limitations. In response to rising nationalism he urged the churches to present to the non-Christian world not a European or American Christianity, but a "pure Christianity" that would identify itself with the "noble national aspirations" of Asia and Africa, and "adapt itself to the people whom it seeks to save." One of the greatest hindrances to missions was the corruption in "so-called Christian civilization," which presented to the East its liquor traffic, government exploitation of indigenous people, and its "infidel and rationalistic ideas and materialist views" presented in "agnostic, atheistic, materialistic, and destructive socialistic literature."[52]

Although Mott believed that the previous century of missionary effort had undermined the other great world religions of Mohammedianism and Hinduism, he concluded his book on a note of urgency. "It is a decisive hour for the non-Christian nations," he wrote, for as they abandon their old faiths they must choose new ones. In the modern world this meant in effect that they would embrace either Christianity or secularism.[53] Ironically, Mott might also have been referring to the West. For Europe and America were also on the verge of abandoning the old faith and, however reluctantly, embracing modern secularism. In his attack on the corrupting influences of the West, and in his preachments about the need of the churches to rise to the occasion of becoming a world religion, it is possible that Mott sensed that he was living through, not the decisive hour of the non-Christian nations, but of the nations of the West.

*   *   *

In the decade and a half before the First World War the SVM produced dozens of books that reflected the missionary thinking of the era. Missionaries were presented in this literature as heroes with the potential to render significant service to non-Christian nations. The danger and difficulty of the task was not underrated, but rather it was presented as part of the larger call to courageous and devoted service. Individual countries, regions, and religions were also presented. The literature was often tainted with racism and an assumption of Western superiority in religion and culture. It implicitly and occasionally explicitly supported both American and Western imperialism. Opposed to the liberalizing tendencies then growing in the West, missionary literature rejected the relativism of the comparative religion school and emphasized the ethical superiority of Christianity and the practical social consequences of non-Christian cultures. With this unquestioned assumption of superiority and the advances already made on the mission fields, all that remained for the missionary sending denominations and nations by the second decade of the new century was to learn to cooperate practically in a great ecumenical effort for world evangelization. This accomplished, the watchword of the SVM would be shortly realized.

In the years immediately preceding the First World War there were some, like Mott, who may have dimly suspected that missions might be entering an era of difficulties, but this was far from the general mood. Certainly in 1914 there was no discernment among missionary leaders that the beliefs that gave the SVM the confidence of moral and religious certitude would be shaken by a world war centered in Christendom itself. In their self congratulatory mood, they little realized that all their assumptions would soon be brought into question by the general culture, and that, on the eve of modernity, they stood as innocents before the storm.

Chapter Seven

THE SOCIAL GOSPEL
AND THE GREAT WAR

"What would Jesus do?" Suppose that were the motto not only of
the churches but of the business men, the politicians, the
newspapers, the workingmen, the society people --- how long
would it take under such a standard of conduct to revolutionize the
world?

Charles M. Sheldon[1]

The late Victorian period was an age of material advancements that came
with such rapidity and far-reaching implications that no aspect of society
was left untouched. It was an age in which nothing seemed impossible, as
railroads crisscrossed the land speeding travel, as the telegraph and then
the telephone created instant communication, as skyscrapers created a new
cityscape, and as belching smokestacks symbolized a burgeoning industrial
might. Yet in the late nineteenth century there were an increasing number
of voices that weighed the human cost of society's remarkable material
progress, such as Edward Bellamy, Upton Sinclair, Frank Norris, and
Henry George. Still, evangelical Christians were, as was the rest of the
nation in the Victorian period, slow to come to a realization of the need for
social reform.

Though the Social Gospel movement was underway during the last
two decades of the nineteenth century, it did not become a mainstream
movement in the major denominations until the first decade of the new
century, and it was not reflected in the SVM until the years immediately
preceding the First World War. During the war, and in some measure
because of it, the Social Gospel became a dominant influence in the SVM.
The unanticipated result, however, was that the Social Gospel began to
undermine the cardinal principles of the movement. By bringing into
question long-held assumptions of the superiority of Western civilization,
the Social Gospel helped to sever for many the link between the Protestant
ethic and the middle-class entrepreneurial ideology that had so fruitfully
been coupled in the Victorian world view and summed up in the word
character. It created a new ethic that looked beyond individual character
formation to the reformation of society as a whole.

The Student Movement
and the Social Gospel

In the decades before 1900 Christian advocates of social reform such
as Washington Gladden and Walter Rauschenbusch were lonely pioneers.
Despite the antebellum reform tradition, Victorian religion was largely
concerned with individual not social religion. Josiah Strong in his widely
popular book *Our Country* noted a number of social concerns ---
immigration, Romanism, Mormonism, intemperance, socialism, the
poverty and blight of the cities --- but his solution, and the point of his
book, was for Christians to invest in home missions, or evangelism.[2]
There were some, however, like the Christian economist Richard Ely, who
took exception to the orientation of Christianity being toward the
individual alone.

Ely argued that the church was very good at fulfilling the first great
commandment of Jesus, to love God, but that His second great
commandment, to love your neighbor as yourself, had largely been
ignored. While the first commandment implied the study of theology, the
second implied the study of sociology. Therefore he believed that "half of
the time of a theological student should be devoted to social science, and
theological seminaries should be the chief intellectual centres of
sociology."[3] In effect, Ely and other liberal Social Gospelers were calling
for a shift in Christian orientation from an emphasis on individual
reformation to social reformation.

In contrast to Ely's social vision, conservative Social Gospelers
attributed social problems, such as the issues involving labor, business,

poverty and crime, to individual moral failings. Solutions therefore did not lie in forcing systemic changes on the political or social structure, but rather in the conversion and sanctification of individuals, from which would naturally follow structural reform. Charles Sheldon's famous Social Gospel novel, *In His Steps*, urged Christians to simply ask themselves what Jesus would do in any given situation. Sheldon was convinced that if all Christians would walk "in His steps," the social order would be transformed. Even in the face of massive social distress in the depression of the 1890s, the church in general continued to emphasize character formation and supported reforms like the temperance movement, which laid the blame for poverty and unemployment on individuals, for both were seen as the just punishment for improvident behavior. Similarly the excesses of business leaders in corrupting politics and "grinding the faces of the poor" were seen merely as problems of personal ethics.

Those who wrote educational books for the SVM, YWCA and YMCA during this period were increasingly influenced by the Social Gospel movement, but it was largely the conservative (individualistic) wing of the movement whose influence they felt. Two writers in particular were referred to with frequency by the Student Movement writers, Shailer Mathews and Francis Greenwood Peabody. In contrast to earlier Social Gospel writers, these two and others around the turn of the century changed the central theological motif of the movement from the bringing in of the Kingdom of God to the social principles taught by Jesus. This development emerged from the growing interest at this time in the scholarly quest for the historical Jesus.[4]

Mathews wrote *The Social Teaching of Jesus*, which argued that the reformation of society would not occur en masse, but rather through "the successive winning of one man after another until there be developed something like a nucleus of a more perfect social life." The approach of Jesus to social reform, he believed, was not to attack existing social evils, but to change individuals: "To aid in the regeneration of a man is to aid in the regeneration of society."[5]

Similarly, Peabody argued in *Jesus Christ and the Social Question* that the Kingdom of God will not be ushered in "by outward force or social organization or apocalyptic dream but by the progressive sanctification of individual human souls." In language that resonates with the masculine culture of the Student Movement, Peabody asserted that Jesus would "have no part in the limp fatalism which regards character as the creature of circumstances. He makes a masculine appeal to a man's own will." For Peabody, the key to sorting out the modern labor problem from a Christian perspective was to understand that Jesus' solution to social problems focused not on social circumstances but on individual character. He was concerned with "moral virility," and "the making of men," and not with sociology.[6] In effect Peabody was arguing for an unswerving continuation of the capitalist laissez faire system. He sympathized with the socialist's ideas of a just and egalitarian society, but he believed that the Christian must oppose socialistic solutions to the labor problem because socialism assumes that good character will arise from the new cooperative system, while Jesus taught just the opposite, that the new socialist system must arise from good character.

By 1906 progressive Christian social thinking had gained sufficient attention and support that the YMCA published a book presenting its own version of the Social Gospel, Jeremiah W. Jenks's *Social Significance of the Teachings of Jesus.*[7] Jenks was a professor at Cornell University who had given a series of Sunday morning talks around the turn of the century to the Cornell University Christian Association. Published as a twelve week study course, Jenks summarized for a whole generation of Progressive Era students the thought of the Social Gospelers on the social principles of Jesus.

Much of what Jenks wrote would have been very reassuring to his middle-class student readers. Jesus was described as a virile, self-reliant, companionable, sympathetic, optimistic person, who was filled with a joy for life and an appreciation for the beauty of nature. Jesus did not encourage the ascetic life, nor did he insist on poverty. According to Jenks, the desire for "social position, riches, fame, [and] power" were all justified for a Christian as long as the higher aim was service to others. Even great wealth was justified as long as its use was "generous, thoughtful and effective."[8]

Jenks, however, warned against "fraudulent poverty" and "habitual paupers." The service that was to be provided must be genuinely helpful. Money must not be given to the poor in such a way as to encourage them to a life of poverty. "As a rule," Jenks explained, "Jesus' exhortations to give are for the sake of the giver. He in no case urges it directly for the sake of society, rarely for the sake of the recipient." The poor to whom Jesus was so conspicuously sympathetic during his life time "were chiefly the blind, deaf, crippled....the worthy poor." The modern Christian needed to avoid giving in such a way as to foster in the poor "the shiftless dependence inevitably blighting to character." Rather, the Christian should practice "a wise helpfulness" that would enable the poor to retain their self respect and achieve "a higher sense of responsible manhood."[9]

Jenks could find no program for political reform in the gospels. Jesus, he believed, had avoided the political issues of his day and parried the political questions that were specifically put to him. Jesus' method of bringing in the Kingdom of God was through the contagion of His

Gospel remained controversial in the major Protestant denominations, it gained an institutional grounding in 1908 with the creation of the Federal Council of Churches.

As the Social Gospel gained momentum in the half dozen years before the First World War, it began to be reflected in missionary thought. It was first expressed in the addresses of missionary leaders at the Edinburgh Conference of 1910 and the British SVM Quadrennial of 1912. In the first explicit indication of the new direction that American SVM missionary thought was taking, the SVM speakers at the quadrennial convention held in Kansas City, December 31, 1913 to January 4, 1914, also demonstrated a strong Social Gospel commitment. As Clifton Phillips has pointed out, the position that missionaries should be primarily concerned with the social transformation of non-Christian cultures, rather than traditional evangelism, represents a decisive change in missionary strategy. The SVM's major contribution to this new approach was in the area of student leadership. Whereas previously the Student Movement's emphasis on developing indigenous Christian leadership was for the purpose of creating evangelists, increasingly it would be for the purpose of Christianizing non-Western societies.[13]

Charles R. Henderson, chaplain and head of the department of sociology at the University of Chicago, made the reassuring case at the Kansas City convention that the Social Gospel was nothing new in Christian history. It began with the Old Testament prophets, and with Jesus, Peter and Paul. It continued with the charity of the early church and was represented in subsequent history by St. Francis of Assisi, Wilberforce, John Wesley, the Earl of Shaftesbury, John Howard, Elizabeth Fry and others that could be named from every century. Turning to the theme of missions, Henderson asserted that the contemporary need for a social gospel was not unique to the West, but was also needed in the Eastern world. The non-Christian nations needed it not only because of their ancient social problems, but because of the urban and industrial problems associated with the modern world. Moreover, because the West had introduced these latter problems to the East, it had a special responsibility to assist in their alleviation.[14]

Continuing the Social Gospel themes of the convention, Shailer Mathews made the argument that the evangelization of America was crucial to the evangelization of the world, for in the U.S. modern social problems — the place of women, ethnic diversity, economic justice – were "focalized." Mathews warned that until America solved its own social problems "we shall not be able to send an unqualified announcement to the world that we have a Christianity that has been tried and tested in the awful alembic of our economic order." Mathews concluded by observing that American democracy was struggling between a view of itself as either based on a "brutalized, aggressive, sensualized wealth," or a spirituality that embraced the "splendid ideal of service for the world."[15] In effect Mathews believed that the struggle to implement the Social Gospel was a struggle for the soul of America, and because America was a harbinger of things to come in the world, if missionaries would evangelize the world they must first Christianize their own country.

This is a strange message to preach to a missionary convention, for it undermines the missionary motivation. In subsequent addresses others would challenge Mathews's single-minded commitment to the domestic Social Gospel, but the argument that the West had first to clean its own house was one that many would come to share in the coming years. One speaker who took exception to Mathew's message was Secretary of State William Jennings Bryan, who pointed out that "if you can convince yourself that you ought never to try to help others until you yourself are perfect, you can postpone until after death any effort whatever to do good. The Bible does not say, `Let the perfect help the imperfect.' It says, `Let the strong help the weak.'"[16]

The Social Gospel theme, sounded so clearly at the 1914 convention by a variety of speakers, was one indication that the superiority of Western civilization would soon be seriously questioned by the new generation of student volunteers. By suggesting, as Mathews did, that the West ought first to Christianize its society before it could effectively take the gospel to non-Christian nations, he was saying in effect that the West and East were not so morally far apart as had previously been assumed by the church and lay missionary leaders. Bryan's retort that such a position would paralyze all benevolent action would not be compelling to those convinced that the West was so in need of a social reformation as to undermine its moral authority in presenting the gospel.

The prevalence of this new uneasiness concerning Western superiority gains in clarity and poignancy when heard in the utterances of the generally recognized titular head of the world missionary establishment, John Mott. Mott's 1914 book, *The Present World Situation*, the bulk of which was originally given as a set of lectures at Harvard University and again at Boston University School of Theology, was dramatically different from his other books up to this time.[17]

While his previous book, *The Decisive Hour of Christian Missions*, pointed to Western moral failings, the virulence of his attack in his new book amounted to a sweeping indictment of the West, making him sound like a modern, but Protestant, Las Casas. The nations of the West, Mott argued, had divided up the continent of Africa, had divided Persia in two, and carved Asia into zones of influence. Western nations had ignored treaties, committed atrocities, and exploited weaker people. They had purveyed opium and more recently cigarettes in China, and introduced alcohol into Asia, Africa, and even Moslem lands. Quoting Lord Byrce, Mott described the Western traders in non-Christian lands as "the foul scum upon the advancing wave of civilization." Waxing indignant against Western traders, Mott detailed their crimes against the indigenous populations of the East: it was they who had often "despoiled or tricked them out of their lands, who have exploited their mines, who have grown rich upon their labor, who have ruined them by strong drink, who have treated them with roughness and with scorn, and sometimes even with barbarity..."[18]

On a more personal level, Mott assailed the practice of Western traders in keeping concubines as a notorious offence, as were, he added, the number of illegitimate births. Western soldiers and sailors, he continued, differed little from the traders in their immoral practices on shore leave in foreign lands. Even Western tourists in non-Christian lands, in Mott's opinion, had also undermined Christianity by their "attitude of superiority" and their lack of interest in Christian missionary activity. Also non-Christians who came to the West as workers, tourists or students often encountered racial attitudes that belied the universal message of Christianity. The West, he argued, needed to give greater heed to the message conveyed about its Christianity when an African from "beyond the Zambezi" visits South Africa, or an Indian visits British Columbia, or a Chinese or Japanese person visits California. With bitter irony, Mott noted the comment of a Hindu on the Western treatment of Asiatics, "Wherein is it better than the treatment given the pariah by the Brahman?"[19]

More subtly, Mott pointed to the unfortunate impact that the West often had on non-Western cultures. As Western culture met Eastern culture, the latter often broke down, he observed. Not only were indigenous religions swept away, but traditional social restrains were also neglected. And before Christianity could establish itself, "materialistic, agnostic and rationalistic" influences often set in, leaving people "without any restraint; that is, without any substitute for that which they have given up." For Mott the practical consequences of this were frightful. As the moral order in Eastern societies broke down, he believed that women would be particularly vulnerable, for influenced by Western feminism they would gain freedoms before they had "received the protection of laws and conventions which alone make possible the safeguarding of that freedom."[20]

Given the seriousness and extent of Western sins, Mott gave vent to what for him was an unprecedented skepticism: "At times we may seriously question whether we have a Christianity worth propagating over the world," he mused. The catalogue of crimes committed by the West against the East that he observed was not new, but being vigorously stated by a major Christian leader on the eve of the First World War, it appears prophetic. The onslaught of the First World War only added to his dour mood. Though the content of this book was delivered during or before April 1914, Mott wrote the preface in December, four months after the start of the war. "What a colossal exhibition the War affords," he lamented, "of the unchristian character of much of our so-called Christian civilization!"[21]

While the First World War is often seen as the point in which the legitimacy of the missionary movement was undermined in the eyes of the coming generation, it is clear from the 1914 convention speeches and from Mott's 1914 book that the belief in Western cultural and religious superiority that undergirded the missionary enterprise was already being seriously questioned even before the war began. Among Protestant Christians the Social Gospel was both an admission that reforms were needed and a spur to the growing belief that West and East were equally in need of Christianization. It is important to note that at this point these ruminations were directed at Western society and not at Christianity per se. Mott specifically exculpated the Christian religion for the guilt of Western sins, arguing that Christianity, properly applied, would lead to cultural redemption. However, through the crucible of war that lay ahead, many would draw the logical conclusion that a failed culture indicated a failed religion.

The Student Movement's Attitude Towards the War

When in 1914 the "guns of August" first reverberated across the Atlantic to the shores of the United States, Woodrow Wilson asked the American people to remain "impartial in thought as well as deed." During the two and a half years before America too entered the war, the journals of the student Christian movement had little difficulty following Wilson's entreaty and maintained a high-minded neutrality.

Editorials and articles cast no aspersions on Germany. One writer for *The North American Student*, at that time the organ of the Student Movement, argued that the causes of the war were too complex either to assign blame or to take sides. Rather, he called America to play the role of a "constructive neutral," supplying food to all the war-weary populations of Europe and toys to the children.[22] Another writer quoted a German soldier to the effect that the war was a divinely assigned penance for past neglect of social problems. He then urged Americans to take up the cross of social service.[23] Other writers took the opportunity to condemn war in general, one referring to it as "a custom which has come down from the age of the cave man."[24] After the American entry into the war, Harry F. Ward, generously recalled the words of the prophet of Israel, who remarked of Assyria before its attack on Israel, "A day shall come when these two shall come into fellowship with the children of God."[25]

On the eve of the American declaration of war, after Germany had commenced its campaign of unrestricted submarine warfare, two editorials in *The North American Student* directly addressed the question of the morality of military service. The first, after an anguished discourse, finally concluded that the Christian is justified in taking up the sword "to repel aggression and criminal lawlessness."[26] The second, with far less moral agonizing, and drawing on history, nature and the gospels also argued that war is justified.[27] He called especial attention to the example of Jesus scourging the money-changers as a justification for the use of violence in a righteous cause.

Despite their two and a half years of carefully maintained neutrality, as soon as America entered the war the editors of *The North American Student* revealed that "from the beginning of this conflict we have felt that the Allies were in a holy cause." And after attacking the immorality and selfishness of the enemy and praising the patience and high-minded principles of the Allies, the editors urged their readers to "earnestly seek to know in what way each may give his or her life in this war service."[28] Yet the leaders and writers of the student Christian movement never engaged in the vicious anti-German propaganda that characterized so much of the Christian pro-war rhetoric of the period, nor did they espouse that super-patriotism marked by the phrase "one-hundred percent Americanism."

Taking the high road of Christian idealism, a number of articles, both before the American entry into the war and afterwards, saw in the world-wide conflict the possibilities for a better future, and some even believed they detected glimmerings of the Providential purpose. An editorial in the first issue of *The North American Student* to appear after the war began expressed the hope that the war would "usher in a new and better order among men." It would discredit the nations' reliance on militarism and promote "brotherly love and human kindness," the very ideals, the editorialist pointed out, for which the World's Student Christian Federation and the American student movements had been working all along.[29]

Three years after the beginning of The Great War, Edward Bosworth believed that it was leading directly to the establishment of a "Christian World-civilization." "God is forcing the world forward," he declared, "and we ought to be alive to God in the glad recognition of and participation in this forward movement." Bosworth believed that God was teaching the world that the "Christian enterprise" was about more than world evangelization, but involved world Christianization. He asserted that the war showed the need to Christianize race relations, international politics, class prejudice, and other evils that had led to the conflict.

Other editorials and articles in Student Movement journals maintained the same idealism. Shailer Mathews advocated practicing the golden rule in international relations as well as individuals lives.[30] Former President William Howard Taft urged the creation of a "league to enforce peace," a recognizably liberal Christian position by this time.[31] The emphasis on Christian idealism and the avoidance of war-mongering and anti-German rhetoric that characterized the Student Movement during the war did not remove it from controversy. The movement's very moderation in a period of emotional excess left at least one of its leaders open to attack, Robert Speer.

Since his days as a traveling secretary for the SVM in 1888-89, Speer had worked tirelessly in the cause of missions. In addition to regular speaking engagements and book publications, Speer had served on the Executive Committee of the Student Volunteer Movement for most of the first three decades of the new century and he had served as the secretary of the Board of Foreign Missions of the Presbyterian Church in the U.S.A. from the conclusion of his second year at Princeton Seminary in 1889 until his retirement in 1937. By the time of the war he was a nationally prominent leader in the missionary enterprise. Moreover, as the chairman of the Federal Council of Churches' General War-Time Commission of the Churches, Speer was a recognized leader of American Protestantism. However, as a voice for moderation in an era of over-heated patriotism, Speer would be hard pressed.

Speaking in the gymnasium of Columbia University on February 18, 1918 for the Intercollegiate YMCA of New York City, Speer spoke on "World Democracy and America's Obligation to Her Neighbors." He pinpointed a number of the causes of the war, including an overwrought nationalism, race prejudice, and failure of democracy. His remarks would have been unremarkable except that to illustrate his points he used not only Germany, but also the United States. Americans, he charged, were guilty of racism toward the Japanese and American Indians.

Speer was quickly attacked as a pacifist in a number of letters and editorials in the *New York Times*, but he was not a pacifist, and he supported the war effort against Germany. However, he did oppose an unreflective patriotism that would deny America's past sins. Writing in defense of his statements in the *Times*, Speer averred that whoever "requires of the man who would be loyal that he must deny facts or tolerate in America what he is warring against elsewhere comes perilously near to the 'insidious disloyalty'" of which he himself had been accused.[32]

But despite his misgivings about war in general and specific injustices in American history, Speer embraced the high ideals for which Americans told themselves they were fighting the war. For Speer, the war was justified because it was a war to end wars, and, he asked, was "it not as right to use war to stop war as it was for Jesus Christ to use death to stop death?" He also believed that it was necessary to oppose "aggressive autocracy." Germany had in effect claimed exemption from the moral law given by God by which all nations must live. By implication, Germany claimed that "power is its own warrant," and thereby justified any action.[33] Speer believed in a universal moral order, which, being violated by the Central Powers, justified American military action.

Last, and perhaps most important, Speer believed that American involvement in the First World War was directed toward the same goal that had animated Christian missions for a century, the creation of "a new human order" that would be based on righteousness, justice and brotherhood. What missionaries had been doing "peacefully, constructively, unselfishly, [and] quietly for a hundred years [was] exactly the thing that now in a great outburst of titanic and necessarily destructive struggle we are seeking to do by war."[34] When the war was over, Speer explained, thousands of those who had fought in France should go in peace to Asia, Africa and Latin America as foreign missionaries – there to finish the task they had begun in war.

While his artless candor was not widely practiced by many Christian leaders during the First World War, Speer's evenhanded approach to the war did represent the general thinking of the writers and speakers of the Student Movement. Perhaps in large part due to the influence of the Social Gospel, the leaders of the Student Movement could not ignore America's past sins, but neither did this blind them to the faults most saw in Germany. Consequently, they supported the war as readily as did most Americans. Also, Speer's link between the Wilsonian goals of the war and the longstanding goals of the missionary movement was a commonplace among Christian missionary leaders in the Student Movement. In an era of excess, their patriotism was restrained and temperate.

The Northfield Volunteer Conference, 1918

The First World War acted as a catalyst for the growth of the Social Gospel among students as it shifted the interest of Christian students away from traditional religious concerns to foreign affairs, specifically the goals of international peace, cooperation, and the establishment of a federation of nations. The Social Gospel became so much a part of student thought during the war that Shailer Mathews, an avid Social Gospeler, felt constrained to remind students that "social service [is] not a substitute for religion."[35] As early as 1915 Mathews feared that concern for social issues was beginning to undermine the traditional emphasis on personal religion.

The war had an even more powerful effect on those directly exposed to it. For Sherwood Eddy the war was one of the great turning points in his life. After spending most of the period from 1896 to 1914 in the field of Asian missions, Eddy worked, among other things, as an evangelist among the troops during the war. "The war did something to me," he wrote two decades later in his autobiographical work *A Pilgrimage of Ideas*. "I could never be quite the same again. Like a burst shell or the upheaval of a mine, it shattered the easy, optimistic complacency of my previous ideas of a fictitious evolutionary social development toward millennial utopias."[36] Exposure to the war led Eddy to change his evangel from a message of personal religion to a declaration of the Social Gospel. After the war he became one of the leading evangelists of the Social Gospel among student Christians.

Perhaps the clearest indication of the new social emphasis of the student movement, and specifically of the Student Volunteer Movement, was the 1918 Northfield Conference. Due to the exigencies of war, it was not possible to hold the SVM quadrennial during the 1917-1918 college winter break. Instead, the SVM leadership decided to hold a small student conference at Northfield, January 3 to 6, 1918. Of the 768 participants, there were 404 college students, 304 members of missionary boards, and 60 faculty members. Characteristic of war-time generosity, participants in the conference pledged $22,000 annually for four years. One writer noted that this was more money than had been subscribed at the Kansas City Convention with its 5,000 delegates.[37]

The significance of this conference lay in the ideological shift in the SVM that it clearly demonstrated. The balance between personal and social religion, maintained at the 1914 quadrennial convention, was noticeably lacking.[38] The theme adopted by the conference was the creation of a "Christian world democracy." This construct included the concept of an interracial "world brotherhood," which was described as a "genuine, unpatronizing and unpatronized fraternity."[39] The establishment of democracy was seen as the political expression of Christian principles. And only Christianity constituted an "adequate religion," one that could create the individual character needed to sustain a democratic form of government.[40]

The speakers at the convention sounded an unmistakable Social Gospel note. In raising the issues of race and class, speakers often sought to link the social problems of North America to those suggested by the war and sometimes also make them directly applicable to student life. Weatherford, for example, chose to discuss "anti-social" college behavior, which he also labeled "anti-Christian." In attacking racism, he asserted that those students who use the terms "Jap," "nigger," and "Dago," have "not the spirit of Jesus Christ."[41] Channing H. Tobias, a noted black student Christian leader, used the opportunity of the war to compare atrocities committed by the Germans in Belgium to those committed in the United States against blacks. He referred specifically to the East St. Louis massacre, where perhaps over 500 blacks were killed.[42] Harry F. Ward of the Boston University School of Theology delivered an impassioned plea for those doing "the humble toil of this country," those working in the mills, factories, mines and lumber camps, and those doing seasonal work.[43] He sympathized with the socialist symbol of the red flag, he explained, because it had much in common with "the blood stained banner of the cross." Both stood for human brotherhood. Neither of them, he was convinced, would triumph "until each absorbs the content of the other."[44] Ward of course was at the radical end of the political spectrum in the SVM. Still his message was heard and later reprinted in *The North American Student*. Clearly, the Social Gospel in all its hues was being heard in the movement.

To begin to achieve the lofty goals of the Social Gospel at home and in the world, the conference unanimously agreed to a four point program for students that included Christian education, calls for personal commitment, recruitment of missionaries and a fund rasing goal of one-half million dollars for the 1918-19 academic year to fund foreign missions. Also, whatever additional funds were need for war relief were to be raised.

The first goal of Christian education envisioned a heavy concentration on the Social Gospel message in volunteer college classes. The books recommended for study included Bosworth's *About Jesus*, T. R. Glover's *The Jesus of History*, Rauschenbusch's *The Social Principles of Jesus*, J. Lovell Murray's yet to be written *The Call of a World Task*, Edmund D. Soper's *Faiths of Mankind*, Ward and Edwards's *Christianizing Community Life*, and Weatherford's *Negro Life in the South*.[45]

Most clearly expressing the new direction of the Student Movement was Murray's *The Call of a World Task*.[46] Written in the month following the Northfield Conference, it summarized much of the spirit and thought of the SVM that was expressed at the student gathering. In the first part of the book, Murray faced squarely the challenge that the world war presented to the Christian faith. "We cannot ignore the fact that this is a war of so-called Christendom," he conceded, pointing out that all but four of the then 23 belligerent nations were part of Christendom. Murray cited people from the Asian and African nations who questioned the superiority of Western Civilization and the efficacy of the Christian religion. And he noted a particularly apt cartoon in the London Punch "showing two barbarians, very fierce and very black, in their crude war regalia, singing together a lusty duet. The caption of the cartoon was "The Black Man's Burden"; beneath was written, "Refrain by natives of South Africa and Kikuyu," and the title on the song sheet was "Why do the Christians rage?"[47]

The problem that missionary apologists faced was the logical correlation that they had always insisted upon for non-Christian nations, the connection between a society's religion and its moral performance. Despite all the arguments that Murray was able to muster for foreign missions, he never adequately addressed the key question: if Christianity was a superior religion, how could it have produced a civilization that would subject two-thirds of the world's people to total war? His answer, and the standard answer at the time, was that the West had not truly been Christianized, and therefore Western civilization was not a reflection of the religion of Christ. But if this last point were true, could Christian leaders make any meaningful distinction between East and West? If not, what did this portend for the missionary enterprise?

Other books recommended at the Northfield Conference also sounded a Social Gospel note and offered a new vision of missions, and one at least offered a solution to the implicit questions raised by Murray. The books by Rauschenbush, Ward, Edwards, and Soper were part of a four-year study program established by the Committee on Voluntary Study of the Council of North American Student Movements, which included the YMCA, YWCA, SVM and the Sub-Committee on College Courses of the Sunday School Council of Evangelical Denominations (comprising 29 denominations).

Soper's *The Faiths of Mankind* was a comparative study of the world's great religions, which embraced Christianity as the one true and unique religion. Yet Soper began his study by explaining that he felt that "in every religion men have been trying to find the true God and are reaching out after Him....Realizing this, the only attitude of a Christian is that of sympathy..."[48]   While this maintains the position of exclusiveness traditionally claimed by Christians, it is far removed from the demonizing of non-Christian religions by earlier Student Christian writers. This suggests that the critiques of Western society by the Social Gospel and the embarrassment of a world war between Christians had helped to produce a new sensitivity to the world's other great religions.

Rauschenbusch's *The Social Principles of Jesus* urged a greater sympathy for the poor, whom middle-class evangelicals had long spurned as suffering the just deserts of their own improvidence. Arguing against the Social Darwinist ideas of "eliminating the unfit" and not coddling the weak in the best "interest of the future of the race,"[49] Rauschenbush embraced the principle that humanity is unified in a moral and spiritual solidarity. This suggested that no aspect of life, no class or race or nation of people, was beyond the concern of the Christian. Rauschenbusch's book attempted to move Christians beyond the emphasis on individual character formation as a solution to social problems to the notion that bringing in the Kingdom of God required changing the social order. When America was a collection of small towns, he reasoned, the Christian churches were able to check evil in their communities. But now that evil had become more complex because society was more complex, "We can not restrict the modern conflict with evil to the defensive tactics of a wholly different age."[50]

While Soper and Rauschenbusch's books promoted a greater sympathy for those outside the world of white middle-class Americans, Edwards and Ward's *Christianizing Community Life* broke down all the walls traditionally separating the insiders and outsiders of the Christian world. Asserting a new vision of missions, it made clear that as there were social problems in non-Christian lands, so there were also social problems in Christian lands. In India there was the problem of recurrent famine, but in the "prosperous Central States [of the U.S.] at least one-tenth of the population is not adequately fed, clothed, nor sheltered." While missionaries had brought modern medicine to Africa and the Orient, "more than six hundred thousand lives are needlessly sacrificed every year in the United States from disease which modern science knows how to prevent." The East still maintained the caste system, slavery and polygamy, but Europe currently served "the Iron God of Battle" and America the god of "Mammon."[51]

Edwards and Ward proposed a Social-Gospel-inspired reorientation of missions that made no distinctions between Christian and non-Christian lands. Rather, they saw the world as a collection of communities, which the new industrial system was making increasingly uniform; thus in the new world "Osaka... Manchester and Hankow becomes like Pittsburgh." If the world was one, then a single comprehensive Christian vision for the world was now possible. Edwards and Ward favored a Christian social movement that abandoned philanthropy in favor of social justice, where labor became the owners of industry. They also saw a crucial need for governmental action in the social sphere. No important reform movement, they believed, had ever succeeded without involving government.[52]

Although the book offered a vague socialist vision and looked forward to the New Deal in its advocacy of government activism, it still largely belonged to the Victorian era in that its optimism about the human potential did not exclude a utopian future. Taking stock of the social progress of the previous three decades, Ward and Edwards pointed to favorable changes in industrial conditions, business standards, prison practices, and other indications of progress toward a Christianized nation. Moreover, pointing specifically to the work of the WSCF in more than 40 nations, they believed that "the tools and materials are at hand to build the road that leads into the city of God."[53]

Taking Stock

With 24 million casualties, shattered economies, extensive physical damage, and massive political dislocations, the First World War was a disaster that was then unparalleled in modern European history. Yet in relative terms America came out of the war quite well. Only 112,000 Americans soldiers had died, the nation endured no domestic damage or civilian casualties, and its economy boomed during the war, making the U.S. the world's leading creditor nation. But the reaction of American Christian leaders to the war was mixed, for the war both inspired and rocked the Christian church.

After the war at the Foreign Missions Conference of North America in January 1919, the Rev. Charles R. Watson noted the many physical disruptions of the missionary enterprise that the war had caused. But at a more profound level another problem that occurred due to the war was the questioning of Western moral and spiritual superiority by non-Westerners. Watson reported that in the early days of the war a Mohammedan preaching in the Mosque of St. Sophia at Constantinople noted gleefully that "twenty millions of Christians in Europe were cutting each other's throats, and he prayed that their number might increase. He said, `That is Christian civilization,' and added, `We spit in the face of such civilization.'" Watson noted, too, that Christian claims to producing "superior character" were undermined by the war. Had the magnificent courage and determination of non-Christian soldiers demonstrated in the war, he asked, "somehow unconsciously created the impression upon many that the great fundamental qualities of courage, devotion, and sacrifice are not exclusively nor even distinctively the fruitage of Christianity?"[54] In other words, the war worked not only to discredit Western superiority, but also the indispensability of Christianity for character formation.

Despite the difficulties brought on by the war, Watson noted a number of areas in which missions benefited by the war. He estimated that nine-tenths of the mission work continued despite war-time disruptions and that the opportunities to work with soldiers "deepened interest in the message of Christianity to non-Christian life." Perhaps most significant, contributions to foreign missions by Americans actually grew during the war, from $16 million in 1915 to $20.7 million in 1918. In the light of the increased generosity of the American people as demonstrated not only in missions giving but more generally in war relief – Congress alone voted $100 million for relief work – Watson concluded that Christians in the past had been mistaken not in asking too much from the American people, but in asking too little.[55]

Mott had drawn similar conclusions as early as 1915. He believed that the war mobilization showed that Christian leaders had underestimated the potential of the West to mobilize for world evangelization. Mott estimated that Christianity needed 20,000 missionaries working for 30 years to complete the evangelization of the world. Previous to the war, college professors and other leaders calculated that this would impose too great a burden on the West to maintain. Yet the massive mobilization of troops for the war suggested otherwise.

Mott and Watson were not alone in their wonder at the potential generosity of the American people once properly organized and inspired. While a previous generation of Christians had been inspired by the business organization of the new industrial era, the generation that lived through the war was inspired, even awed, by the war time mobilization of the West in the world's first "total war." "I will never let off the colleges as easily in the future," Mott declared. "I will never again make such small demands upon the students."[56]

*   *   *

The Victorian era was characterized by optimism, a belief in Western superiority and progress, and a belief that success or failure in life was fundamentally based on individual character. At first much of the Social Gospel movement affirmed these beliefs, but by the time of the First World War Social Gospelers began to question these cardinal tenets that constituted the Victorian consensus. The war helped to bring into focus the implications of the Social Gospel for Victorian ideas and pointed to a new moral order where state power would be used to address the human suffering of the under classes, and where nations would meet in a world community based on terms of a cultural, if not a material, equality.

For the leaders of the Christian churches in general and the missionary movement in particular, the war pointed in two directions. The undermining of the assumption of Western superiority and the belief that the West was generally a Christian society suggested that missions as a priority of the Western churches needed to be rethought. If both East and West were in need of Christianization, then advancing a domestic social gospel and sending missionaries abroad for the purpose of world evangelization became competing goals. Given the limited resources of the Protestant community, the churches would have to make a difficult choice between two worthy goals. Yet, because of the tremendous war-time giving and the exciting example of war-time mobilization, missionary leaders convinced themselves that the churches could pursue both goals simultaneously. Their calculations, however, did not take into consideration the new mood among students that appeared following the war.

Chapter Eight

FROM FOREIGN MISSIONS TO WORLD MISSIONS

We can not hypocritically profess to be a "superior" race
with all our lynching, our lawlessness, our mob violence,
our sordid materialism, our un-Christian politics, industry
and race relations.

Sherwood Eddy[1]

The SVM leaders were unprepared for the extent of the disillusionment of
the younger generation following the First World War and the peace of
Versailles. The war as a moral crusade, as a means to "make the world
safe for democracy," as a "war to end all wars," had proved to be illusory.
In the aftermath of the slaughter of the western front and the politics as
usual at Versailles, the idealism of the Victorian era suddenly seemed
naive if not tawdry. The general optimism and steady belief in progress
that characterized the Victorian era appeared now to be built on little more
than Western arrogance. Americans entered a decade of critical self-
examination, youthful rebellion against traditional social and moral
restraints, and abandonment of the heady idealism of Wilson for the
normalcy of Harding.[2]

Though Student Movement leaders were increasingly committed to
the Social Gospel and to the need to Christianize both East and West,

Protestant leaders in general emerged from World War I largely insensitive to the coming cultural revolution. John Mott epitomized the optimistic mood of the older generation. In the decade following the Edinburgh Conference Mott had scaled to ever higher heights of popular acclaim and worldly honors. In 1910 he was offered the presidency of Princeton, after Woodrow Wilson became the Governor of New Jersey. And in 1913 Wilson asked Mott to be his ambassador to China. Mott declined both positions, finding his Student Movement work more important. Nevertheless, Mott later served temporary assignments on diplomatic missions to Mexico in 1916 and to Russia in 1917. Moreover, his leadership of the American YMCA's war work in Europe and his efforts in the United War Work Campaign brought him much national attention. Also, during the war Mott resigned as head of the intercollegiate YMCA and became the head of the national YMCA.

Mott's personal success paralleled the apparent success of the Christian churches in America, whose leadership seemed to believe that their star was now rising quickly in the nation and in the world. Unchastened by the war, they were confident and aggressive concerning the prospects of their faith in the world. Awed by the charitable giving of Americans during the war, they wanted to continue the war-time fund-raising efforts of the churches. The most outstanding expression of their boundless optimism was the launching in 1919 of the Interchurch World Movement (IWM), which was a nation-wide ecumenical movement to raise $300 million in its first year and $1.5 billion in five years for the purpose of advancing the Social Gospel at home and world missions abroad. It arrived at its day of reckoning in May 1920 when only $200 million was pledged. By pre-war standards this should have been a tremendous accomplishment, but in the extravagant post-war expectations the IWM fell $100 million short of expectations and left the denominations with the organization's debts, which took several years to pay. Consequently, the IWM collapsed. The churches had counted on the support of "friendly citizens" – those sympathetic to the Christian cause but not themselves church members. This hope was premised on the conviction that America was a Protestant country, whose citizens, whether church members or not, would support Protestant causes. The failure of the IWM gave a tremendous check to Protestant sense of triumph, and the churches had to conclude that their religion was no longer synonymous with America, which by the 1920s was a pluralistic society.

Similarly, the Student Volunteer Movement, which had gone from strength to strength throughout its history, suffered its first reverses in the 1920s. It was plagued by a series of controversies, many of which were a reflection of the larger cultural confusion of the period. Born in the

Victorian era, the SVM flourished in the cultural and religious consensus that existed up to about 1920. During the transition to the new pluralistic culture that would constitute the "modern" era, the SVM was faced with the need to appeal to a new student generation and to adjust its vision of missions to meet the new post-war realities of the world.

Des Moines Convention

In the years before the First World War Robert Wilder served as Foreign Students' Secretary of the British Student Christian Movement. Wilder had been one of the original organizers of the British movement, and after leaving the mission field of India for health reasons, he found working with European students congenial. He also served the WSCF as its representative for Lands without National Organizations. During the war Mott asked Wilder to serve as the head of the YMCA's Religious Work Department at its New York headquarters. Wilder accepted. And in 1919, when Fennell P. Turner stepped down from the position of General Secretary of the SVM, Mott asked Wilder to replace him. Wilder accepted the position, his career having now gone full circle by returning to head the organization he had helped to found at the Mount Hermon Conference 33 years before.

Wilder's first task as General Secretary was to organize the 1920 Quadrennial Convention to be held in Des Moines. That the 1920 Quadrennial Convention was a success could be supported by a variety of statistical evidence. Six thousand eight hundred ninety delegates gathered for this convention, the largest to date, and 400 of them represented 39 foreign countries. The number of new missionary volunteers reached its apogee the following year when 637 volunteers sailed for foreign mission fields. Individual convention delegates pledged themselves to contribute $195,600 in four annual installments.[3] Yet statistics do not tell the story of the Des Moines Convention. SVM leaders then and later agreed that the 1920 convention, despite its apparent success, was a major turning point in the history of the SVM.

John Mott inaugurated the Convention with a soaring address on "The World Opportunity." Flanked by a large map of the world that was marked to show the nations where a generation of student volunteers had gone, framed on either side with large flags of the United States and Canada, and printed with large letters spelling out the watchword of the movement - "The Evangelization of the World in this Generation" - Mott began with stirring words, "We stand on the threshold of the greatest opportunity which North American students have ever confronted." Mott described a world that had greatly changed because of the terrible destruction of the war and the existence, by his estimate, of 11 million freshly dug graves. The nations were torn by class strife, the threat of Bolshevism, and death by starvation and exposure in Europe. "It is a humbled world," Mott concluded. "What nation today," he asked, "gives one the impression of pride and self-sufficiency, as was true of not a few nations but six years ago?"[4]

While this address struck the right notes with regard to the failure and humility of Western civilization, and the need to emphasize the social and ethical ideals of the gospel, it failed to capture the angst of the new generation or to offer any self-criticism for the failure of Christianity to prevent the war. For the students the zeitgeist of the postwar era was one of bewilderment, alienation, outrage. Rather than confronting this new reality, Mott spoke in the old optimistic language of the Victorian era. For him progress was still possible, the world was still "plastic," and all the pillars of civilization may have crumbled but an unaltered Christianity was still pointing the way to a bright, peaceful future. And among convention speakers, Mott was not alone in his approach.

For many students at the convention this rhetoric sounded hollow. The youth of America who had responded to the war as a great moral crusade were not yet prepared once again to so easily strap on their armor. Moreover, many of the students attending were not committed to the missionary cause. David Porter, in an article describing the convention, commented that many of the delegates did not seem to understand the missionary purpose of the convention. Despite advertisements that made the missionary emphasis clear, "About all some students seemed to hear," Porter explained, "...was something about making the world over."[5]

Having come to what they believed was a general Christian convention, many delegates were disappointed by the missionary emphasis, and preferred to discuss Wilson's "Fourteen Points," or other matters relating to international relations. Others would have preferred a frank discussion of America's own domestic ills. Still others objected to the traditional religious language of the convention and in their disillusionment even questioned the missionary purpose of Christianity. Ad hoc conferences within the convention appeared among the students in order to discuss issues of greater immediate importance to them. Some of the student leaders, such as Henry P. Van Dusen and even Mott's own son, John L. Mott, attempted to present the new student mood to the leaders of the movement. The business sessions of the convention became stormy affairs as two generations struggled to understand one another and vied for dominance. Sherwood Eddy referred to the change in student attitude towards missions that first appeared at Des Moines as an "insurgent revolution."[6] At the very least the Des Moines Convention marked a new departure for the movement.[7]

Robert Speer, who had been scheduled to speak on the inadequacy of non-Christian faiths, told the convention that an hour or two before he had decided rather to speak on the issues that were being "expressed and unexpressed in group after group" as to whether American Christianity or the Christianity expressed in the Convention was itself an adequate faith, whether it was worth taking abroad, or if American Christians ought first to attend to their own domestic problems. "We are not here to evade anything," Speer explained defensively. "We did not gather in this convention to repeat ancient shibboleths. We did not come here to thrash old straw."[8]

Speer summarized the complaints of what he clearly believed to be the more obstreperous students. They believed, according to Speer, that American Christianity was a failure because it was not engaging the great social, political and economic issues of the day. This group would have the convention pass resolutions endorsing the League of Nations and social radicalism. In contrast, Speer embraced those students of a decidedly different nature, who disdained the passing of "impotent resolutions," but nevertheless believed that "our Christianity is just a mockery today, and this convention is unreal, because we can admire heroism that is gone by, but we cannot display that heroism in our own lives now."[9]

Toward the end of the convention Sherwood Eddy also addressed the complaints of students concerning the messages they were hearing at the convention. Students had asked him, he explained, "Why do you bring us this piffle, these old shibboleths, these old worn-out phrases, why are you talking to us about the living God and the divine Christ?" For Eddy the problem was not in the adequacy of Christianity to meet the great political and social problems that vexed the students, but rather in the spiritual condition of the students themselves. Eddy asked the students to measure themselves against "the four great tests of character." He asked them if they were pure, honest, surrendered to Christ, and dedicated to service. Perhaps their problem, he suggested, was that they had yet to discover the living Christ in their lives. Furthermore, if they were more engaged in bringing in the Kingdom of God, then they would have no time for criticizing others. "The man who is playing the game, who is covered with sweat and mud and blood has not time to criticize his fellow players."[10]

The shift in generational values and the consequent misunderstandings and mutual recriminations between the students of the twenties and the traditional SVM leaders is reflected in Eddy's address. For Eddy Christians who did not emphasize a personal gospel must be sinful, unconsecrated, nominal believers. For the students of the post-war era the approach of the personal gospel alone seemed inadequate at a time when their civilization itself was being questioned. On the other hand, it is not clear that the students really knew what they wanted. Clearly they were dissatisfied with the old rhetoric of an individual gospel and of character formation and wanted a more frank discussion of Christianity's failures, but new leaders with a message that spoke to the new generation were not yet being heard. The 1920s, then, would be a time of confusion, conflict, and painful transition.

A Turbulent Half Decade

The years between the Des Moines convention in 1920 and the Indianapolis convention four years later were among the most vexing the SVM leadership ever experienced. Problems arose concerning the nature of the leadership, finances, Canadian-American relations, the demands of blacks in the movement, and a question about whether the SVM should include home missions among its evangelistic efforts.

The need to make the SVM a more democratic and therefore a more truly student movement was apparent for some time before the Des Moines Convention. The YMCA began to discuss democratizing its student department as early as 1913, and set up a student "committee of counsel" in 1917 to ensure student participation in the governance of its organization.[11] But it was not until February 1919 that the Executive Committee agreed to alter the form of government to achieve the goal of greater student participation. The Executive Committee would be expanded from six to thirty members, and meet three times a year. One-half of the members would be students, and the other half would include five from the mission boards, four from the YMCA and YWCA, and six at-large members. In addition there would be a Student Council that would include a male and female representative from all the Unions, which in 1920 numbered 40. The council would meet once a year, make recommendations to the Executive Committee, and elect student members to the Executive Committee. It would have no executive or legislative power, but merely provide a student perspective.[12]

Seven Student Councils met from 1920 to 1926, after which the SVM organization was again reorganized. While the councils generally filled their reports with uncritical remarks about the SVM and did not attempt to alter the general direction of the organization, the councils did make some practical contributions, such as in raising funds, the location of the 1924 convention, requiring all new volunteers to obtain physical examinations,[13] and recommending a new wording of the movement's purpose to reflect the broadened vision of "world missions" that students held by the mid-1920s.

Perhaps more important than any practical suggestions that the councils may have made, they helped to restore a sense of proprietorship over the movement to the students, which may have given some volunteers a more sympathetic attitude towards the leaders of the movement. Council member Lucile Gibson wrote in the *Bulletin* that the leaders were attempting to overcome the problem of intergenerational communication by listening carefully to the council members. "They seek to learn what we are thinking; what problems we are facing; the crises through which we are passing."[14]

While the volunteers were facing a crisis of the spirit, the leaders of the SVM were facing a far more tangible crisis. Throughout the 1920s the SVM had difficulty meeting its budget. In part this was due, in the early 1920s, to a brief national recession. Also, following the war, the SVM expanded its budget to an all-time high, from $62,240 in 1918-19 to $95,850 in 1923-24. Wilder justified the larger budget in 1920 because of the increase in the demand of mission boards for missionaries after the war. They were asking for 2000 volunteers, which Wilder calculated to be a 25 percent increase over the previous year. Also there were specific expenses that needed to be met. The Des Moines Convention ran a deficit of $5,600. Publishing the Convention report cost more than anticipated due to increased material and production costs. And the *Bulletin* was expanded from an annual to a quarterly journal --- later it became a monthly.[15]

Wilder commented that "nearly half of the time of the General Secretary has gone to raising money for the Movement." "Like the poor this problem of finance is always with us."[16] The budget of the SVM was enormous for its time. It was not of course as extravagant as the Interchurch World Movement's budget, which for 1919 alone had been $2 million, but the IWM was exceptional. The SVM expanded its budget by about 20 percent immediately following the war, when the churches' fund-raising optimism was at its height. Later in the early 1920s, when denominations were having difficulty meeting their own missions budgets, the SVM became a victim, like the IWM before it, of its own overheated expectations. It is little wonder that Wilder had so much difficulty keeping the organization out of the red.

In addition to financial woes, Wilder also faced a split in the movement. Early in 1921 Canadian Christians formed the Student Christian Movement (SCM), which united men and women in one college organization. The Canadian Student Volunteer Committee now considered separating from the American SVM and either joining the SCM or operating independently.

After three years of rancorous negotiations, it was finally agreed between the two organizations that a plebiscite would be held on the options of Canadian autonomy or continued union with the American SVM. At the meeting, when the votes were taken, it was discovered that the Canadian volunteers were overwhelmingly in favor of remaining in principle a part of the American SVM. Wilder noted that only 2 or 3 voted against it. The agreement reached, however, made the Canadian movement essentially autonomous. The Canadian volunteers agreed to recognize the American General Secretary as their head, send delegates to the Student Volunteer Council and the Quadrennial Conventions, but retained the right to elect their executive committee, appoint their own secretaries, and provide for their own budget.[17] The separation of the Canadian and American movements was representative of the growing nationalism within the WSCF countries and the fragmentation of the movement in the 1920s.

While Canadian volunteers wanted a larger measure of autonomy within the movement, black Americans, who had a long history with the Student Movement, began to make increasingly insistent demands for greater inclusion in the SVM. Following the war the rise of the Ku Klux Klan and the increase of lynchings brought the racial question to the forefront of student social thinking.[18] Thirty-six black students at the Des Moines Convention signed a request asking the SVM to cooperate with them in securing a secretary to organize a student movement in Africa and North America for blacks. The Executive Committee gave the task of forming a movement in North America to the Committee on Friendly Relations with Foreign Students, and the task of forming a movement in Africa was turned over to the WSCF.[19] Also, the Secretary of the Colored Men's Department of the YMCA, C.H. Tobias, requested that the SVM include black students on the Student Volunteer Council. Wilder responded that these appointments were made by the Unions and therefore were out of his hands. In effect he was saying that the SVM would not aggressively lead on this issue.[20]

At the February 1923 Executive Committee meeting, Wilder reported on a conference of four black student leaders held at the SVM headquarters. The SVM's failure to appoint a black traveling secretary and to "establish forums and study classes in the colleges to discuss problems of racial adjustment" was the source of much disappointment among black students and their leaders, Wilder noted. They also complained of the mission boards' unwillingness to appoint black volunteers as missionaries to African nations. Due to the boards' position, the SVM did not appoint a black traveling secretary because, as Wilder explained, "to recruit a large number of colored Volunteers when there is at present no hope of their entering Africa might lead to an unfortunate reaction."[21]

Potential black missionaries were hindered by the internal logic of colonialism. European powers in Africa, who controlled the entire continent by 1920, tended to view black American missionaries as disruptive. They believed that the Christianizing and educating of indigenous Africans by black Americans would foment social discontent and eventual political revolt. Therefore European colonial policy was to discourage sending black missionaries. Consequently in the 1920s black missionaries were largely withdrawn by the sending agencies in the U.S., although black churches continued to send some missionaries as they were able. It was not until decolonialization in the 1960s that blacks again began to be sent in appreciable numbers to Africa. That the SVM could have solved this racial problem in the 1920s seems unlikely, but the issue at least continued to be raised by both black and white students and by Christian leaders throughout this period.[22]

One of the most critical questions faced by the SVM in the 1920s was over the expansion of its evangelistic goals to include unchurched Americans. Home missions departments of the major denominations existed throughout most of the nineteenth and early twentieth centuries, but the effort never enjoyed a student recruitment organization equivalent to the SVM. By the 1920s The Home Missions Council was concerned with immigrants, mountaineers, and people in isolated areas such as on the Western plains. The appeal of home missions, if lacking the glamour of foreign cultures and faraway places, was in many ways similar to that of foreign missions.

The SVM until this time had cooperated with the home missions movement by annually printing its job listings in the *Bulletin*. The Home Missions Council passed a resolution at their September 1920 Wichita, Kansas, convention calling upon the SVM "to give as adequate a place to Home Missions in their program as they are now giving to Foreign Missions," adding that if the SVM found this inconsistent with its organizational goals then the Home Missions Council should establish a Student Volunteer Movement for Home Missions.

Faced with the threat of a rival organization appealing to the limited student Christian constituency, the Executive Committee voted to set up a sub-committee to examine the problem, which included Mott, Wilder and four other senior members. The sub-committee recommended that the SVM should include two separate divisions, one for home and one for foreign missions, which would share resources where appropriate in order to avoid redundancy. This startling capitulation to the home missions advocates, and to those who viewed the separation of home and foreign missions as untenable, was largely reversed by the Executive Committee two weeks later.[23]

Wilder presented the meeting with the reasons for and against the SVM becoming a home missions recruiter, but he declined to take a strong stand. Following this failure of leadership by the General Secretary of the organization, Robert Speer made a strong case for the impracticality of the plan, questioning how the dual role of the SVM would effect conventions, student bands, the education program, and how the line could be drawn between the recruitment for home missions and the regular recruitment for home ministers. He recommended instead that the Home Missions Council be offered minimal accommodation. He suggested that three or four home mission enthusiasts be allowed into SVM conferences on an experimental basis, where they could work with SVM workers, and learn from their experience.

Mott responded that the SVM could no longer "continue on the old track " and needed to cooperate in some form with the Home Missions Council; however, he was not decided as to what plan the organization should take. For a man lauded for his natural organizational ability and who referred to the Student Movement as his first love, Mott's apparent passivity and irresolution is perhaps best explained by a rapid emotional detachment from the movement due to the events of the Des Moines Convention.[24] After the Convention he attended few Executive Committee meetings of the SVM and spent much of his time in Europe working with the WSCF and the new International Missionary Council, an ecumenical missionary organization for denominational cooperation. During a crucial decade of transition, Mott's leadership and experience would not be available to the SVM.

Most of the others at the standing committee gravitated to Speer's position, and the committee voted to approach the Home Missions Council with the Speer plan. The upshot was that the Home Missions Council was given office space in the SVM headquarters for a single representative who would learn by observation and consultation, but the SVM would continue to recruit exclusively for the foreign field. Later, when home missions enthusiasts formed the Student Fellowship for Christian Life-Service, the home missions equivalent of the SVM, the new organization was also given office space by the SVM.[25]

While the SVM leadership viewed the proposal of the Home Missions Council as a threat to the traditional purpose of the SVM and as a potential administrative nightmare, the combining of home and foreign missions recruitment was also an opportunity for the SVM to align itself with the growing student belief that both Eastern and Western nations needed to be

Christianized. By remaining an exclusively foreign missions organization, the SVM maintained the integrity of its tradition, but further distanced itself from the new student direction.

The WSCF Enters the Modern Era

While many religious organizations were struggling to adjust to the post-war era, the WSCF had one of the most daunting tasks before it. After the war the WSCF worked to rebuild the unity of its pre-war days. No SCM dropped out of the movement as of 1919. However, Germany needed assuaging after the Versailles Treaty excluded German missionaries from returning to their former mission stations. Also, their worst fears of Anglo-Saxon prejudice in the WSCF were confirmed by Mott's pro-allied activity in Russia in 1917. In general the WSCF was in confusion in many countries after the war. This was true especially of Eastern Europe where the map was completely redrawn at Versailles, creating six new nations divided along ethnic and political cleavages. Also there were war-battered nations, such as France and Holland, that needed food and medical relief.

The Executive Committee met at St. Beatenberg, Switzerland, for the first time since its meeting at Lake Mohonk in 1913. There it agreed that one of its primary aims would be to work for world harmony through the adoption of the principles of Jesus in international relationships. It also accepted a resolution to further the welfare of the whole student, which led to the creation of the European Student Relief program (ESR), that raised $2.5 million from 42 nations between 1920 and 1925 for the European students of 19 nations.

The St. Beatenberg conference also created a more democratic organization. In an attempt to meet the criticism of those nations in mission lands that the WSCF was dominated by the West and to meet the criticism of Europeans that it was dominated by the Anglo-Saxon world, the committee reorganized itself. First, it dropped the international groupings of student movements, such as that of France and Italy, in favor of nationalism. This led immediately to an enlargement of the committee from 12 to 20 members. It agreed to meet in conference every two years, and to insure student representation by appointing two to four students to the Executive Committee. In another indication that the old era of Western domination was over, there were a number of resignations at the conference. Dr. Fries resigned as chairman after 25 years. Mott resigned as General Secretary, but continued in the honorary role of President until

December 1928. And Dr. Walter Seton from Britain resigned as treasurer, a position he had held since 1908.

During the post-war era, the WSCF was buffeted by the same student criticisms that affected the SVM. While the impetus for the formation of the organization had been the advancement of missions, students in WSCF countries were now concerned with the issues of international relations, race, and economic justice. To the extent that they discussed missions, they were concerned with blunting imperialism and empowering indigenous churches. In Australia and New Zealand, immediately after the war, students embraced the union of home and foreign missions with the practical result that the SVM was abandoned in 1921 in both countries and the sending of foreign missionaries slowed to a trickle. The British Student Christian Movement after the war was beset with a creeping religious relativism that undermined the missionary impulse. The SVMU, in appealing to general student interests, split the student movement by alienating the conservative evangelical students. The result was a series of conferences in the 1920s held by the conservative Inter-Varsity Fellowship of Evangelical Student Unions, which set up a formal organization in 1928 and eventually replaced the SVMU as the major missionary recruiter of the nation. Like the SVMs in Australia, New Zealand, and Great Britain, the SVMs in other countries were beset with life threatening problems.

Wilder wrote to Mott that the new Social Gospel emphasis of the WSCF was replacing the personal gospel and would therefore eventually undermine the movement. Calling students to a massive social service campaign before they were grounded in a personal gospel, Wilder warned, would make of the movement "an empty shell with but little real life within it." This new WSCF approach, he believed, was simply an attempt to capitalize on a current student interest; it was a "get-rich-quick" method that was no substitute for traditional religion. That the WSCF should emphasize the social aspects of Christianity at the expense of personal religion was especially inappropriate in Europe, Wilder believed, because students there received little evangelical preparation in either home or church, and the schools either presented Christianity from the dry "wissenshaftlich" approach or from the perspective of destructive criticism.[26] Both perspectives, he believed, were anti-Christian.

The people in mission lands during these years also experienced rising anti-Christian sentiment. In an era of rising nationalism and corresponding anti-colonialist feeling, missionaries were often seen as agents of Western imperialism and became the targets of anti-Western criticism. Non-Christian nations were also becoming more aware of the humanist critique of Christianity, and used the Western rationalist tradition against the missionaries. The tours of John Dewey and Bertrand Russell in

China between 1919 and 1921 symbolized and spread this growing critique.

In an effort to combat the growing and increasingly organized anti-Christian feeling in China, the leaders of the WSCF agreed to hold their 1922 conference in Peking. The conference, held in April, proved to be a watershed in the history of the WSCF. Thirty-two nations were represented, and more than 500 delegates from China attended. To ensure that student concerns were addressed, the conference was broken up into six open forums, discussing as many subjects. However, the group discussing "Christianity and International and Inter-racial Problems" drew most of the delegates. The conference soon divided largely between the East and West, between those who favored pacifism and those who would not renounce war in all circumstances. The debate often led to an attack on the faults of the Western nations and showed that the Anglo-Saxon leadership of the federation could no longer be taken for granted.[27]

The conference, however, did agree on what became known as the "Peking Resolutions," which altered the purpose of the WSCF as stated in its constitution, affirming the equality of races, the need to oppose the causes that lead to war, and enjoining the Federation members to use all the instrumentalities at their disposal to bring these issues before the student world. Before the Peking Conference, Wilder wrote to Mott that, given the British abandonment of the watchword in 1922 and the waning missionary effort in many Federation countries, the Conference should address the missionary work of the WSCF. But this was not to be. Instead the new "international" approach of the WSCF at the conference marked the organization's formal shift away from traditional evangelistic missions to a concern for social issues.

The Peking conference also marked a shift in the emphasis of student groups around the world. In an editorial in the October 1923 issue of *The Student World*, the editors noted that student conferences during the previous two years had been dominated by a discussion of international issues and called for student groups to take even more seriously the "Peking Resolutions" in the light of current international events.[28] David Porter of the YMCA commented in the same issue that it was difficult to separate the momentum of student interest in international issues and the impact of the "Peking Resolutions." At the very least, then, the resolutions symbolized, augmented and helped to direct student interest in this area. In addition, the 1922 Peking Conference helped to shape and prepare student thought for the 1924 Student Volunteer Convention to be held in Indianapolis. The forum technique, and the emphasis on war, race and industrial issues, were all to be repeated there.

The Indianapolis Convention

Writing to the Executive Committee in the summer of 1922, Sherwood Eddy attempted to alert the leaders of the SVM to the remarkable change in the student world. Eddy had spoken at Des Moines and had traveled to many colleges since then. His reading of the student world was that the "progressive students" at the last Convention represented a new college sentiment for the presentation of a social gospel and the amendment of missionary practices to conform to a new sensitivity to non-Christian cultures. The next convention, he counseled, should clearly present the pagan practices of both the East and the West, and in general present missions in the broadest possible terms. The SVM, he warned, "is standing at the parting of the ways." Either it would cling to the past and continue to speak for a generation that was passing, or it would represent the different and broader vision of the majority of the current Christian college students.[29]

At the Executive Committee meeting held on September 23, 1922, Wilder opened a discussion of the next convention by reading Eddy's letter. The question at issue was how broad, or narrow, the convention should be. The Executive Committee voted to limit the convention to foreign missions, but also appointed a convention committee to meet with other interested groups to receive their recommendations.[30] The committee met on November 20-21. There were 95 participants present, which included representatives of the mission boards and the two student associations. Porter of the YMCA moved that the convention consider not only foreign missions, but also "the injustices and wrongs in our own national life," so that the convention would "emphasize the solidarity of the world" and the need of students, both those who went and those who stayed behind, to accept equal responsibility for the Christianization of the world. The conference adopted the motion and left the control and organization of the convention in the hands of the SVM. However, they recommended that the program committee include equal numbers of missionary board leaders who accepted the new view of missions, and also representatives of the YMCA and YWCA.[31]

In the end the Committee on Arrangements, chaired by Kenneth Lautourette, included 36 members from the YMCA, YWCA, SVM, mission boards, and some foreign nationals. They met throughout 1923 and planned a convention that would not only present a broad interpretation of Christian responsibility, but also be open to student contributions that would fundamentally alter the nature of the convention.

In contrast to the speakers at the Des Moines Convention, who had mostly been prominent leaders in the missionary movement, most of the speakers at Indianapolis were either students or foreign nationals. Addressing 6,150 delegates, and flanked by Mott, Wilder, Speer, Harlan Beach and other dignitaries on the platform, Dr. Walter H. Judd, chairman of the fourth Student Volunteer Council, opened the convention with an address that clearly reflected his own sense of inadequacy. "I am young, impetuous, and inexperienced as you might guess by looking at me," he admitted, "and I may fail entirely this afternoon." This was the first convention that Mott had not chaired and given the opening address. In contrast to Mott's maturity, optimism and perfect confidence in presiding over previous conventions, Judd sounded callow and cautious. Judd would later serve for a decade as a medical missionary in China, where he would witness firsthand the atrocities of China's civil war and the Japanese occupation. After returning to the United States, he would eventually serve for two decades as a Republican congressman from Minnesota and become well-known as a China expert and for his staunch anti-Communism.[32] But with this brave future well ahead of him, Judd defensively told the delegates that the convention committee had met for over a year to carefully plan the convention in order to insure that it would reflect student concerns and that the Business Committee that would run the convention included 18 students out of the 24 total members. "This is a student convention. It will be what we make of it," he warned.

There was very little theology discussed at the Convention. During the first day a series of addresses were given on contemporary social issues: capital and labor relations, race relations, and war. Clearly the liberal perspective was presented in every instance. Paul Blanshard, a socialist and leading figure of the American left whose personal religious journey began in Methodist fundamentalism and ended years later in humanist atheism,[33] noted that "if Jesus had worked in the modern factory He might have been discharged as an agitator, for He would stand firmly for the right of the working class."[34] He urged that workers be given a "living wage," the eight hour day, guaranteed employment, union empowerment in industrial relations, and cooperative ownership of industry between employees and employers. Several speakers spoke on racial relations, denouncing "white supremacy," the Ku Klux Klan, lynching, the use of racial epithets, and the scientific racism argued in the books of Madison Grant and Lothrop Stoddard. Newton Rowell, a Canadian representative to the First Assembly of the League of Nations, urged that Christian idealism replace self-interest alone as the rule governing international conduct. He praised the recent Washington Conference on naval disarmament, and urged American cooperation with the League of Nations.

Distressed by the new direction of the movement, Robert Speer presented the case for the good old cause against its modern detractors. He objected to the charge that past missionaries delivered a "narrow, individualistic" gospel. Those "great men....do not deserve the slurs that now and again slip into our references to them. We can thank God if we are one-tenth the men that they were."[35] The earlier missionaries had both a personal and a social gospel, he asserted. Speer also opposed the suggestions being made that the day of missions was over, that modern communications made obsolete the need for a face-to-face witness, or that short-term missionaries could meet the present need. And as for the watchword of the movement, "Don't throw it away too light-heartedly," he admonished his hearers. "The new generation requires it just as the old generation."

After the soaring rhetoric, passionate appeals and introspective thoughts of the speeches are considered, one is left to conclude, as it was nearly universally agreed at the time, that the centerpiece of the five day convention was the three two-hour long student sessions. During the first two sessions the students separated into 49 groups to discuss contemporary problems of their own choosing. Forty-one of the groups discussed racial relationships, 35 discussed war, and eleven considered the rightness of imposing Western civilization and Christianity on foreign peoples. The discussions were generally praised for the frankness of the participants, though S. Ralph Harlow later wrote that the ignorance the students revealed in the discussion groups on the most important issues of the day made them "serious indictments of our entire American educational system and the religious educational program of the churches."[36]

One student noted that the "colored" delegates were indignant at some of the comments of white racists also claiming to be Christians. She quoted several offensive remarks: "'I was one of the mob who hung that Negro in – '; 'We must protect our women'; 'Segregation and ill-treatment are the only means of keeping the Negro in his place.'"[37] Such remarks however appeared to be exceptional as most agreed that there was little rancor and much unanimity among the students.

Student leaders who emerged during the group discussions met in a meeting that lasted into the early hours of the last morning of the convention and selected eight of their group to present to the convention the fruits of their discussions in the third and final student session. The first four speakers would present the student views on race; the second four would present student views on war and its prevention.

The speakers announced that nine groups unanimously and eight by majority vote agreed that there ought to be no distinctions made in society on the basis of race. Four groups unanimously and three others by majority vote agreed with the above, but stipulated that this not include interracial marriage. Many objected to close social relations between the races. Southerners favored segregated or "parallel" education. Others opposed the Ku Klux Klan and lynching. Some favored Federal anti-lynching legislation. And there were a variety of practical suggestions made about how to "eliminate the white superiority complex" in their own colleges, through such means as inter-racial prayer and discussion groups, attempting to integrate college dormitories, social clubs, and athletics, and including college history courses that would present a fairer racial attitude than was then being offered.[38]

The elimination of war was the second major topic taken up by the groups. The positions expressed in the group discussions were reduced to four positions, which were presented by four student speakers and subsequently voted on by the delegates. The positions ranged from absolute pacifism to a deterrence strategy, but the vast majority, an estimated 5,500, agreed that the League of Nations and World Court were the best means to avoid war, but that if these failed Christians should engage in war.

Embracing "World Missions"

The February issue of the *Bulletin* was devoted to reviewing the Indianapolis Convention. T.H.P. Sailer, who had attended all the conventions since 1891, wrote that "The most immediate impression is that the Convention is passing out of the control of the hands of its founders. It came rather as a shock to have anyone but Dr. Mott preside."[39] Most of the student articles that were published, however, praised the convention for its democratic spirit, the visibility of student leadership, and the relevance of the issues discussed. Some comments, however, were quite harsh, reflecting a persistent disagreement with the methods and purposes of the SVM.

The major issue that came into focus following the convention was the shift to a new vision of missions. About two weeks before the convention an article appeared in *The Intercollegian* by John L. Childs, a student volunteer. Childs summarized the leading ideas of modern missions thinking and challenged the SVM to keep pace with the change in the times. He noted the implications of the rise of indigenous Christian movements, such as those in China, Japan and India. This suggested to him that native leaders ought increasingly to direct the Christian work in their own lands. For Childs the emphasis of missionaries should be on "co-operation" between East and West, and an eschewing of their imperialistic tendencies to dominate. Following the Convention, the SVM leaders sent the article to all the members of the first five Student Councils, asking for their responses. Thirty-six replies came back. Many found much to agree with in Child's article, especially with the need to emphasize the whole task of the church.

Similarly, the Fifth Volunteer Council, meeting February 21-24 at Yonkers, New York, discussed the variety of criticisms of the SVM that the delegates brought with them from their respective Unions and concluded that most of the criticisms of the organization were unfounded. What was really at issue, they agreed, was not the superficial criticisms heard throughout the student world, but nothing less than the meaning and purpose of the movement. The Indianapolis Convention presented to the students, as council member Clemmy Miller later summarized it in the *Bulletin*, a vision of "world missions rather than foreign missions."[40]

World missions was a catch-all phrase for the current shift in mission thinking. It meant that missions should now include both the Western and Eastern nations, that missionaries should show a new sensitivity to the positive aspects of Eastern culture and religion, that fraternalism should replace paternalism in the mission field, that indigenous churches should be given a greater share in the determination of how Western missionaries and money should be used, and that missionaries should treat the issues of race, war and industrialism as international problems for which in practice the West was more culpable than the East.[41]

The enlarged vision of "World Missions" led the council to three practical recommendations. First, stronger cooperation was needed with the other three student movements: the YMCA, YWCA and the Student Fellowship for Christian Life Service. A more unified student movement would help to present the vision of "world" missions and to alleviate the opinion expressed by many students that student volunteers regarded a foreign missionary vocation as a higher form of consecration. Second, the Council recommended for the study of the Unions four possible wordings of the declaration card. The first of these was the traditional wording that dedicated the student to foreign missions. The other three wordings included home missions on a parity with foreign missions. Finally, the Council recommended a rewording of the purpose of the movement found in its charter. The key changed enjoined the movement "to lay an equal responsibility on those not led or permitted to work abroad to choose their vocations in the light of Christian missions and the world's needs."[42]

*   *   *

In the four short years between the Des Moines and the Indianapolis conventions the SVM had endured a period of startling transition. Unlike most other religious organizations that enjoy enduring class, ethnic, and cultural stability, and therefore can evolve at a generational pace, the SVM, as a student organization, had to respond immediately to the sea change in student thought that occurred following the First World War. Students, disillusioned by the Great War and informed by the Social Gospel, shifted their attention from the social problems of the non-Christian world that so activated the Victorian era, and focused instead on America's own industrial, racial and international difficulties. Together with the rising nationalistic feelings in the East and Africa, this resulted in the shift in missionary thinking from "foreign" to "World Missions". However, the challenge to the SVM would not be limited to responding to new missiological thinking, but to an even greater transition in the American culture, which was characterized by the term "modernism."

Chapter Nine

IN THIS GENERATION

The slogan of the preceding generation of students was "The evangelization of the world in this generation." I do not say that this new slogan was not also theirs, but in a particular sense our slogan must be, "If any man would come after me, let him deny himself, take up his cross and follow me."

---Reinhold Niebuhr[1]

Victorian culture was built on the belief in progress, the home and family, the truth of Protestant Christianity, the superiority of Western culture and of the Anglo-Saxon race, and the importance of character. All of these constructs came under attack in the 1920s. The American literati was among the most visible iconoclasts. F. Scott Fitzgerald, Theodore Dreiser, Ernest Hemingway, T.S. Eliot, Ezra Pound, Eugene O'Neal, and others spoke for a "lost generation," alienated from traditional American values. Sinclair Lewis's *Main Street* (1920), *Babbitt* (1922), and *Elmer Gantry* (1927) mercilessly revealed the shallowness and banality of American middle-class life. H.L. Mencken did the same thing in the *American Mercury* but with a barbed wit that delighted the "smart set." As early as 1908 Van Wyck Brooks in *The Wine of the Puritans* traced America's repressive and materialistic culture to the nation's Puritan heritage. Brooks also saw in *The Ordeal of Mark Twain* (1920) the stunting hypocrisy of Victorian culture that left Twain an artistically unfulfilled and bitter old man, who became in his latter years the "gloomy prophet of modern civilization."[2]

The social sciences revealed much of the same picture. Robert and Helen Lynd's classic study of an American small town, *Middletown* (1929), revealed an American family life that was deeply unhappy, lonely and unsatisfying for the participants. Margaret Mead's *Coming of Age in Samoa* (1928) showed that in many important ways the life of a primitive tribal community was superior to the sexual repression and over-burdened family life of the typical American home.

In a process that began in the pre-war years, but became widespread after the war, youth were the first to rebel against traditional Victorian restraints. Experiencing the war first-hand, and finding themselves worn-out by idealism and lost crusades, youth sought pleasure, and soon adults were to follow. With the rationale of the "new psychology" that in the 1920s was being called Freudian, and the new freedom that came with the availability of birth control techniques, the automobile, and the autonomous life that came with the growth of cities, America experienced a change in its moral climate in the 1920s. Walter Lippmann's *A Preface to Morals* (1929) frankly discussed the "new hedonism" as a product of modern men and women being "emancipated not only of all fear of divine authority and human custom but of physical and social consequences as well."[3]

As a result of the relaxation of old standards and the increasing acceptance of new ways of understanding the world through the physical and social sciences, and also a generation of immigration from Catholic eastern and southern Europe, American Protestants found themselves in the 1920s dethroned from their preeminent position as the arbiters and exemplars of American culture. Notwithstanding the importance of the shift in missionary thinking in the first half of the 1920s and the growing rumblings of the Fundamentalist-Modernist controversy, the most important problem facing the SVM in this decade was the transition of American society from the Protestant hegemony of the Victorian era to the pluralism and growing secularity of the modern world.

Change in the Student Christian World

Despite the SVM's attempts in the 1920s to accommodate its promotion of missions to the new vision of "World Missions," their appeals to students seemed increasingly less effective. As early as 1921, when more volunteers were sailing abroad than at any other time in the SVM's history, the *Bulletin* noted a recent survey of fifty Western colleges, the traditional heart of student volunteer strength, that indicated a declining interest not only in missions but also in Christianity among the students.[4]

A sounding of international student opinion conducted by *The Student World* for the WSCF in 1921 produced similar results.[5] Christian leaders of student movements from around the world reported a student revolt against traditional standards of Christian morality and belief. Australasian students were caught up in a materialistic age, and finding their own leaders com-promising between God and mammon, wondered if the Christian message was either right or relevant. In France, students once hostile to Christianity were now simply indifferent. German students, reading Nietzsche, Schopenhauer and Spengler, were caught in a morass of moral and religious relativism. The Austrian students ignored Christianity and were lost in an aimless chase after the latest -isms – "pacifism, anarchism, Tolstoyism, nationalism, all grades of idealism, monism, anthroposophy, mysticism and even occultism."[6] Italian students were indifferent to Christianity, and indulged in sensuality and materialism. In the East matters were little different. Japan reported rampant hedonism and a rejection of all religions as inadequate in the present day. The Chinese, though generally still favorable to the missionaries, found the clergy intellectually deficient and the conduct of church members and the Western nations immoral by even pagan standards. In India, Christianity, long associated with the Western nations, was discredited by the excesses of the war and by the rising demand for home rule being led by Mahatma Gandhi.

In the same article the spokesman for the United States reported that the students were increasingly under one of two influences. The first was fundamentalism, which the writer described as "an ultra-conservative moral and theological attitude which frowns upon certain amusements and magnifies certain extremes of Christian doctrine." The second influence was not theological modernism as one might guess, but rather "a very liberal, not to say, lax view of Christianity and traditional moral standards as repressive of that free satisfaction of individual appetite and ability." This position, the writer noted, was endorsed and supported by modern psychology, social science, and professors who teach moral and epistemological relativism. These new teachings, the writer explained, led "students to believe that the old sanctions have no rational authority."[7]

From Austria to Japan and from India to Canada, it seemed that students in the postwar world were caught up in an age in which the claims of Christianity could be discarded with all the thought that one normally reserves for a change of clothes. To civilians who had experienced the irksome privations of war, to the soldiers who had endured the horrors of world-wide conflagration, and to everyone who had recoiled in bitter disillusionment at the cynical peace made at Versailles, the 1920s was not a time for high ideals, but for self-indulgence. In such an environment the contest was not between Fundamentalism and Modernism, or even belief and unbelief, but between belief and indifference.

One result of the cultural sea change of the 1920s was a decline in the number of missionaries being sent abroad, a decline that was also reflected in the number of sailed SVM missionaries. In 1920 the U.S. sent out 1,731 missionaries, but within eight years that number was reduced by two-thirds, to 550. In his final report to the General Council in 1927, Wilder offered a number of reasons for the decline in missionaries sent.[8] The missionary boards of the denominations, he explained, experienced a financial pinch in this period, so that potential volunteers demurred for fear that the boards could neither afford to send them nor to maintain them once they were in the field. He cited the inadequacy of the Indianapolis Convention in sounding the missionary call and urged the SVM to return to an exclusively missionary agenda in its next convention. Wilder also found the Fundamentalist-Modernist controversy to be an "acute" problem for the SVM, as four educational institutions had already withdrawn from the movement.

In addition to these intramural concerns, Wilder also believed that students were negatively influenced by the number of trends and critiques of Christianity predominant in the general culture of the postwar era: the general anti-missionary sentiment, the charges of imperialism, the demands for indigenous churches, the need for domestic religious work, and the religious relativism taught in the schools. Many concluded, Wilder believed, "that the day of the foreign missionary is rapidly drawing to a close."[9]

Wilder was particularly concerned about the religious relativism promoted in the schools, which taught the excellence of such non-Christian religions as "High Hinduism" or "High Buddhism," and ignored the popular religion of the East or the continuing social consequences and needs in non-Christian lands. By emphasizing the limited good in other cultures and not the overwhelming evidence of social evil, Wilder believed that many Christian students became concerned with "world fellowship," rather than becoming "prophets who are burning with zeal for Christian civic righteousness and Christian social reform."[10]

Wilder bemoaned the spiritual declension of the era. Students, in his estimation, showed little acquaintance with the Bible and gave little time to Bible study and prayer. Their faith in the reliability of the Scriptures, he believed, was undermined by their reading of Higher Criticism: "Jesus is accepted by them not as _the_ way, but as _one_ of the ways to God" (his emphasis). As a consequence of these developments, he reasoned, students emphasized meetings, conferences, and discussion groups, that did not lead to consecrated lives but rather "a vague interest in international questions." The students, he mused, were more sinned against than sinning, for they were the victims of the modern teachings of psychology, comparative religion, and of the general materialism of the times.[11]

Wilder was not alone in his appraisal of the student world. Following the Indianapolis Convention, several Student Movement leaders wrote in the February edition of the *Bulletin* of a spiritual aridity among the students. While most of the comments on the Indianapolis Convention concerned either the generational conflict or the new "world" missions perspective, Henry Van Dusen, then a student volunteer, wrote ominously of a spiritual declension evident at the convention. Traditional spiritual disciplines, he noted, were not evident, and discussion groups seem to have taken the place of Bible study. Students were respectful during the Convention when spiritual subjects were raised from the platform, but spiritual experience was not something with which the students were familiar, nor did they feel the need of it. The Convention, he believed, was an accurate "thermometer of the spiritual life in undergraduate circles, a revelation of conditions which have long existed but of which we have not become fully conscious before."[12]

A Canadian student James Endicott writing for the *Bulletin* believed he detected not simply a lack of spirituality, but a general religious relativism dominant among the students. Students, he commented, listened more carefully to Fay Campbell's address than to any other that attempted to deliver a personal message. Campbell sounded the traditional holiness themes of surrender, consecration, and empowerment, "But there was not any expression of conviction on the part of the students that the way of Jesus is the way. One did not feel any very vital expression of belief on the part of the average student, that in Jesus we can receive a power to change our own lives..."[13]

T.H.P. Sailer, now on the Presbyterian Board of Foreign Missions and also writing for the February edition of the *Bulletin*, noted the same lack of spirituality at the Convention. He heard no theological discussions and suggested that the topics of war and race were discussed because the students were not prepared to discuss foreign missions due to their ignorance of the subject. He noted further that, in contrast to other conventions, the negative aspects of Western civilization and Christianity were criticized, while the positive side of Eastern civilization and "heathenism" were commended. He also noted that the watchword "lacks voltage" for most of the students and suggested that this was due to the change in missionary thinking. The task as now conceived, he reasoned, was not evangelization but world reconstruction. Because this could not be accomplished in a single generation, the watchword "fails to strike fire as it once did."[14] In fact this was the last convention to display the watchword above the convention platform. Never officially repudiated, the watchword was allowed to simply fade away.

Student leaders in general were also very aware of the spiritual change that had occurred in their generation. The Sixth National Council (Student Volunteer Council), reacting to the decline in membership and the continuing criticism of the movement in their February 1926 meeting, concluded that the heart of the problem must be in the individual volunteers themselves. They were ignorant of the ideas and traditions of the SVM and the broader missionary movement. Therefore the Council recommended that the Executive Committee gradually shift the educational emphasis in the movement from an "extensive" to an "intensive" emphasis on missions. It reasoned that the other student movements should be left to educate students on the general issues confronting Christians in the world, so that the SVM could devote itself exclusively to educating its volunteers in missions. Furthermore, the Council recommended that students not be allowed to sign the declaration card until they thoroughly understood its meaning. To accomplish this, literature on the movement would be provided for their perusal, and consultations with other volunteers would take place to ensure that they understood the meaning of being a volunteer.

The sixth Council, however, believed that it detected an even greater failing in the then current student population. Writing in the *Bulletin*, Council member J. Davidson Taylor concluded that "The basic fault among Volunteers is not lack of knowledge nor of ambition; it is lack of power. We have attempted an impossibility -- the substitution of high ideals for a personal relationship with Jesus Christ."[15] The Council's findings committee concluded "that the Volunteers have in large part failed spiritually," because they were not completely consecrated or surrendered to Christ. They commended "Bible study, morning watch, and private devotions" to the volunteers, and suggested that the *Bulletin* place an article on spirituality in each issue.[16]

Perhaps the most sensitive and perceptive of the explanations for the apparent student declension in faith was given by Walter Judd in his opening address at the 1924 convention. After paying obeisance to the new conventional wisdom that all the world is a mission field, including "pagan" America and Canada, Judd proceeded to make some searching remarks about his own student generation. Like a seventeenth-century Puritan minister delivering a Jeremiad, Judd compared his generation to the founding generation represented by the men sitting behind him, which included Mott, Wilder, Speer and others. "Are we presenting the Christ as effectively today, we as students, are we moving our student generation as those men did?" he asked the delegates. "If they were to step out today who of us could step in and move this, our generation, as they have moved theirs?" Then with a series of rhetorical questions Judd mused over what might be wrong with his generation. Perhaps they were too "coldly scientific" to experience the warmth of the old religion? Perhaps the Mount Hermon student of 1886 was "able, more or less, to hypnotize himself into a state where he thought he was conscious of the presence of Jesus Christ, whereas all that he experienced was a reflex effect of his own abnormal psychological processes?" Perhaps students have not experienced Christ or the power He can bring to bear on the world's problems? Perhaps the church had so emasculated its teaching and demonstration of Christ that it had "lost its prophetic vision and spiritual power?" Perhaps modern students had not completely surrendered their wills to Christ? Judd's questions suggest what was undoubtedly true, that his generation admired the older generation, but could not follow precisely in their footsteps.

Above all believing that his generation lacked commitment, Judd returned to the fountainhead of evangelical spiritualism, the great motif of the holiness or higher life movement, which was the emphasis on the will. Referring to the venerable leaders of the SVM seated behind him, Judd asked, "What is the secret of the success of the men who have lived Christ, however imperfectly, before our eyes?"

> ...seeing with trained and informed minds and feeling with educated and sensitive hearts, we need cultured and consecrated wills that will slip in like automatic clutches and hold fast to the thing that we know we ought to do.[17]

His reference to "trained and informed minds", "educated ...hearts" and "cultured wills" was clearly meant to distinguish what he believed to be the sophisticated modern generation from the naive older generation. His automobile metaphor is also an attempt to update an older theology. The secret of the founders was the decisiveness of their wills, according to Judd. But Judd had managed in these words to present a holiness doctrine without mentioning the Holy Spirit, and without saying specifically that the power he referred to was to come from God. Judd implied that the older generation's experience of God was simply self-hypnosis. Shorn of any supernaturalism, he seemed to be saying, in effect, that the secret of the older generation's power was simply their decisiveness of will.

At the end of the address he quoted the Gospel of John 7:17, "He that willeth to do His will shall know." Judd used this verse as a proof text for experiential religion, arguing that "if I will to do His will, step by step as this is revealed, gradually the whole purpose of God for my life will stand revealed before me."[18]   However, knowing God's will is not the same as having the power to do His will. In place of a theology of power, Judd had substituted a providence revealed gradually through experience.   Judd concluded his address using derivations of all the key holiness terms --- surrender, consecration, victory --- yet all the power he referred to was simply will power.

Ironically, having jettisoned all of the holiness movement but its language and its focus on the will, even these seemed hopelessly anachronistic in the 1920s, because they were premised upon an outdated psychology. This was the decade when many Americans suddenly became aware of Freudian psychology.   Most important for the Student Movement, as the words "suppression," "subconscious," and "libido" became part of the American vocabulary, was that the new psychology appeared to render passe traditional notions of character formation, self-control, and the will.

Pre-Freudian psychology had taught that human conscious perception informed people of all their important needs and desires.[19] Based on this information, their minds made conscious commands that their wills would carry out. In opposition to this, Freud taught that conscious perception, the ego, was not actually informed of all a person needs. Rather, there are subconscious depths in the mind of which the ego is only dimly aware and of which it cannot completely fathom even if it wanted to.   Furthermore, Freud argued that the will is incapable of completely taming sexual instincts and that the suppression of sexual drives might lead in some to neurosis. Freud summed up his position succinctly, "the ego is not master in its own house."[20]

While the new psychology undermined the Student Movement's emphasis on character, there were other factors that also contributed to its downfall. The logic of the Social Gospel and the Progressive era policies moved from an emphasis on character formation to an emphasis on systemic reform of society's problems. Moreover, the solution offered by individual character reformation seemed trifling and out of step in an age that had witnessed the massive mobilization of entire nations for war, an age beset by an increasing number of union strikes and a new militancy among educated black Americans, and an age that was more interested in self-expression than in self-control. Clearly a kingdom based on character would not be suited to the "modern" world.

Judd may have spoken for the student mind of the 1920s better than he realized. The words of his address reflected both the awe his generation felt for the generation of the 1890s that had pioneered the movement, and its sense of the inadequacy of the verities of that generation for the new times. His generation wanted to believe in the old religion, perhaps they even wanted to embrace the old shibboleths, but the best many of them could do was to parrot some of the old words without really embracing their full meaning. The banner of evangelical religion was clearly in tatters, but, not yet having a reinterpretation of their religion to meet the new situation, students were forced to use remnants of the slogans and ideas that they had rejected four years before.

Attacks on the SVM Leadership

Faced with a massive cultural transition and an apparent generational conflict in missionary and Christian thinking, it was inevitable that the leadership of the SVM would come under attack. While there was an initial revolt at the Des Moines Convention in 1920, the attacks following the Indianapolis Convention were more open and more far-reaching in their results. Writing in *The Intercollegian*, Paul Harrison criticized the SVM for its "most unsuitable mass of administrative machinery" that he felt impeded its purpose. He observed that the Executive Committee and the volunteers were frequently in disagreement, and that the 90 thousand dollar budget, of which the students supplied only a third, undermined its mission as a student movement. He recommended that the Council become the legislative head of the movement, and that the budget be dramatically trimmed to a level that students could themselves fund. In this atmosphere, his article suggested, perhaps spiritual life would flourish and the General Secretary's time would be freed up for more important things than raising money.[21]

Writing for the *Bulletin*, T.T. Brumbaugh, secretary on the Third Student Council, wrote an even more scathing article. He also served on the Business Committee that ran the Indianapolis Convention and acted as an aide to Joseph Robbins, Chairman of the Convention. Brumbaugh felt that the convention's five day presentation of the world's problems was so packed with eloquent speakers making specific appeals that the students were overwhelmed with information, resulting in "mental indigestion." He believed that the final day of the convention should have been a time of summation and reflection on what had gone before, but instead it was the occasion for the presentation of even more and varied issues, which he described as a "Colossal blunder!" Rather than being inspired by the presentations, Brumbaugh felt "insignificant" and "depressed" in the light of the world's problems. He argued that this was the result of the SVM's aging leadership being insensitive to student needs. The SVM he argued, must again "become a `student' movement or we shall cease to be a worth while Movement at all."[22]

The "Old Guard," he believed, dominated the movement and the convention despite the Student Volunteer Council. Student leaders, notwithstanding their numerical majority on the Executive Committee and other committees, were often overawed by the older leaders. What student, Brumbaugh asked "has not felt the repressing force back of remarks from the Chair or other older member[s] of the committee such as the following: `Now, there you have the plan as outlined; we should like to have some student opinion.'" The veneer of student leadership often results in decisions otherwise "odious to students!" More than simply a call for further student representation, Brumbaugh attacked the venerable leaders of the movement in derisive language, much of which was not reprinted in the *Bulletin*. He reported that it was generally held at the Indianapolis Convention that "the `Higher ups' were too much in evidence." Brumbaugh reported that a foreign speaker remarked to him that despite their limited appearance on the platform,

> "The conservative and restraining hand of the Old Guard was there. It was a great Convention, but they were out of touch with its greatness, and consequently its greatness didn't go far enough. Leaders in a day that is past, they now can't think things through. It's too bad the Convention wasn't left in the hands of the young."

Brumbaugh referred specially to the "Big Four" as he says Mott, Speer, Eddy and Wilder were generally known among the students. Speer's address, he complained, contained no new ideas. He missed Mott's address but the next day's newspaper account gave him no surprise. While he lauded Eddy's outspoken commitment to the Social Gospel, he was perplexed at how Eddy could argue in his address, "Intellectual Unrest and the Youth Movement," that the current world-wide student dissatisfaction and desire for change was organizationally expressed in the American Student Christian movement. Wilder, he believed, was "hardly in a position to reflect student sentiment." Brumbaugh held Wilder, as head of the convention's Business Committee, responsible for the inflexibility of the convention program and unresponsiveness to student desires that led to the over-crowded program.

Brumbaugh's comments made explicit what many SVM leaders sensed after the Des Moines Convention. Confronted with the new student generation's restiveness and shift in theological orientation, the older generation of leaders seemed to gradually drift away. In the years before the war's end, the SVM enjoyed great stability in its leadership. Mott had been the chairman of the movement since 1888, and Fennell Turner had been General Secretary since 1898. Others had served nearly as long. Educational Secretary J. Lovell Murray, Business Secretary William McCulloch, and Executive Secretary Thomas Sharp had all been serving since the decade of the 1900s. In rapid secession all these men retired in the first half of the 1920s: Turner in 1919, Mott in 1920, Murray in 1921, McCulloch in 1922, and Sharp in 1925.

Sharp/Baker Scandal - Reorganization

A scandal within the SVM organization, which was buried in the SVM archives and never made public, had important implications for the organization and leadership of the movement and revealed growing tensions among the staff over the theological direction the movement should take.

Tom Sharp, the Executive Secretary of the organization, who among other tasks scheduled the itineraries of the traveling secretaries and ran the office in the absence of Wilder, allegedly had an affair with Mary Baker, one of the traveling secretaries. Sharp, a married man, initiated the hiring of Baker in 1922. As early as the Spring of 1923 the other staff workers began to notice that Sharp and Baker were spending a conspicuous amount of time together. By the time of the Indianapolis Convention one worker, who had also attended the Des Moines Convention, felt that the spirit of the workers had changed, and that "something seemed wrong with the whole bunch."[23] The office gossip continued, finally coming to a head at a leadership conference at Westtown in September 1924. Wilder explained that the matter came to his attention about the time of the Indianapolis Convention, but "reached a climax when every member of our headquarter's Staff asked to be excused from attending the Setting up Conference for our traveling and headquarter's Secretaries at Westtown if Tom was to be there."[24] Wilder persuaded them to change their minds, but later regretted that he did not simply fire Sharp at that time.

Wilder worked with Sharp and Baker for about a year, apparently hoping to quietly mend the harmony of the organization and restore the errant couple. Nevertheless the affair continued, and probably out of resentment Sharp began to criticize Wilder's leadership both to his face and among the staff. "Mr. Sharp has told me," Wilder explained to J. Lovell Murray, "that Dr. Mott rendered me a great unkindness by inviting me to become General Secretary of the Student Volunteer Movement since my gifts do not lie in that direction. How can a General Secretary have on his Staff a man who regards him as not fit for his job?"[25]

The situation came to a head on October 31, 1925 at a Standing Committee meeting when Wilder presented Sharp's letter of resignation and another asking for its immediate acceptance. The committee asked the staff members to leave while it considered the situation, and minutes were not kept of their deliberations. The committee decided to accept Sharp's resignation but to keep him on in a temporary position with the staff. The committee may not have known of the personal behavior that resulted in Sharp's resignation, or perhaps they chose to disregard it as rumor. In fact the only information that the committee had before it were the two letters from Sharp, which may have led the committee to believe the reasons for Sharp's resignation were largely due to a personal rift between Wilder and Sharp over the leadership and direction of the movement. Consequently Wilder was not allowed to give his point of view. The committee then voted to form a committee of inquiry to consider "the future policy, program and staff" of the movement.[26]

Wilder took these actions to be a vote of no confidence in his leadership and tendered his resignation the next day. Nothing came of this, but later Wilder reproduced letters from Mott written to him when offered the Position of General Secretary, which confirmed that he would have the right to determine his own staff. Mott also wrote to confirm this understanding. The Executive Committee subsequently declined to offer Sharp a temporary position. At a meeting of the Executive Committee in November, Wilder read a letter to the Committee intimating if not fully disclosing Sharp's dalliance. In a letter to Wilder that was also sent to all the committee members, Sharp threatened a slander suit if such "insinuation and inferences" continue.[27] They did not, at least openly, and, as Sharp was now gone, there was now no reason to further discuss his probable indiscretions.

This minor tempest, however, did issue in the formation of a Commission of Ten to study the future course of the SVM. The Standing Committee appointed five senior and five junior members of the movement to the commission.[28] The committee asked the vice-chairman of the Executive Committee, J. Lovell Murray, to convene the first meeting. At that meeting Robert Speer was elected chairman. Speer had the confidence of everyone, but his steady conservative qualities insured not only that the commission findings would be accepted but that they would probably not be very far-reaching.

Meeting individually with the members of the headquarters staff, with two members of the candidate departments of the Baptist and Methodist Boards, and with nine former traveling secretaries of the movement, including Mary Baker and Tom Sharp, the commission came to some broad conclusions regarding the current state of missionary theory and practice. Recognizing the growth of indigenous churches and the oft-heard complaint that foreign missionaries were no longer needed in large numbers, the Commission questioned whether, nearly four decades after its founding, the SVM was still needed. They concluded that with the denominational boards calling for large numbers of missionary recruits, 1,400 in 1924, and with the indigenous churches continuing to call for Western missionaries, the SVM was still a vital necessity as a recruiter of missionaries.

The Commission dealt thoughtfully with the relationship of the SVM to broader denominational and student worlds, asking important organizational questions. Was it necessary that the SVM be an independent organization? Might it not be better if it was run directly by the foreign mission boards or subsumed by the intercollegiate organizations of the YMCA and YWCA? Should the SVM broaden its goals to include the contemporary belief that there should be no distinction between home and foreign missions?

The Commission rejected amalgamation with the missionary boards on the grounds that doing so would mean that the SVM would no longer be a distinctively student movement. The SVM, the report averred, "has been a living activity of students themselves and ought to remain so."[29] The commission rejected becoming an organizational part of the larger student movement of the YMCA and YWCA because of its belief in the "necessity of continued specialization of interest and care" for the missionary enterprise.[30] The Commission urged that the SVM work at a closer relationship with the broader student movement and that it continue to avoid becoming a rival of other student organizations. The Commission conceived of the SVM as an organization that stood between the denominational boards and the student organizations with its own distinctive task. Finally the commission summarily rejected the broadening of the SVM's task to include home missions simply because they believed that this was the task of the Student Christian Organizations.

The Commission was most effective in its suggestions on how the SVM should reorganize itself. The original conception of an Executive Committee to decide policy matters and a small staff of secretaries to implement those policies worked well while Mott was chairman, when there was a broad consensus about the purpose of the movement and when the leadership was closely in tune with the student world. This arrangement worked less well during Wilder's tenure. The formation of the Student Council in 1920, a tacit admission that the SVM had been out of touch with the student world, added redundancy to the governmental structure and implicitly raised the question of whether the SVM was actually a student movement after all.

The Commission recommended that the Executive Committee, Student Council, Headquarters staff, and traveling secretaries be combined into a single General Council, which would include representatives from the Unions, the foreign mission boards, and the YMCA and YWCA. Meeting for several days once each year, the council would form the policies of the organization and elect an interim Administrative Committee to meet quarterly.

The Commission indirectly addressed Robert Wilder's leadership of the SVM. Without any overt criticism of the General Secretary, the Commission recommended that a plan to obtain an understudy for Wilder, originally discussed in 1920 and embraced by Wilder but rejected by Sharp at that time, now be accepted by the SVM. The report explained that the understudy was needed "against the time when he lays down his work as will be inevitable in view of the age consideration alone." Former SVM Business Secretary W. P. McCulloch pointed out that the word "alone" suggested that something other than age was also being taken into consideration. "In view of what has been said in and out of the Commission," McCulloch explained in a letter to Speer, "this slight inference [sic] to something besides age can do no good and is very apt to be taken by Mr. Wilder as a bit of a thrust."[31]   The current Business Secretary Stanhope R. Pier saw the possibility that the Commission's recommendation of an understudy for Wilder was "an easy way of politely putting Mr. Wilder on the shelf." Pier objected to this, writing that "I for one don't want any polite diplomacy to step in and superannuate him before God calls him out of the job."[32]

There were at least two issues involved in the controversy over Wilder's leadership. First, according to Pier, Sharp was letting it be known that Wilder was not giving adequate attention to the job of administering the organization and consequently Sharp had been forced to take on this added burden. Sharp's resignation, according to this scenario, was a deliberate attempt to force to a head the issue of Wilder's administrative neglect. A second reason was given in a series of letters written by another headquarters staff worker Fay Campbell.

Campbell wrote to Wilder shortly after his appearance before the Commission to explain what he had said, and thus began with Wilder a revealing correspondence concerning the growing theological division within the SVM. Campbell first expressed his fear that the SVM was moving in a theologically conservative direction. Based on his observations at student meetings, he believed that the student volunteers were beginning to separate from the mainstream of the more liberal student associations and predicted that within a few years the SVM would be a conservative counterpart to the liberal YMCAs and YWCAs on college campuses. Wilder responded that he was aware of conservative missionary developments in Great Britain and Norway, but that this was unlikely in the American SVM. In fact his experience pointed to the opposite. He knew of two conservative institutions where the students had voted to separate from the SVM because of its liberal tendencies. He knew of two others that were close to separation for the same reason. Wilder noted that there were about 200 institutions with SVMs but without Student Associations. "Many of these are conservative and are watching every move of our Executive Committee."

This division between liberal and conservative thinking also found expression in the Commission report. The Commission members listened to a variety of views concerning the possible purposes and functions of the SVM, and their report listed a number of dual options, which without saying so suggested a Fundamentalist-Modernist division of thinking among those interviewed. For example, some saw the need to stress personal character, others modern thought; some wanted a stronger faith requirement for membership, others accepted the current standard of evangelical church membership as adequate; some would reemphasize the urgency of the watchword, others wanted to assert Social Gospel issues. Finally, some of those interviewed would avoid all theological issues by confining the SVM to missionary recruitment and leaving the broader issues to the mission boards and the missionaries themselves to decide.

The End of an Age

As Robert Wilder later commented, the Commission of Ten was successful in having "clarified the atmosphere" -- at least for the moment.[33] It confirmed the traditional missionary motivation of the movement, glossed over theological debates that would later be revisited, and reorganized the structure of the movement, enhancing its claims to be a student movement by placing students directly on the General Council and yet maintaining much of the traditional leadership to provide the wisdom and stability necessary for smooth operations.

Earlier in the year Jesse R. Wilson accepted the invitation of the SVM leadership to become the Associate General Secretary, Wilder's understudy. Wilson had been a student volunteer, a Student YMCA Secretary, an SVM

Traveling Secretary, served as a student member of the Executive Committee, and then served in Japan as a missionary for four years. After Wilder's retirement, he would serve as General Secretary of the movement for ten years, leading it through the turbulent period of the Fundamentalist-Modernist controversy, whose divisiveness for the movement had as yet only been suspected.

At the very time that the SVM was celebrating its fortieth anniversary in the December 1926 issue of the *Bulletin*, the National Council of Christian Associations (CCA), which included the YMCA and YWCA, held its first National Student Convention. The only national Christian student conventions previous to this had been the SVM's. Despite the SVM's attempts at accommodating the social agenda of the other student movement organizations, the CCA concluded unanimously in a meeting at Lake Forest College in Illinois during the summer of 1925 that the student world needed a non-missionary national convention.

Held at Milwaukee, the 1926 convention heard new voices that would come to dominate the student world of the next generation such as Kirby Page and Reinhold Niebuhr. To a generation that disparaged the easy slogans of the past and invented the word "debunk", Niebuhr warned that "the real enemy of religion never has been skepticism; the real enemy of religion is cynicism." Niebuhr explained that while the previous generation of Christian students had been galvanized by the task of world evangelization, the current generation had a new task: "Our business is no longer merely to Christianize the nominally non-Christian world but to Christianize the world which is nominally Christian. Western civilization, you see, has become a missionary territory."[34]

Niebuhr, however, did not speak for all of the student world. Fundamentalists would always see the Neo-orthodox theology that Niebuhr would come to represent in America as simply a more insidious form of the old liberalism. Fundamentalists, as Wilder feared, gradually disengaged themselves from the SVM, whose policies and ideas it associated with the liberal CCA.

As one of the original student volunteers at the Mount Hermon conference, it was fitting that Wilder resigned his position as General Secretary in order to spend his last three working years as a missionary in the field. He accepted the position of Executive Secretary of the Christian Council of Western Asia and Northern Africa. With John Mott acting as intermediary, Wilder agreed to do what he did best, provide leadership and inspiration to his fellow evangelicals. This he did for the missionaries of Turkey, the Levant and Egypt.

Why Wilder resigned is not difficult to conclude. In a letter to McCulloch he confessed, "The experience of the past three months has

been about the hardest in my life. It has dogged and stunned me." He
endured the ordeal of the commission, he said, because, in Paul's words,
"The Lord stood by me and strengthened me," and because of the support
of his family, and, he added, "your support, Mac."[35]

But there were other hardships beside the ordeal of the Commission of
Ten. As the General Secretary, Wilder had had to deal with a number of
vexing problems: the general student revolt of the period, the Canadian
conflict, black demands, and the home missions controversy. Being out of
the country so long before be became General Secretary, Wilder had few
contacts from which to solicit money; consequently much of his time was
unavoidably taken up with fund raising. He was in great demand as a
speaker, and therefore spent many months away from the New York
headquarters, even going abroad. But as a result Sharp was right: Wilder
neglected administration. Also Wilder was theologically conservative, yet
the *Bulletin* was filled with Social Gospel articles and much of his staff and
many vocal students were theologically liberal. This must have made him
at times feel at very least uncomfortable. Wilder also had an
organizational difficulty. Both he and Mott had been the charismatic
leaders of the SVM during their separate eras of leadership, but the
difference was that Mott sat on the policy-making Executive Committee,
while Wilder as General Secretary was officially an administrator. And, as
with the Sharp/Baker scandal, there could be considerable friction between
the staff and the committee. By the summer of 1927, however, Wilder was
once again on the mission field; and, relieved of the onerous burdens of
fund raising and trouble-shooting, he was once again the inspirational
leader and evangelist that he had always wanted to be.

Wilder was the first of his generation to lead the SVM and the last.
His passing from leadership marks the end of an era. The leadership of the
American missionary enterprise, having sent out 11,531 student volunteers
by the end of 1926, now passed to the younger generation.[36] Of course the
sense that one generation was setting aside the burden for another to take
up had long been in the air. Several months before, the SVM devoted the
December 1926 issue of the *Bulletin* to marking the fortieth anniversary of
the founding of the movement at Mount Hermon. It recorded a speech by
Robert Speer at a YMCA Student Conference at Northfield during the
summer before. Standing in the room at Mount Hermon where forty years
before the "Meeting of the 10 Nations" had occurred, the meeting that had
that propelled Robert Wilder's dream of a missionary student movement
into a reality, Speer asked the youthful audience a series of questions that
were for him more than merely rhetorical:

Now we put it to you. It is forty years that we have been at it. Will you take it over for the forty years to come? Are you going to throw over what has been won so toilfully across these years? Or are you going to do what men ought to do – take the best and carry it on, keep all that is good and real of it, and make that something richer and greater and more wonderful still?[37]

Despite Speer's eloquent plea, with the older generation no longer leading the SVM, the organization began to distance itself from the missionary ideas that had launched it. At the 1928 SVM convention in Detroit Sherwood Eddy, *The Christian Century* reported, "finally and publicly repudiated that famous war-cry: 'The evangelization of the world in this generation.' No one challenged him; no one attempted to maintain that what is still needed is --- to use the Eddyian phrase --- 'a Paul Revere's ride across the world.'"[38] Yet, despite the *Christian Century*'s assertion of a final repudiation, the reproduction of Eddy's address in the 1928 convention book did not include Eddy's explicit denial of the watchword, suggesting a lingering reluctance on the part of the leadership of the SVM to break completely with the past. Nevertheless, it was clear that the corpse was now quite cold and that Eddy had only issued a long delayed certificate of death.

*   *   *

The painful transition endured by the SVM in the 1920s reflected the new student attitude toward religion as well as the new intellectual and cultural trends of the period. Ironically, the SVM prided itself on its worldly acuity, but it owed much of its success to the very innocence and naivete that many today find alternately so charming and appalling. Student volunteers harnessed modern science and technology to advance the spread of the gospel, but did not anticipate that these forces would eventually undermine their movement. Missionaries hitched their wagon to the meteor of Western colonial expansion and cultural optimism, but were severely chastened when that meteor suddenly plunged earthward in the fiery cataclysm of world war. Provincial Americans went abroad in the firm conviction of having the one sure truth, but quickly discovered that others also had claims to truth, which seemed on closer inspection not to be altogether unreasonable.

In the student world the milieu of the 1920s was largely one of either indifference to Christianity or open hostility to the forms and assumptions for which it was generally known before and during the war. The association of missions with Western imperialism, the spreading acceptance of cultural and religious relativism, the flagrant materialism of the West, and the rising demand of Christians in the East for truly indigenous churches all worked to undermine the traditional vision of an Anglo-American-led Western missionary movement. In the meantime, the rise of the Social Gospel, the general impact of the First World War, and the acceptance of Freudian psychology removed the intellectual undergirding of the pietistic religion and social vision that characterized the movement. By the 1920s, the preponderance of weight given by society to the first half of Peabody's question asked in the introduction to this history – "Does the world make the person, or does the person make the world?" – was so pronounced as to make the vision of a kingdom of character a hopeless relic of the past.

Epilogue

As American Protestantism in the 1920s adjusted to being only one part of a larger pluralistic society, it suffered the further humiliation of internecine fighting. The Fundamentalist-Modernist controversy had been smoldering in American society at least since the 1870s, but it was not until the 1920s, when modernists had gained sufficient strength in the Northern Presbyterian and Baptist churches, that the conflict burst into flames. Though the book series *The Fundamentals* had been published between 1910 and 1915, the term "Fundamentalism" was coined in 1920, and the movement gained great notoriety and respect in the first half of the decade before it was discredited in the general culture by the Scopes "Monkey Trial" in the summer of 1925.

Aside from the teaching of evolution in the schools, no where were the practical implications of the debate more apparent than in the mission fields. The famous 1932 Report of the Laymen's Foreign Mission Enquiry, concluding with *Re-Thinking Missions*, embraced the extreme relativist wing of modernist thought when it took the position that Christians should stop competing with other religions and cooperate with them in social reform and against secularism. Moreover, it argued that all religions can learn from each other and should strive together toward "unity in the complete religious truth."[1] In this view, there are many roads to Heaven, and therefore Christianity should cease to make claims to an exclusive truth.

The SVM attempted at first to rise above the controversy, believing that if it focused on the imperative of both humanitarian and evangelistic missions it could hold together the Christian consensus of the previous age. But this was not possible in the polarized atmosphere of the mid-1920s through the 1930s. While the top leadership of the SVM, first Wilder and then Wilson, were conservative, the lower echelons of the leadership of the movement were clearly committed to the primacy of the Social Gospel and to a theologically liberal view of missions. The liberal leaning of the SVM was obvious to observers by the speakers it invited to its conventions, the articles it published in its journals, and its continued association with the liberal YMCA and YWCA. To give just one example, Daniel Johnson Fleming, perhaps the most outspoken of liberal missiologists in the 1920s, whose work anticipated *Re-Thinking Missions*, was invited to speak at the 1924 SVM convention. His books were published by the YMCA and YWCA and were favorably reviewed in *The Intercollegian*. Later he had articles published in *The Student Volunteer Movement Bulletin*.[2] Symbolic of the growing split, the conservative Moody Bible Institute, where the SVM had had one of its first headquarters, quietly declined to continue supporting the movement in 1928.

As the mainline denominations moved in an increasingly liberal direction, and as their financial wherewithal declined, the numbers it sent as missionaries also declined, by two-thirds in the 1920s alone. During this period, faith missions began to replace the denominations as the primary senders of missionaries. Faith missions were non-denominational, independent missionary organizations. They tended to be conservative, and therefore had little use for the SVM. By identifying itself with the denominations and with theological liberalism, the SVM was slowly relegating itself to irrelevancy in the larger missionary enterprise. Moreover, during the 1920s and 1930s, the denominations set up their own student organizations on college campuses, further reducing the need for a non-denominational, liberal, missionary recruiting organization.

The 1930s were especially difficult years for the SVM, not only because of the struggle to find its way in new theological and culture territory, but also because of the financial pressures caused by the depression. In the 1940s it was further challenged by the Inter-Varsity Christian Fellowship (IVCF), established in the U.S. in 1939 as a conservative organization for college students. Nevertheless the SVM still enjoyed some recruiting success. By 1936 it had recruited over 13,000 volunteers, and in the 1950s over 20,000.[3] Still, the faith missions organizations and the conservative denominations increasingly relied on IVCF for missionary recruitment.

In 1936 the SVM held its last independently sponsored quadrennial convention. Those that followed were sponsored by the YMCA, YWCA, and other student organizations. The 1939 and 1943 conventions were small consultative conferences, limited to about 500 people. The traditionally large SVM conventions did resume after World War II, with for example about 2,500 delegates in 1952 and 3,500 in 1956. Congressman Walter Judd made the 1952 convention memorable when in the opening address he called on students to send aid to Chiang Kai Shek's Chinese nationalist government.[4] The conventions also continued to draw some important speakers, such as Martin Luther King in 1960. Notwithstanding some renewed vigor after World War II, the SVM conventions after the 1920s were increasingly distant from the center of Protestant missionary recruitment, and they never achieved the level of prestige they had attained in the Victorian era.

Finding itself buffeted on every side, the last thirty years of the SVM can be told as a history of mergers and consolidations in an ever elusive struggle to find a niche in the larger Protestant missionary enterprise. In 1939 the SVM General Secretary became a member of the Administrative Committee of the National Intercollegiate Christian Council (a YMCA-YWCA organization). When in 1944 the YMCA, YWCA and the denominational organizations on college campuses created a new organization, the United Student Christian Council (USCC), the SVM served at its Missionary Committee, which in 1954 was reorganized as the Commission on World Mission of the USCC. In 1959 the USCC joined with the SVM and the Interseminary Committee to create the National Student Christian Federation (NSCF), and the SVM became its Commission on World Mission. The SVM ceased to be an independent organization in 1966 when the NSCF was reorganized as the University Christian Movement, an alliance of various groups including the Roman Catholic National Newman Student Federation. The SVM became simply the missions department of the new organization. When this ecumenical student alliance voted itself out of existence in 1969, the history of the SVM came to a close.[5]

From the mid-1930s onward, the SVM was an organization dedicated, for all practical purposes, to the recruitment of liberal missionaries, but its secondary motivation was to advance the cause of ecumenism among the mainline denominations. The WSCF, the offspring of the YMCA and SVM, also adopted this new goal, but its transition from an emphasis on missionary evangelism to liberal ecumenism was much smoother and more natural than the bumpy road followed by the SVM. As early as the General Committee meeting in 1924 at High Liegh, England, the WSCF took a dramatic step away from its origins in missions by emphasizing its commitment to the ecumenical movement. The organizing principle of the WSCF from its origins through the First World War had been the missionary agenda. Its new organizing principle would now come to be characterized by its longstanding motto: "Ut omnes unum sint" – that they all may be one (John 17:21).

The WSCF educated an entire generation of leaders in the principles and spirit of ecumenism. And as the missionary enterprise began to ebb in the 1920s, many of these leaders found their way into the ecumenical movement.[6] Mott's efforts on the Continuation Committee, which followed the Edinburgh Conference, led after the war to the creation of the International Missionary Council. This organization combined with the Faith and Order movement begun by Charles H. Brent, Episcopal Bishop of the Philippines, led directly to the founding of the World Council of Churches in 1948. For Mott's generation-long efforts in the cause of Christian ecumenism, he received the Nobel Peace Prize in 1946.

While the SVM did not succeed in achieving its principle goal, the evangelization the world in a single generation, the student volunteers did succeed in launching the modern American Protestant missionary enterprise and a growing world-wide missionary movement. Though the SVM was largely moribund by the 1930s, its legacy is treasured and carried on by numerous Protestant organizations around the world that are currently supporting about 121 thousand missionaries.[7]

The consensus-oriented evangelicalism of the Victorian period, which spawned the SVM and was largely destroyed in the Fundamentalist-Modernist controversy, has been making a slow comeback in America and in turn has given impetus to a new missions enthusiasm. The rise of Neo-evangelicalism with the formation of the National Association of Evangelicals (1942), Fuller Theological Seminary (1947), the journal *Christianity Today* (1956) and the evangelistic ministry of Billy Graham that became a veritable national institution in the 1950s, has laid claim to the legacy of Dwight Moody and dreams of recapturing the mainstream of American culture for evangelical religion.

The development of missions as a science gained new impetus when Donald A. McGavran published *The Bridges of God* in 1955. An old student volunteer recruited by Robert Wilder in 1919, McGavran helped to create the modern "church growth" movement and developed a new paradigm of mission strategy, "people movements." To give his ideas an institutional base, he started the Institute of Church Growth at Northwest Christian College in Eugene, Oregon, in 1961. In 1965 he was invited to form the School of World Mission at Fuller Theological Seminary. The school attracts hundreds of students and has become a major center of missiological research, which in turn has spawned a number of other mission schools associated with seminaries and Christian colleges. In the 1960s when "postcolonial" thought seemed to suggest the end of the missionary enterprise, McGavran declared that "we stand in the sunrise of missions!" The Fuller school continues to teach innovative strategies for evangelization and has highlighted the concept of "unreached peoples" in part as a way to combat the idea that the need for cross-cultural missions is past.[8]

In another attempt to awaken in modern evangelical leaders the vision of Moody and Mott of a Protestant evangelization of the world, *Christianity Today* sponsored the World Congress on Evangelism in Berlin in 1966. Under the leadership of Billy Graham, 1,200 evangelical leaders from 104 nations arrived for a ten day conference on mission strategy and world evangelization. Like their Victorian predecessors, the convention speakers urged Christian leaders to proclaim the traditional gospel message and use the latest technological and mass media techniques. The Convention concluded with a statement of purpose that strongly suggested the influence of the SVM watchword: "Our goal is nothing short of the evangelization of the human race in this generation."[9]

The 1974 International Congress on World Evangelism held in Lausanne, Switzerland, a convention summoned, financed and largely organized by Billy Graham, included 2,400 Evangelical leaders from 150 nations. The purpose of the convention was to develop specific strategies to implement world evangelization within a generation.[10] The congress launched the Lausanne Committee for World Evangelization (LCWE), which continues to promote missions around the world, with its most enthusiastic supporters being in the churches of the third world. At Lausanne Ralph Winter help to popularize some of the ideas being taught at Fuller regarding cross-cultural evangelism, and Winter shortly afterwards founded the U.S. Center for World Mission, which has become one of the major centers of evangelical missions in the world today.

The centennial of the SVM in 1986 found the missionary movement as optimistic as at any time in the Victorian period. From its low point in 1935 of only 11,000 American missionaries, the number of missionaries had been steadily growing since the Second World War.[11] By 1953 the total number of missionaries from North America had grown to 18,599, by 1968 it increased to 34,150, and by 1985 it reached 39,309.[12] Ralph Winter observed that the years 1886 and 1986 were pointedly comparable in that missionary enthusiasm seemed to be mounting to new heights at both times.[13]

Not least on Winter's mind was the growing success of the regular Student Missionary Conventions at Urbana, Illinois, which in 1984 and 1987 reached attendances of well over 18,000.[14] The Urbana conventions are a product of the Student Foreign Missions Fellowship (SFMF), formed in 1936, the last year of the independent SVM conventions. The SFMF merged with the Inter-Varsity Christian Fellowship in 1945, becoming its missionary arm. They held their first missionary convention in Toronto in 1946, and then moved to Urbana in 1948 and have held triennial conventions ever since. Attendance at the conventions has steadily grown until they are now nearly three times as large as the most successful SVM convention in 1920.[15] But perhaps as important as the growing student interest in missions was a return to the nearly unbounded optimism that characterized Mott's generation.

Like their Victorian predecessors, Protestant missionary leaders in the 1980s looked hopefully to the turn of the new century as the potential closure date of missionary efforts. As the SVM was initiated with the hope that world evangelization would be completed by 1900, so evangelicals in the 1980s launched what would seem to be a wildly sanguine endeavor, the A.D. 2000 Movement.[16] By one estimate there were by the end of the 1980s 33 organizations in the process of spending more than $1 billion each to achieve world evangelization, and 11 of them had set A.D. 2000 as their target date.[17] With less money but more visibility, the 2,500 participants from more than 150 countries at the 1989 International Congress on World Evangelization, or "Lausanne II in Manila," included in their "Manila Manifesto" the possibility of completing the task of world evangelization by the end of the century. The group expounding this position at the convention adopted the equivocally worded slogan "World Evangelization by AD 2000 and Beyond."[18] Nevertheless, their intentions were obvious, and the agenda for the 1990s was clearly set. To mark the progress of the movement at the halfway point of the decade, nearly 4,000 mission enthusiasts from 186 nations gathered in Seoul, Korea, for the Global Conference on World Evangelization (GCOWE) in 1995. Apparently undaunted by the huge task before them, they met to strategize, network, and pray for the achievement of their goal before the close of the millenium.[19]

Mott, Wilder, Speer and Eddy would surely have appreciated the growing student interest in missions and the optimism of modern evangelicals about the possibility of a near fulfillment of the Great Commission. They undoubtedly would have recognized the current movement as nothing less than a continuation of the practical approach and evangelical spirit of the student volunteers. The difference, of course, is that the while the SVM was at the center of American culture, A.D. 2000 and Beyond barely registers in popular awareness. On the other hand, while evangelical Protestants have lost status and power in the United States, they can perhaps claim to have gained at least a proportionate strength in lands that were formerly mission fields. By one estimate, at the end of this century, 58 percent of all Christians will be in the third world.[20] Moreover, missionaries today are no longer being sent exclusively from Western countries. Third-world missionaries are steadily growing in numbers and now constitute about one-third of all Protestant missionaries, so that some are predicting that, if current growth rates continue, before the end of the 1990s they will actually outnumber missionaries from the United States and Europe.[21] It would seem that Mott's and Wishard's dream at the end of the nineteenth century, that the non-Western nations would produce an indigenous missionary force to complete the evangelization of the world, may be coming about at the end of the twentieth century.

Aside from its long-term effect on the ecumenical movement and its inspiration for later efforts at world evangelization among Protestant evangelicals, the broader cultural significance of the Student Volunteer Movement is in the role it played in the Victorian era. The movement represented the best of the Victorian religious culture. It was optimistic, benevolent, and dedicated to serving God by serving humanity. Less to its credit, it also accepted the hierarchy of races concept that characterized the age, but its racialism rarely issued in the arrogant, exclusionist, paranoid, or hate-filled thinking that is often seen now as the dark side of Victorianism. Rather, the student volunteers generally embraced a benevolent version of the "white man's burden," dedicating their lives to uplifting non-Christian civilizations and sometimes believing that their efforts at world evangelization would not only result in an eventual equality of races but in ushering in the kingdom of God on earth.

This high-minded internationalism came at a crucial time in American history. The SVM emerged in the 1880s and 1890s just when Americans were beginning to look beyond their own shores to a more active engagement in the world. During the first four decades of its history, the importance of the SVM as the embodiment of the highest ideals of Victorianism cannot be underestimated. For a generation of Americans becoming for the first time conditioned to their nation taking on important international obligations, the SVM offered a vision of American involvement that was noble and inspiring. At very least, the SVM played the same role for idealistic young Americans that the Peace Corps did in the 1960s: In a frightening world of dangerous international rivalries, the SVM offered a humanitarian alternative that saw itself as the fulfillment of William James's "moral equivalent of war." With its maps, books, lectures, and inspiring rhetoric, the SVM eased America's transition from insularity to accepting world responsibilities.

Another aspect of the cultural significance of the SVM lies in its relationship to women. The women's movement within missions, so crucial for the Protestant denominations' success in missionary recruitment and fund raising, largely died out in the 1920s. In part the movement faltered because of its very success. Most of the worst abuses against women in the East, such as footbinding or the sati, had been largely abolished as a result of Western and specifically Christian influence. Consequently the motivation for women to become missionaries in order to help liberate their sisters in other lands ceased to have great resonance. At the same time in the United States, as women claimed equality with men, they lost the rationale for separate women's auxiliaries within the denominations. Between 1910 and 1940 most of the major auxiliaries were merged into the mission depart-ments of the various denominations, giving women a much diminished institutional role in the missions movement. Also, women in the 1920s, following their success in the passage of the Nineteenth Amendment, largely abandoned the political activism that led them to seek protective legislation for themselves and children in the Progressive era. Women in the 1920s accepted a new paradigm of womanhood, which elevated them as "companions" to their husbands, but abandoned the gender-based arguments of the Victorian era that justified a distinctive role for women in the public sphere.[22]

Questions of gender, which preoccupied Victorian culture, have persisted into our own time. Certainly manliness, as an aspect of character, continues to have cultural currency as Christian rallies still feature sports celebrities as role models. One group organized to deal with modern male anxiety and feelings of inadequacy is Promise Keepers. Founded by the former coach of the University of Colorado football team Bill McCartney, Promise Keepers is a conservative Christian organization that seeks to promote among men greater responsibility for Christian families and marriages, as well as involvement in the life of the church. In 1994 Promise Keepers organized six summertime rallies that had an aggregate attendance of 234,000 men, and in 1995 it held 13 rallies with an estimated attendance of 711,000. Held in sports stadiums in regions all over the country, these massive gatherings are pep rallies for modern manhood. Speakers load their addresses with sports metaphors and male-oriented aphorisms. And McCartney usually concludes the rallies with fighting words reminiscent of an earlier age: "We're calling men of God to battle – we will retreat no more."[23] But concern about the meaning of manhood is far from a purely Christian concern. The "wild man" craze of the 1980s and the success of Robert Bly's best seller, *Iron John: A Book About Men*, betrays the ongoing felt needs and obvious insecurities of men in the general culture and suggests that we are not as far removed from our Victorian past as is sometimes believed.[24]

Manliness, of course, is only one aspect of the broader theme of character, as we have been using the term. The key theme of the Victorian era and the organizing principle of the Student Movement, character seemed passe in the roaring twenties. But it was quickly missed. As early as 1931, F. Scott Fitzgerald has one of his protagonists, a recently reformed alcoholic, lamenting the passing of character:

> He believed in character; he wanted to jump back a whole generation and trust in character again as the eternally valuable element. Everything else wore out.[25]

Franklin Roosevelt would probably have agreed; for the New Deal, though an experiment in large government programs that seemed to abandon character, was actually very concerned not to create permanent programs that would undermine individual responsibility. Rather, the New Deal, as the embodiment of both the liberal and conservative Social Gospels, attempted to achieve a balance between the desire to assuage the human costs of modern industrial society with the need to support the traditional middle-class values of hard work, self-control, and self-reliance that make modern society possible. The imbalance perceived in our own time between social and individual responsibility, as well as the existence of massive and persistent budget deficits, is leading to the recovery of at least some of the Victorian emphasis on character.

Character as a term, or its surrogates, has even begun to appear again in our public discourse. For example, William Bennett's recently released anthology of moral tales, *The Book of Virtues*, whatever immediate political purposes it may have been produced to serve, was written to underscore the indispensability of good character for a free society.[26] And, as it was in the Victorian era, character also continues to be bound up with questions of race. Long the hobby horse of white conservatives, black leaders are now also beginning to emphasize character in addition to civil rights as a means to racial advancement, as can be seen in Shellby Steele's influential book *The Content of Our Character* (1990).[27]

The inevitable down-sizing of government and the reappearance of character in our public lexicon does not mean that we are entering a new Gilded Age. Having become more sophisticated about sociology and psychology, and having grown far too use to the social safety net and other entitlements created since the 1930s, it is inconceivable that Americans living now in the post-modern age could return to the simplistic (and demanding) convictions that our pre-modern ancestors held regarding the paramount importance of character. However, modern Jeremiads against relativism, such as Allan Bloom's *The Closing of the American Mind*, remind us of the fragility of democratic society and the possibility of devolution in a culture in which anything goes.[28] And so Americans are maintaining a uneasy tension between individual and collective solutions to social problems. We still appreciate the uncluttered vision of that simpler Victorian age, but like our first ancestors, we have been driven from the garden of our primal innocence, and, as if barred by an angel with flaming sword, we can never return to the mentality of an age that would found a kingdom solely on character.

Endnotes

Introduction

1. Luther D. Wishard, *The Beginning of the Student's Era in Christian History*, 1917, TMS., 116. Yale Divinity School Library.

2. Charles W. Forman, "II. The Americans," *International Bulletin of Missionary Research* 6 (April 1982): 54. William R. Hutchison, *Errand to the World* (Chicago: The University of Chicago Press, 1987), 45, 176.

3. "Sailed Volunteers for 1926," *The Student Volunteer Movement Bulletin* VII (May 1927): 287.

4. *The Works of President Edwards*, vol. III, *Thoughts on the Revival of Religion in New England*, 1740 (New York: Leavitt, Trow and Co., 1844), 313-316.

5. Jonathan Edwards, *A History of the Work of Redemption* in Edward Hickman, *The Works of Jonathan Edwards*, A.M., vol. 1 (London: F. Westley, and A.H. Davis, Stationer's Court, 1834), 609. **6**. Paul E. Johnson, *A Shopkeeper's Millennium: Society and Revivals in Rochester, New York, 1815-1837* (New York: Hill and Wang, 1978), 1009-113.

7. Nathan Hatch, *The Democratization of American Christianity* (New Haven: Yale University Press, 1989).

8. Hutchison, *Errand to the World*, 44, 91.

9. Clifton J. Phillips, "The Student Volunteer Movement and Its Role in China Missions, 1886-1920," *The Missionary Enterprise in China and America*, ed. John K. Fairbank, 91-109 (Cambridge: Harvard University Press, 1974), 101.

10. Kenneth Scott Latourette, *A History of the Expansion of Christianity*, vol. 4, *The Great Century* (New York: Harper and Brothers, 1941), 18, 45-46.

11. Sydney E. Ahlstrom, *A Religious History of the American People* (New Haven: Yale University Press, 1972), 733.

12. Robert Handy, *A Christian America: Protestant Hopes and Historical Realities*, 2nd ed., revised (New York: Oxford University Press, 1984), 134.

13. Valentine H. Rabe, *The Home Base of American China Missions 1880-1920* (Cambridge: Harvard University Press, 1978), 4-5.

14. See introduction to William R. Hutchinson, *Errand to the World, American Protestant Thought and Foreign Missions* (Chicago: The University of Chicago Press, 1987).

15. Francis Greenwood Peabody, *Jesus Christ and the Christian Character* (New York: The MacMillian Company, 1905), 9.

Chapter One

1. Charles Grandison Finney, *Lectures on Revivals of Religion*, ed., William G. McLaughlin (Cambridge: The Belknap Press of Harvard University Press, 1960), 19-20.

2. *Springfield Daily Republican*, August 2, 1866, 1. See SVM Archives, Series V.

3. Ober, *Exploring a Continent*, (New York: Association Press, 1929), 81 passim.

4. Mott, *Five Decades and a Forward View*, 3.

5. Summaries of these speeches are recorded in the *Missionary Review*, 1886.

6. *Springfield Daily Republican*, August 2, 1886, 5.

7. Robert P. Wilder, *The Student Volunteer Movement: Its Origin and Early History*, 16. See SVM Archives, Series VII.

8. Clyde Binfield, *George Williams and the U.M.C.A.: A Study in Victorian Social Attitudes* (London: Heincimann, 1973).

9. C. Howard Hopkins, *History of the Y.M.C.A. in North America* (New York: Association Press, 1951), 11-19.

10. The best biography on D.L. Moody is James F. Findlay, Jr., *Dwight L. Moody: American Evangelist 1837-1899* (Chicago: The University of Chicago Press, 1969).

11. Both Moody's and Whitefield's appeals were also based largely on their celebrity status. For this interpretation see Jon Butler, *Awash in a Sea of Faith: Christianizing the American People* (Cambridge: Harvard University Press, 1990), 186-191.

12. For a good description of Finney's "new measures" see Whitney R. Cross, "New Measures," Chap. in *The Burned-over District: The Social and Intellectual History of Enthusiastic Religion in Western New York, 1800-1850* (Ithaca: Cornell University Press, 1950). For an older but durable interpretation of Finney as a revivalist see chapters 4 and 5 in Bernard A. Weisberger, *They Gathered at the River: The Story of the Great Revivalists and their impact upon religion in America* (Boston: Little, Brown and Company, 1958). For a more recent interpretation of Finney, using a social control model, see Paul E. Johnson, *A*

Shopkeeper's Millennium: Society and Revivals in Rochester, New York, 1815-1837, American Century Series (New York: Hill and Wang, 1978).

13. Jonathan Edwards, *A Faithful Narrative of the Surprising Work of God*, in *The Works of Jonathan Edwards*, ed. Sereno E. Dwight, vol. IV, (New York: S. Converse, 1829-1830), 27.

14. Findlay, *Moody*, 204.

15. Ibid., 300.

16. C. Howard Hopkins, *History of the U.M.C.A. in North America* (New York: Association Press, 1951), 272-3.

17. Ibid., 273-275.

18. Wishard, *College Bulletin III* (November 1880): 1.

19. Clarence P. Shedd, *Two Centuries of Student Christian Movements*, (New York: Association Press, 1934), 219.

20. Inter-Seminary Alliance Convention Report, 1886.

21. Wishard, *The College Bulletin*, VII (March 1885): 18-19.

22. Findlay, 143.

23. Wishard, *College Bulletin*, VIII (April 1886): 1.

24. Ibid., 140, 148.

25. For background on Mott see C. Howard Hopkins, *John R. Mott: 1865-1955: A Biography* (Grand Rapids: William B. Eerdmans Publishing Company, 1979).

26. For background on Wilder see Ruth Wilder Braisted, *In This Generation* (New York: Friendship Press, 1941), 15; Robert P. Wilder, *The Great Commission: The Missionary Response of the Student Volunteer Movements in North America and Europe* (London: Oliphants Ltd., 1936), 14. For an analysis of Royal Wilder's controversial career in India see Robert A. Schneider, "Royal G. Wilder: New School Missionary in the ABCFM, 1846-1871," *American Presbyterians: Journal of Presbyterian History* 64 (Summer 1986), 73-82.

27. The MHMA adopted the pledge, "We hold ourselves willing and desirous to do the Lord's work wherever He may call us, even if it be on foreign land." Thirty-four young women signed this pledge, many of whom later became missionaries. Grace graduated in 1883, the same year that Robert helped to found his own missionary society at Princeton. The influence of Grace on her brother, and the importance of the MHMA as a model for the Princeton society, should not be underestimated. For the MHMA and the importance of Grace Wilder see Mary L. Matthews, "The Story of Mount Holyoke Missionary Association, 1878-1884," *The Missionary Review of the World*, LVII (December 1934): 565.

28. Wilder, 18.

29. John R. Mott, *Five Decades and a Forward View* (New York: Harper and Brothers, 1939), 4.

30. Wilder, *The Student Volunteer Movement*, 14.

31. John R. Mott, quoted from Basil Mathews, *John R. Mott, World Citizen* (New York: Harper, 1934), 46-47.

32. John R. Mott, "The Beginnings of the Student Volunteer Movement," in *The Student Volunteer Movement After Twenty-Five Years, 1886-1911* (no editor given) (New York: Student Volunteer Movement, 1911), 10-11. See SVM Archives, Series VII.

33. The Mount Hermon One Hundred consisted of students from a variety of institutions and denominational backgrounds. Twenty-five were students at the Mount Hermon School itself, only four of whom were registered as delegates. The rest presumably were staying on during the summer months to work on the grounds and help with the conference. Nine of the 10 delegates from Princeton volunteered. The colleges of Cornell and Rutgers produced 5 volunteers each. Williams contributed 4. Amherst, Dartmouth, Madison, (N.Y.), Randolph-Macon, and Yale each contributed 3 volunteers. Fully 63 of the volunteers came from denominational schools. There were 31 Presbyterians or those from the reformed tradition, 26 Congregationalists, 11 Baptists, 9 Methodists, 4 Episcopalians, 2 Lutherans, and 7 undesignated — the later were Mount Hermon students and therefore doubtlessly evangelicals.

34. Wilder, *The Great Commission*, 23.

35. Ibid., 37.

36. Wilder, *The Great Commission*, 40.

37. Ober, *Exploring a Continent*, 87.

38. The advisory committee as of 1891 consisted of the Rev. George Alexander, Bishop M.S. Baldwin, Miss Abbie B. Child, Pres. Merrill E. Gates, the Rev. A.J. Gordon, and the Rev. A.T. Pierson.

39. SVM Archives, Series V, Executive Report, 1891, 5, 7.

40. SVM Archives, Series V, Executive Report, 1898, 5, 7.

41. *The First Two Decades of the Student Volunteer Movement* (New York: Student Volunteer Movement for Foreign Missions, 1906), 7-8.

42. For background on Pitkin see Robert E. Speer, *A Memorial of Horace Tracy Pitkin* (New York: Fleming H. Revell Company, 1903), 70, and George Sherwood Eddy, *Horace Tracy Pitkin: Missionary Advocate and Martyr*, 9 — pamphlet without publisher or date found in the SVM Archives, Series VII. For Borden see Mary Geraldine Taylor, *Borden of Yale* (London: China Inland Mission, Newington Green, 1926; revised edition 1952 by David Bentley-Taylor) 7; see also Charles R. Eerdman, "An Ideal Missionary Volunteer," *The Missionary Review of the World*, 36 (old series) 26 (new series) (August 1913): 567-577; and Charles Soutter Campbell, *William Whiting Borden: A Short Life* Complete in Christ, a pamphlet found in the Miscellaneous Person Papers: William Whiting Borden, Yale Divinity School Archives. Other traveling secretaries who later became famous or important in the movement include Robert E. Speer, W. H. Cossum, W. J. Wanless, M.D., 1895-96, 1904-5, Ruth Rouse, 1897-98, 1904-98, 1904-5, Sophia Lyon (Mrs. Fahs), 1899-1900, 1900-01, S. Earl Taylor, 1899-1901, Pauline Root, M.D., 1902-04, Una M. Saunders,

1905-06, S.M. Zwemer 1905-07, K.S. Latourette, 1909-10. See Beahm, "Factors in the Development," 226.

43. Wilder, *The Pledge of the Student Volunteer Movement for Foreign Missions* (New York: Student Volunteer Movement for Foreign Missions, 1890).

44. The SVM archives contain the minutes of only one of its regional unions during the Movement's early years, The Student Volunteer Union of New York City and Brooklyn. See SVM Archives, Series VI.

45. At the 1924 quadrennial convention Joseph Robbins reported 39 state conferences in the previous year, with an estimated attendance of about 10,000 students. See Joseph C. Robbins, "Report of the Executive Committee of the Student Volunteer Movement for Foreign Missions," in *Christian Students and World Problems*, ed. Milton Stauffer (New York: Student Volunteer Movement for Foreign Missions, 1924), 70-71.

46. *Report of the First International Convention of the Student Volunteer Movement for Foreign Missions* (Boston: Press of T.O. Metcalf & Co., 1891), 3, 193-205.

47. "Prefatory Note," in *Report of the First International Convention*, 3.

48. Max Wood Moorhead, ed., *The Student Missionary Enterprise* (Boston: Press of T.O. Metcalf & Col, 1894), 362-4.

49. *Association Men: The Young Men's Christian Association Magazine*, XVII (April 1902). See SVM Archives, Series VIII.

50. For the finances of the SVM, 1886-1891 see John R. Mott, "Report of the Executive Committee," in *Report of the First International Convention*, 30-31. The general overview of the 1904 annual budget is contained in the Executive Committee minutes for 12 September, 1904.

Despite the growing financial needs of the SVM, Mott did not over use the students for the aggrandizement of the organization he led. Rather, from the beginning of the movement the emphasis of the SVM was to organize and encourage students to raise money not for themselves, but for the direct support of missionaries. In the 1891 report of the executive committee it was reported that 40 colleges and 32 seminaries had contributed an estimated $30,000 over the previous two years for the support of missionaries under the aegis of the missionary boards. By 1909/10 1,477 educational institutions were giving $96,053 for foreign missions and $37,708 for city and home missions. By 1918 the total mission giving from educational institutions was $300,000. Also, during the war years the students were encouraged to contribute to a "Student Friendship Fund" to provide aid to the war-torn parts of the globe. The SVM together with others within the Student Movement contributed $200,000 in 1916/17, $1,295,000 in 1917/18, and 2,300,000 in 1918/19 for a total of $3,795,000. See SVM Archives, Series V, Report of the Executive Committee, 1891, 7. Fennell P. Turner, *A Year of the Student Volunteer Movement for Foreign Missions* (New York: Student Volunteer Movement for Foreign Missions). *The Achievements of the Student Volunteer Movement for Foreign Missions During the*

First Generation of its History 1886-1919, (New York: Student Volunteer Movement for Foreign Missions, 1919), 9.

51. In the three decades that the SVM contribution record covers (1901-1932), there were only 789 people contributing to the movement. Together they donated $748,489 over the entire period. Of this total figure, $313,830 or about 42 percent was obtained from only 13 people, and in the first decade for which records survive, about 78 percent of the total contributions were given by only 5 people. Throughout this period the number of contributors grew steadily. By 1910 100 people were contributing to the movement. In the second decade of the century 444 people contributed, and in the 1920s 641 people contributed. Yet the bulk of the contributions were still coming from a tiny number of people. Between 1911 and 1920 15 people produced 55 percent of the total receipts, and in the 1920s 34 people produced 59 percent of the total.

52. Although the SVM consistently published the number of volunteers who sailed, after 1891 it ceased to publish the total numbers of volunteers enlisted. In large measure this was due to the great number of volunteers who dropped out of the movement and to the criticism the organization received for touting its 6,200 volunteers while by 1891 seeing only 320 sail as missionaries. Apparently many had made commitments under the pressure of the moment that they were not prepared to keep upon further consideration. Examining the years between 1893 and 1920, out of 33,726 volunteers fully 22 percent sailed as missionaries. However, this figure is low because many of those who volunteered in the last few years of this period, still being in school, would not have yet sailed as missionaries. Looking at the total number of sailed volunteers from 1893 to 1912, who sailed by 1920, shows that fully 26.5 percent of the volunteers eventually became missionaries.

53. The Directory's information on volunteers listed by state is further corroborated by the statistics of the first three SVM conventions. Of the 558 student delegates at the 1891 convention, 478 came from 9 of the 27 states represented. Of that number fully 66 percent wee midwestern states, and nearly half of the total delegates came from Ohio alone, which sent 272 student delegates. At the 1894 convention 600 of the 1,082 student delegates, or 55 percent, came from the three midwestern states of Illinois, Michigan and Ohio, and from the province of Ontario. At the 1898 convention 695 of the 1, 598 student delegates, or nearly 50 percent, came from the same three states and Canadian province.

The educational institutions listed in the Directory for 1892-1904 show that the top four schools for volunteer recruits were the Moody Bible Institute, Chicago, Illinois with 379 volunteers, Northwestern University and Garrett (Seminary), Evanston, Illinois with 155 volunteers, Ohio Wesleyan College, Delaware,, Ohio, with 166 volunteers, and Mount Hermon School, East Northfield, Massachusetts with 102 volunteers. The convention reports during these years also confirm the conclusion that the bulk of the students volunteers came from midwestern Christian colleges and seminaries.

For the Director see William M. Beahm, "Factors in the Development of the Student Volunteer Movement for Foreign Missions" (Ph.D. Dissertation, University of Chicago, 1941), 127-129. Beahm had access to the *College Volunteer Enrollment D Directory*, which can no longer be found in the SVM archives.

54. All volunteer "banks" can be found in the SVM Archives, Series I, Application Blanks.

55. Beginning with the 1906 convention report, the SVM published an "Honor Roll" of those volunteers who had died as missionaries, which by the 1924 report came to 300 martyrs. In the 1920 report, however, included only those who died while serving in the military.

56. Perry Miller, *The New England Mind: The Seventeenth Century* (Cambridge, The Belknap Press of Harvard University Press, 1939), 3-5.

57. For the classic critique of Weber see R.H. Tawney, *Religion and the Rise of Capitalism* (Harcourt, Brace & Company Inc., 1926; reprint Gloucester: Peter Smith, 1962).

58. For the classic treatment of status anxiety as an impetus for social reform see chapter IV, "The Status Revolution and Progressive Leaders," in Richard Hofstadter *The Age of Reform: From Bryan to F.D.R.* (New York: Alfred A. Knopf, 1955).

Chapter Two

1. George Sherwood Eddy, *The Maker of Men* (New York: Association Press, 1917), 3.

2. Brother Lawrence's spiritual classic *The Practice of the Presence of God* was first published in French in 1692. For a recent translation see Brother Lawrence, *Practicing His Presence* (Goleta, California: Christian Books, 1973).

3. Ralph Waldo Emerson, "Divinity School Address," *Selected Writings of Ralph Waldo Emerson* (New York: Signet Classic, 1965), 250.

4. Mark Twain, *The Unabridged Mark Twain*, vol. 1, *The Adventures of Tom Sawyer* (Philadelphia: Running Press, 1976), 460.

5. Ann Douglas, *The Feminization of American Culture* (New York: Alfred A. Knopf, 1977).

6. For a fuller explanation for the shift from a theology-centered to a devotional-centered clergy see Donald Scott, *From Office to Profession: The New England Ministry, 1750-1850* (Philadelphia: University of Pennsylvania, 1978). In examining the evangelical clergy of New England in the first half of the nineteenth century, Scott placed the clergy's move toward a more devotional Christianity in the broader context of their transition from holding a "public office" to practicing a profession. He argued that the key transitional years occurred in the 1830s and 40s when doctrinal issues and abolitionism were at a height.

In the face of much opposition and controversy, the clergy largely retreated from political and denominational partisanship and satisfied themselves with more general pronouncements about theology and the application of Christian principles to public life. In Scott's view the clergy by the 1850s were not less influential than their eighteenth-century counterparts, but they were influential in different ways. Moreover, as professionals, they saw themselves as primarily responsible for the "cure of souls;" hence, they focused on the pastoral aspects of the ministry.

7. Douglas, 77.

8. E. Anthony Rotundo, *American Manhood: Transformations in Masculinity from the Revolution to the Modern Era* (New York: Basic Books, 1993), 171.

9. Gail Bederman, "'The Women Have Had Charge of the Church Work Long Enough': The Men and Religion Forward Movement of 1911-1912 and the Masculinization of Middle-Class Protestantism," *American Quarterly* 41 (January 1993): 438.

10. Lew Wallace, *Ben-Hur: A Tale of the Christ* (New York: The Heritage Press, 1960 [1881]), 409, 447. For the importance of *Ben-Hur* to Victorian culture see Paul A. Carter, *The Spiritual Crisis of the Gilded Age* (DeKalb: Northern Illinois University Press, 1971), 65-79.

11. Bederman, passim.

12. William E. Winn, "Tom Brown's School Days and the Development of 'Muscular Christianity,'" *Church History*, XXXIX (March, 1960), 64-73.

13. Norman Vance, *The Sinews of the Spirit: The Ideal of Christian Manliness in Victorian Literature and Religious Thought* (Cambridge: Cambridge University Press, 1985), 86.

14. John J. MacAloon, *This Great Symbol: Pierre de Coubertin and the Origins of the Modern Olympic Games* (Chicago: University of Chicago Press, 1981). Donald N. MacMillian, "The Presbyterian Who Invented Basketball," *Presbyterian Record* CXVII (January 1993): 20-22. Michael Rosenthal, *The Character Factory: Baden-Powell and the Origins of the Boy Scout Movement* (New York: Pantheon Books, 1986).

15. Thomas Hughes, *The Manliness of Christ* (London: MacMillian & Col, 1880), 5.

16. Ibid., 59-60, 149.

17. Ernest Renan, *The Life of Jesus* trans. Charles Edwin Wilbour (New York: Carleton, 1864), 102, 108, 148, and 168.

18. See chapter 3 in David Leverenz, *Manhood and the American Renaissance* (Ithaca: Cornell University Press, 1989).

19. See Speer, *Studies of the Man Christ Jesus*, (New York: Young Men's Christian Association Press, 1896), 119-128; Harry Emerson Fosdick, *The Manhood of the Master* (New York: Association Press, 1913); T.R. Glover, *The Jesus of History* (New York: Association Press, 1921).

20. Glover, 130-131.

21. See chapter 14 "'Personality' and the Making of Twentieth-Century Culture in Warren I. Susman, *Culture as History* (New York: Pantheon Books, 1984), 171-185.

22. George M. Marsden, *The Soul of the American University: From Protestant Establishment to Established Nonbelief* (New York; Oxford: Oxford University Press, 1994), 82 and passim.

23. Henry Churchill King, *How To Make a Rational Fight for Character* (New York: The International Committee of Young Men's Christian Association, 1902), 6.

24. Ibid., 32, 33.

25. George Sherwood Eddy, *The Maker of Men* (New York: Association Press, 1917), 6.

26. Ibid., 23-29.

27. Wishard, *The Student Era*, 90.

28. Ober, *Exploring a Continent*, 32.

29. Ibid., 35.

30. Alfred D. Chandler, Jr., *The Visible Hand: The Managerial Revolution in American Business* (Cambridge: The Belknap Press of Harvard University Press, 1977).

31. John R. Mott, "Our Responsibility for the Extension of Christ's Kingdom into the Regions Beyond," *The Churchman* (22 Jan. 1898): 116-117.

32. Arthur Pierson, "Student Volunteers' Convention," *Missionary Review* (1891): 357.

33. Ibid.

34. Valentin H. Rabe, *The Home Base of American China Missions 1880-1920* (Cambridge: Harvard University Press, 1978).

35. "Volunteers Enter Canada," *New York Observer* (16 March 1902): 301.

36. H.A.B., "Aftermath from Toronto," *The Congregationalist and Christian World* (15 March 1902): no page number given. Found in SVM Archives, Series VIII, oversized record book, 1.

37. *The Missionary*, (April 1902): 165. Found in the SVM Archives, Series VIII, oversized record book, 1.

38. "Student Volunteer Movement Quadrennial Convention," *American Friend*, 249. Found in the SVM Archives, Series VIII, oversized record book, 1.

39. *The Baptist Union*, XII (Chicago, 1902): 244. Found in the SVM Archives, Series VIII, oversized record book, 1.

40. Marsden, *Fundamentalism and American Culture*, 80.

41. The Scriptural proof text for this position is usually given as Acts 2:17: "'And it shall be in the last days,' God says, 'That I will pour forth of My Spirit upon all mankind: and your sons and your daughters shall prophesy...'"

42. A.G. Dickens, *The English Reformation* 2nd. ed. (London: Batsford, 1989), 133-138.

43. Marsden, *Fundamentalism and American Culture*, 72-80.

44. Ibid.

45. C. Howard Hopkins, *John R. Mott: A Biography* (Grand Rapids: William B. Eerdmans Publishing Co., 1979), 15, 18-21.

46. Mott Papers, John R. Mott, "Spiritual Atrophy."

47. Mott Papers, John R. Mott, "The Spread of Christ's Kingdom Among Men — `Nearer to Christ,'" 91.

48. Mott Papers, John R. Mott, "Christ A Reality."

49. John Foster, *Decision of Character*, abridged, with an introduction by John R. Mott (New York: 1907), 55-58.

50. Mott Papers, John R. Mott, "The Power of Jesus Christ in the Life of the Student," 3-4.

51. Mott Paper, John R. Mott, "The Power of Jesus Christ in the Life of the Student," 4.

52. Ruth Wilder Braisted, *In This Generation: The Story of Robert P. Wilder* (New York: Friendship Press, 1941), 96.

53. Ibid., 84-85.

54. John F. Piper, Jr., "Robert E. Speer: His Call and the Missionary Impulse, 1890-1900," *American Presbyterians: Journal of Presbyterian History* 65 (Summer 1987): 102.

55. Sherwood Eddy, *Pathfinders of the World Missionary Crusade* (New York: Abingdon-Cokesbury Press, 1945), 259.

56. Quoted in W. Reginald Wheeler, *A Man Sent From God: A Biography of Robert E. Speer* (New York: Fleming H. Revell Co., 1956), 42-45.

57. Eddy, *Pathfinders*, 260.

58. Robert E. Speer, "The Keswick Conventions of 1894," in *Northfield Echoes* (East Northfield: Rastell and McKinley, 1895), 25-32.

59. Speer, "Faith in God," in *Northfield Echoes* (East Northfield, E.S. Rastell, 1896), 42-43.

60. Ibid., 44.

61. Jane Hunter, *The Gospel of Gentility: American Women Missionaries in Turn-of-the-Century China* (New Haven: Yale University Press, 1984), 14.

62. Bederman, 457.

Chapter Three

1. Helen Barrett Montgomery, *Western Women in Eastern Lands: An Outline Study of Fifty Years of Woman's Work in Foreign Missions* (New York: Macmillan, 1910), 206.

2. *Report of the Executive Committee of the Student Volunteer Movement for Foreign Mission*, 1891, SVM Archives, Series I, 10.

3. I am largely indebted for the early history of the YWCA to Elizabeth Wilson, *Fifty Years of Association Work Among Young Women 1866-1916* (New York: National Board of the YWCA of the USA, 1916).

4. Montgomery, *Western Women in Eastern Lands*, 10.

5. This institution was renamed Illinois State University in 1964.

6. Margaret E. Burton, "The Women's Student Christian Movement," *The North American Student* IV (January 1916): 142-143.

7. Ibid., 162.

8. C.K. Ober, *Luther D. Wishard: Projector of World Movements* (New York: Association Press, 1927), 70-72.

9. Mary S. Sims, *The Natural History of a Social Institution - The Young Women's Christian Association* (New York: The Woman's Press, 1936), 23.

10. Elizabeth Wilson, "Twenty-Five Years of Summer Conferences," *The North American Student* V (October 1916): 16-17. Louise W. Brooks, "The Women's Conferences 1916," *The North American Student* V (October 1916): 19-20. Helen Thoburn, "The Women's Conferences," *The North American Student* VI (October 1917): 9.

11. Lee C. Deighton, ed., *The Encyclopedia of Education* (New York: The Macmillan Company and the Free Press, 1971), s.v. "Education of Women: History," by Kathryn Kish Sklar.

12. Ibid., and also Berth Conde, "The Women Students of the United States," *The Intercollegian* XXIII (April 1901): 148-150.

13. For YWCA statistics see Margaret E. Burton, "The Women's Student Christian Movement," 141. For YMCA statistics see *Year Book of the Young Men's Christian Associations of North America for the Year 1902* (New York: International Committee, 1902), 101, and *Year Book of the Young Men's Christian Association of North America*, May 1, 1915 to April 30, 1916 (New York: Association Press, 1916), 57.

14. Hutchinson, *Errand to the World*, 102.

15. R. Pierce Beaver, *American Protestant Women in World Missions: History of the First Feminist Movement in North America* (Grand Rapids: William B. Eerdman's Publishing Co., 1980), 111.

16. For the ideology of women's missions see Patricia Hill, *The World Their Household: The American Woman's Foreign Mission Movement and Cultural Transformation, 1870-1920* (Ann Arbor: University of Michigan Press, 1984).

17. Bishop Thoburn, "India's Call to Women," in *Northfield Echoes* I, ed. Delavan L. Pierson (East Northfield: The Conference Bookstore, 1894), 168.

18. Ibid., 171.

19. A.J. Gordon, "Women as Evangelists," in *Northfield Echoes* I ed. Delavan L. Pierson (East Northfield: The Conference Bookstore, 1894), 148.

20. Ibid., 150.

21. Ibid., 149.

22. Harry Emerson Fosdick, *The Manhood of the Master* (New York: Association Press, 1913), 13, 39, 54, 55, 57, 66 and 67.

23. "Conferences on Association Work," in *Northfield Echoes* I, ed. Delavan L. Pierson (East Northfield: The Conference Bookstore, 1894), 200.

24. Miss Zehring, "The Missionary Department of the College Young Women's Christian Association," *Northfield Echoes* I, ed. Delavan L. Pierson (East Northfield: The Conference Bookstore, 1894), 202.

25. Pauline Root, "Woman's Medical Work in India," *Northfield Echoes* I, ed. Delavan L. Person (East Northfield, The Conference Bookstore, 1894), 178.

26. Dr. Pauline Root, "Life and Work in India," in *Northfield Echoes* I, ed. Delavan L. Person (East Northfield: The Conference Bookstore, 1894), 142.

27. Ibid., 41, 43 and 45.

28. Ibid., 53, 28.

29. Ibid., 69, 25.

30. Hutchison, 107-110.

31. Montgomery, *Western Women in Eastern Lands*, 24.

32. Ibid., 45.

33. Ibid., 60.

34. Ibid., 86.

35. Ibid., 205-206.

36. W.A. Montgomery, "The Failure of the Non-Christian Religious in Relation to Women," in *North American Students and World Advance*, ed. Burton St. John (New York: Student Volunteer Movement for Foreign Missions, 1920), 175.

37. See for example Ruth Rouse, "An Appeal to Women Students for Missionary Decision," *The Intercollegian* XXIII (April 1901): 151-153, and continued in *The Intercollegian* XXIII (May 1901): 174-175.

38. Mrs. Henry W. Peabody, "Missions and the World's Womanhood," *The Student Volunteer Movement Bulletin* I (March 1920): 24 and 25.

39. "The Missionary Campaign by Dr. and Mrs. Howard Taylor," *The Intercollegian* XXIII (May 1901): 180-182.

40. Lucy Guinness, ed., *In the Far East: Letters from Geraldine Guinness in China* (New York: Fleming H. Revel, 1889), and M. Geraldine Guinness, *The Story of the China Inland Mission* (London: The China Inland Mission, 1894).

41. John Mott, in *The Student Missionary Enterprise*, ed. Max Wood Moorhead, (Boston: T.O. Metcalf and Co., 1894), 54.

42. For more on Guinness see Joy Guinness, *Mrs. Howard Taylor: Her Web of Time* (London: China Inland Mission, 1949).

43. For this brief summary of Rouse's career I am indebted to Ruth Franzen, "The Legacy of Ruth Rouse," *International Bulletin of Missionary Research* 17 (October 1993): 154-158. For works by Rouse see especially Ruth Rouse, *The World's Student Christian Federation: A History of the First Thirty Years* (London: Student Christian Movement

Press, 1948). For information on Rouse in this book note especially chapter X, "An Autobiographical Interlude," 111-123. Also see Ruth Rouse and Stephen Charles Neill, ed., *A History of the Ecumenical Movement*, 1517-1948 (Philadelphia: Westminster Press, 1954).
44. Jane Hunter, *The Gospel of Gentility: American Women Missionaries in Turn-of-the-Century China* (New Haven: Yale University Press, 1984), XV, 38.

Chapter Four

1. William James, quoted in John R. Mott, "The Power of Jesus Christ in the Life of the Student," 27; Mott Papers.
2. "This World's Evangelization not an Easy or Short Work," *The Foreign Missionary* XXXV (January 1878): 230-233.
3. Royal Gould Wilder, "To Our Readers," *The Missionary Review* (January-February 1878): 3-12.
4. Royal Gould Wilder, "Who Will Go For Us?" *The Missionary Review* (January-February 1878): 12-19.
5. Royal Gould Wilder, "Answer to the Foreign Board Required by the General Assembly—Presented to the Board October 30, 1877," *The Missionary Review* (March-April 1878): 125.
6. In 1906 this was the position of Ruth Rouse as to the understanding of those attending the Liverpool Conference and why they accepted the watchword for the SVMU held Dec. 22nd. 1906 in the C.M.S. Committee Room, Salisbury Square, E.C." SVM Archives, Series V.
7. Arthur T. Pierson, *The Crisis of Missions* (New York: Robert Carter and Brothers, 1886).
8. Ibid., 273, 276.
9. Ibid., 274, 279; Biblical references are Mt. 12:45 and Lk. 11:24-26.
10. Ibid., 283-4.
11. Ibid., 322, 325.
12. C.A. Clark, *An Appeal from Japan*, Student Volunteer Series, No. 11 (New York: Student Volunteer Movement for Foreign Missions, ca. 1890), 11.
13. Sherwood Eddy, *The Supreme Decision of the Christian Student*, (Chicago: The Student Volunteer Movement for Foreign Missions, 1893).
14. Ibid., 8.
15. Ibid., 18.
16. Ibid., 30.
17. SVM Archives, Series V, "Material Related to Student Volunteer Movement Watchword, 1896-1909."
18. "Dr. [Gustave] Warneck on "The Modern Theory of the Evangelization of the World," *Missionary Record of the United Presbyterian Church*, (October 1897): 297-299.
19. SVM Archives, Series V, letter from Warneck to the 1900 New York Ecumenical Conference on Foreign Missions.

20. John R. Mott, *The Evangelization of the World in This Generation* (New York: Student Volunteer Movement for Foreign Missions, 1901), 3, 8 and 10.

21. Ibid., 9.

22. Ibid., 200.

23. Frank Lenwood, "Concerning the Watchword of the Student Volunteer Missionary Union," *The Student Movement* 11 (Oct. 1908): 55-58.

24. John R. Mott, "The Missionary Uprising Among the Young." An address delivered at the Fourteenth Christian Endeavor Convention, Boston, Massachusetts, 1895. Found in Mott Papers.

25. John R. Mott, "Our Responsibility for the Extension of Christ's Kingdom into the Regions Beyond," *The Churchman*, 22 June 1898, 116. Found in the Mott Papers, Series V.

26. John R. Mott, *The Call of the Non-Christian World* (Laymen's Missionary Movement, 1907), 15, 16.

27. John R. Mott, *Modern World Movement: God's Challenge to the Church* (London: Student Christian Movement, 1908), 29.

28. John R. Mott, "Wanted-Men for Foreign Missions," *St. Andrew's Cross* IX (December 1894), 79.

29. John R. Mott, "The College Students' Obligation to the Young Men of Rural Communities," (1902), 9, Mott Papers.

30. John R. Mott, speech given before the Greater New York Convention National Missionary Campaign, Laymen's Missionary Movement, 1, Mott Papers.

31. Ibid., 113.

32. Ibid., 115, 118.

33. John R. Mott, "The Missionary Problem in Its Relation to the College and University," 1905, Mott Papers.

34. Mott, *The Call of the Non-Christian World*, 15.

35. John R. Mott, "The Larger Co-Operation of Laymen Imperative," 1, Mott Papers.

36. John R. Mott, "The Call to a Great Advance," 107, Mott Papers.

37. John R. Mott, "Modern World Movement," 26.

38. Mott, "The Call to a Great Advance," 109.

39. Mott, *The Call of the Non-Christian World*, 16-17.

40. Ibid., 7.

41. Robert Speer in at least one address at Mt. Hermon in 1895 disagreed with Mott about a special providential role for the Anglo-Saxon race. See John F. Piper, Jr., "Robert E. Speer on Christianity and Race," *Journal of Presbyterian History* 61 (Summer 1983): 230.

42. Ibid., 17-18.

43. Mott, Greater New York Convention, 12.

44. John Mott, "Wanted - Men for Foreign Missions," 78-79.

45. John R. Mott, *Modern World Movements*, 14.

46. Ibid., 14, 16.

47. Ibid., 26, 27.

Chapter Five

1. Lyman Beecher, *A Plea for the West* (Cincinnati: Truman and Smith, 1845), 12.

2. Wishard's account of his involvement in the WSCF is given in Wishard, *Beginnings of the Student Movement*, 193-194.

3. C.K. Ober, *Luther D. Wishard: Projector of World Movement*, (New York: Association Press, 1927), 104-106. Contains a letter from Sanders to Ober describing the importance of his relationship to Wishard.

4. Ibid., 106-7.

5. Wishard, 168-9.

6. Ibid., 199.

7. Ibid., 201-202.

8. The standard biography is George Adam Smith, *The Life of Henry Drummond* (New York: Doubleday & McClure Company, 1898).

9. T. J. Shanks, ed., *A College of Colleges* (Chicago: Fleming H. Revell, 1887), 33, 6.

10. For a discussion of the anti-intellectual tendencies of American revivalism see Richard Hofstadter, *Anti-intellectualism in American Life* (New York: Alfred A. Knopf, 1963). See especially "Part II: the Religion of the Heart."

11. Wishard, 171.

12. Shanks, 227.

13. Wishard, 171.

14. John R. Mott, *The World's Student Christian Federation: Origin, Achievements, Forecast* (New York: World's Student Christian Federation, 1920), 2.

15. Wishard, 172.

16. Wishard, 175-180.

17. Mott, *The World's Student Christian Federation*, 3.

18. James B. Reynolds, *Facts and Forces in the Religious Life of the Universities of Europe* (1893), World Student Christian Federation Archives, Yale Divinity School Library.

19. For Wanamaker's Christian activities see William R. Leach, *Land of Desire: From the Department Store to the Department of Commerce: The Rise of America's Commercial Culture* (New York: Pantheon Books, 1993).

20. Wishard, 263-4.

21. Luther D. Wishard, "College Work in Japan III," XII *The Intercollegian* (October 1889): 7-9.

22. Luther D. Wishard, *The Intercollegian*, XIII (October 1890): 5-6.

23. Wishard, *Beginnings of the Student Movement*, 170.

24. Luther D. Wishard, *The Intercollegian* XIII (November 1890): 21-23.

25. Luther D. Wishard, *A New Program of Missions* (New York: Fleming H. Revell Company, 1895).

26. Ibid., 16.

27. Ruth Rouse, *The World's Student Christian Federation* (London: Student Christian Movement Press Ltd., 1948), 45.

28. Mott, *The World's Student Christian Federation*, 3.

29. John R. Mott, *Strategic Points in the World's Conquest* (New York: Fleming H. Revell Company, 1897), 15-16.

30. Mott, *The World's Student Christian Federation*, 4.

31. Ibid., 7.

32. Hopkins, John R. Mott, 133.

33. *The Student Volunteer Movement of South Africa* (Lovedale Mission Press, 1916), 5-6.

34. The total number of SVM missionaries by 1920, according to WSCF records by country:

SVM Missionaries from Countries in the WSCF

Denmark	15
Finland	23
France	2
Germany	60
Britain	2,322
Netherlands	100
Norway	29
South Africa	161
Sweden	23
Switzerland	23+
U.S. and Canada	8,140
Australasia	181
Total	11,079

35. WSCF annual reports, 1897-1926, 1935-1938, are in the WSCF Archives, Yale Divinity School Library.

36. See the 1899/1900 WSCF report, 120.

37. For the connection between the WSCF and the ecumenical movement see Herbert Reece Coston, *The World's Student Christian Federation as an Ecumenical Training Ground* (Northwestern University Ph.D. dissertation, 1963).

38. Wishard, *Beginnings of the Student Movement*, 258.

39. John R. Mott, "The Influence of Dwight L. Moody on the Student Movement, *The Intercollegian* XXII (Jan. 1900): 87.

Chapter Six

1. John R. Mott, *The Decisive Hour of Missions* (New York: Student Volunteer Movement for Foreign Missions, 1910), 146.

2. Hutchinson, *Errand to the World*, 91-95.

3. John Comaroff and Jean Comaroff, *Ethnography and the Historical Imagination* (Oxford: Westview Press, 1992). See especially 34-42.

4. See for example Paul E. Johnson, *A Shopkeeper's Millennium: Society and Revivals in Rochester*, New York, 1815-1837 (New York: Hill and Wang, 1978).

5. For an overview of the development of racialist ideas in American history see Thomas Gossett, *The History of an Idea in America* (Dallas: Southern Methodist University Press, 1963). For a more recent discussion of racalism as an ideology see Barbara J. Fields, "Ideology and Race in American History," in *Region, Race, and Reconstruction: Essays in Honor of C. Vann Woodward* eds., Morgan Kousser and James McPherson, 143-177 (New York: Oxford University Press, 1982).

6. Harlan P. Beach, "The educational Policy of the American Volunteer Movement," in *Make Jesus King: The Report of the International Student's Missionary Conference*, Liverpool, January 1-5, 1896 (New York: Fleming H. Revell Col, 1896), 135-139.

7. Archives of the Student Volunteer Movement for Foreign Missions, Series V., Report of the Executive Committee, 1904/5, 5.

8. Following his work at the SVM, Beach taught mission history at Yale and founded and successfully promoted the Day Missions Library, now at the Yale Divinity School Library, and the source for much of the research in this dissertation.

9. SVM Archives, Series V, Report of the Executive Committee, 1898, 6.

10. SVM Archives, Series VII, "The First Two Decades of the Student Volunteer Movement," 46.

11. SVM Archives, Series V, Report of the Executive Committee, 1898, 6.

12. A perusal of the mission study materials over time also gives the reader an interesting overview of the evolving thought of the SVM. There were 22 books published by the SVM between 1894 and 1901. At the end of the first four year cycle, Beach tabulated the number of books sold by the SVM and used in the study classes in 447 participating institutions. It came to 25,217 books. The total number of books sold by the SVM for the entire period up to 1901 came to 84,000. Of these six books account for nearly 60 percent of the total sales, and all of them continued to be recommended for use at least through the first decade of the new century. The books by Beach were always popular, and Mott's *The Evangelization of the World in this Generation* was among the SVM's best all time sellers. By 1901 it had already sold 20,000 copies in America, was reprinted in England, and was translated for use in Norway, Germany and Sweden. See SVM Archives, Series III, Executive Committee Minutes, April 23, 1901, 2.

John R. Mott, *The Evangelization of the World* (1901), 15,000; Harlan Beach, *Dawn on the Hills of T'ang* (1898), 13,000; Otis Cary, *Japan and Its Regeneration* (1899), 8,200; Harlan Beach, *Knights of the Labarum*

(1895), 4,800; Harlan Beach, *Cross in the Land of the Trident* (1895), 4,500; A.C. Thompson, et. al., *Modern Apostles of MissionaryByways* (1899), 4,000. Total: 49,700.
Book sales for 1894-1901 period were found in the SVM Archives, Series V.

13. Harlan P. Beach, *Dawn on the Hills of T'ang* (1898)
Robert E. Speer, *South American Problems* (1912)
Samuel M. Zwemer, *The Unoccupied Mission Fields* (1911)
Douglas M. Thornton, *Africa Waiting* (1897, 1906)
Samuel M. Zwemer, *Islam, a Challenge to Faith* (1907)
John R. Mott, *The Evangelization of the World in This Generation* (1901)
James S. Dennis, *Social Evils of the Non-Christian World* (1897)
J. Rutter Williamson, *The Healing of the Nations* (1899)
James L. Barton, *Educational Missions* (1913)
Arthur J. Brown, *The Foreign Missionary* (1907)
John R. Mott, *The Decisive Hour of Christian   Missions* (1910)
Harlan P. Beach, *Geography and Atlas of Protestant Missions* (1901)
Harlan P. Beach, *World Atlas of Christian Missions* (1910)
J. Lovell Murray, *The Call of a World Task* (1918)

14. Harlan P. Beach, *Knights of the Labarum, Being Studies in the lives of Judson, Duff, MacKenzie and MacKay* (Chicago: Student Volunteer Movement for Foreign Missions, 1896).

15. Ibid., 19.

16. Ibid., 34.

17. Ibid., 51.

18. A.C. Thompson and others, *Modern Apostle of Missionary Byways* (New York: Student Volunteer Movement for Foreign Missions, 1889).

19. Arthur J. Brown, *The Foreign Missionary* (New York: Student Volunteer Movement for Foreign Missions, 1907).

20. R. Park Johnson, "The Legacy of Arthur Judson Brown," *International Bulletin of Missionary Research* 10 (April 1986): 72.

21. Ibid., 67.

22. Ibid., 67, 369.

23. Ibid., 73.

24. Douglas M. Thronton, *Africa Waiting: or the Problem of Africa's Evangelization* (London: 1897; reprint, New York: Student Volunteer Movement for Foreign Missions, 1906).

25. Harlan P. Beach, *The Cross in the Land of the Trident* (New York: International Committee of the YMCA, 1895). The trident is the symbol of the three principle Hindu gods, Brahma, Vishnu and Shiva.

26. Ibid., 61, 62.

27. Ibid., 16.

28. Harlan P. Beach, *Dawn on the Hills of T'ang; or Missions in China*, revised edition (New York: Young People's Missionary Movement, 1907), 141.

29. Ibid., 147.

30. Otis Cary, *Japan and Its Regeneration* (New York: Student Volunteer Movement for Foreign Missions, 1899), 21-23.

31. Ibid., 38.

32. Ibid., 92-93.

33. Arthur J. Brown, *The New Era in the Philippines* (New York: Student Volunteer Movement for Foreign Missions, Fleming H. Revell Company, 1903).

34. Ibid., 23.

35. Ibid., 27.

36. Ibid., 50, 52.

37. Ibid., 127, 128, 137, 138 and 132.

38. Robert E. Speer, *South American Problems* (New York: Student Volunteer Movement for Foreign Missions, 1912).

39. Ibid., 108.

40. Ibid., 73, 74, and 81.

41. Samuel M. Zwemer, *Islam, A Challenge to Faith* (New York: Student Volunteer Movement for Foreign Missions, 1907).

42. Ibid., 24, 124, 125, 86, 111 and 112.

43. Ibid., 42-45.

44. S. H. Kellogg, *A Handbook of Comparative Religion* (New York: Student Volunteer Movement for Foreign Missions, 1907; reprint from 1899).

45. Ibid., 156.

46. James S. Dennis, *Social Evils of the Non-Christian World* (New York: Student Volunteer Movement for Foreign Missions, Fleming H. Revell Company, 1897).

47. Ibid., 132.

48. Ibid., 112, 114, 118 and 121.

49. John R. Mott, *The Decisive Hour of Christian Missions* (New York: Student Volunteer Movement, 1915).

50. Ibid., 230, 108.

51. Ibid., 35.

52. Ibid., 36, 62 and 45.

53. Ibid., 229, 238 and 239.

Chapter Seven

1. Charles M. Sheldon, *In His Steps* (New Jersey: Barbour and Company, Inc. Westwood, 1984), 224.

2. Josiah Strong, *Our Country* (Cambridge: The Belknap Press of Harvard University Press, 1963).

3. Richard T. Ely, *Social Aspects of Christianity, and Other Essays* (New York: Thomas Y. Crowell and Company, 1889), 17.

214

4. For the standard work on the Social Gospel see Charles Howard Hopkins, *The Rise of the Social Gospel in American Protestantism 1865-1915* (New Haven: Yale University Press, 1940). For a fuller discussion of the standard works on the social principles see 206-206 & 213.

5. Shailer Forward, *The Social Teaching of Jesus: An Essay in Christian Sociology* (New York: Hodeder & Stoughton, George H. Doran Company, 1897), 211, 225.

6. Francis Greenwood Peabody, *Jesus Christ and the Social Question* (New York: Grosset and Dunlap Publishers, 1900), 101, 117, 281 and 310.

7. Jeremiah W. Jenks, *The Political and Social Significance of the Life and Teachings of Jesus* (New York: Young Men's Christian Association Press, 1908).

8. Ibid., 89, 93.

9. Ibid., 111, 103, 101 and 115.

10. Willis Duke Weatherford, *Negro Life in the South* (New York: Young Men's Christian Association Press, 1910).

11. Ibid.

12. Walter Rauschenbusch, *Christianity and the Social Crisis* (New York: Macmillan, 1907).

13. Clifton J. Phillips, "The Student Volunteer Movement and Its Role in China Missions, 1886-1920," in *The Missionary Enterprise in China and America*, ed. John K. Fairbank (Cambridge: Harvard University Press, 1974), 104-105.

14. Charles R. Henderson, "Social Study and Social Service Indispensable in the Preparation of the Modern Missionary," in *Students and the World-Wide Expansion of Christianity*, ed. Fennell P. Turner (New York: Student Volunteer Movement for Foreign Missions, 1914), 143-147.

15. Shailer Forward, "Evangelization of the Constructive Forces of Civilization in America," in *Students and the World-Wide Expansion*, ed. Fennell P. Turner (New York: Student Volunteer Movement for Foreign Missions, 1914), 159-162.

16. William Jennings Bryan, "The Importance of Foreign Missionary Work," in *Students and the World-Wide Expansion*, ed. Fennell P. Turner (New York: Student Volunteer Movement for Foreign Missions), 169-178.

17. Mott' book also included his description of his world tour given at the SVM Kansas Convention and an article that appeared in the *International Review of Missions* (April 1914).

18. John R. Mott, *The Present World Situation* (New York: Student Volunteer Movement for Foreign Missions, 1914), 107, 108.

19. Ibid., 119.

20. Ibid., 114, 116-118.

21. Ibid., vi, 227.

22. Edward A. Steiner, "A Constructive Neutrality," *The North American Student* III (March 1915): 235-238.

23. C.V. Hibbard, "Crusaders of Today," *The North American Student* IV (January 1916): 152-155.

24. Charles E. Jefferson, "Seeds of War in American Life," *The North American Student* IV (March 1916): 236.

25. Harry F. Ward, "Social Duties in War Time," *The North American Student* VI (October 1917): 23.

26. "Should a Christian Fight," *The North American Student* V (April 1917): 277-278.

27. Charles W. Gordon "The Sword of God," *The North American Student* V (April 1917): 281-284.

28. "At war," *The North American Student* V (May 1917): 323-324.

29. George Irving, "The Student Movement and the War," *The North American Student* III (October 1914): 23.

30. Shailer Forward, "Shall We Take Jesus Seriously? *The North American* Student V (January 1917): 146-148.

31. William Howard Taft, "What Is the League to Enforce Peace?" *The North American Student* V (February 1917): 189-193.

32. John F. Piper, "Robert E. Speer: Christian Statesman in War and Peace," *Journal of Presbyterian History* 47 (September 1969): 208.

33. Robert E. Speer, "The War Aims and Foreign Missions," *The Intercollegian* 26 (October 1918): 2.

34. Ibid., 3.

35. Shailer Forward, "Social Service Not a Substitute for Religion," *The North American Student* III (February 1915): 204-208.

36. Sherwood Eddy, *A Pilgrimage of Ideas, or The Re-Education of Sherwood Eddy* (New York: Farrar & Rinehart Publisher, 1934).

37. Olive MacKay, "Northfield Student Volunteer Conference," *The Association Outlook* XVII (February 1918): 24.

38. "The Northfield Volunteer Conference," *The North American Student* VI (February 1918): 189.

39. "The Northfield Conference," *The North American Student* VI (February 1918): 190.

40. Winnifred F. Thomas, "North American Students Mobilizing for Christian World Democracy," *The Association Outlook* XVII (February 1918): 20-21.

41. W.D. Weatherford, "Promoting the Spirit of Evangelism," *The North American Student* VI (February 1918): 225.

42. Channing H. Tobias, "Shall America Be Made Safe for Black Men?" *The North American Student* VI (March 1918): 266-267.

43. Harry F. Ward, "Tell Your Church People That!" *The North American Student* VI (March 1918): 260.

44. Ibid., 261.

45. "Following Northfield," *The North American Student* VI (February 1918): 192.

46. J. Lovell Murray, *The Call of a World Task* (New York: Association Press, 1918), 21, 36.

47. Ibid., 2, 29.

48. Edwund Davison Soper, *The Faiths of Mankind*, College Volunteer Study Courses, Third Year-Part II (New York: The Women's Press, 1920), viii.

49. Walter Rauschenbusch, *The Social Principles of Jesus* (New York: Association Press, 1916), 13.

50. Ibid., 164-165.

51. Harry F. Ward and Richard H. Edwards, *Christianizing Community Life* (New York: Association Press, 1919), 69, 71, 74, 131 and 11.

52. Ibid., 10, 121.

53. Ibid., 174.

54. Charles R. Watson, "The Gains, Losses, and Handicaps of Foreign Missions Occasioned by the War," in *Foreign Missions Conference of North America*, ed. Fennell P. Turner (New York: Foreign Missions Conference, 1919), 116-127.

55. Ibid., 121, 126.

56. John R. Mott, "Present World Conflict and Its Relation to Christian Missions," *The Outlook of Missions* VII (December 1915): 579, 580.

Chapter Eight

1. Sherwood Eddy, "Present Day Social and Intellectual Unrest" in *Christian Students and World Problems*, ed. Milton Stauffer (New York: Student Volunteer Movement for Foreign Missions, 1924), 126.

2. For good introductions to the culture of the 1920s begin with Frederick Lewis Allen, *Only Yesterday: An Informal History of the 1920's* (New York: Harper and Row Publishers, 1931); William E. Leuchtenburg, *The Perils of Prosperity 1914-32* (Chicago: The University of Chicago Press, 1958); and Stanley Coben, *Rebellion Against Victorianism: The Impetus for Cultural Change in 1920s America* (New York: Oxford University Press, 1991).

3. David R. Porter, "The Des Moines Convention," *The Student World* XII (January 1920): 67.

4. John R. Mott, "The World Opportunity," in *North American Students and World Advance*, ed. Burton St. John (New York: Student Volunteer Movement for Foreign Missions, 1920), 18, 21.

5. David R. Porter, "The Des Moines Convention," *The Student World* XIII (January 1920): 59.

6. Sherwood Eddy, letter to the Executive Committee, July 17, 1922, SVM Archives, Series V.

7. For the background to the student revolt at Des Moines see Hopkins, *John R. Mott*, 567-568. and Morgan, *Student Religion During Fifty Years* (New York: Association Press, 1935), 135-136.

8. Robert E. Speer, "The Personal Worth or Failure of Christianity," in *North American Students and World Advance* ed. Burton St. John (New York: Student Volunteer Movement for Foreign Missions, 1920), 176.

9. Ibid., 177.

10. Sherwood Eddy, "The Gospel Indispensable to the Students of North America," in *North American Students and World Advance*, ed. Burton St. John (New York: Student Volunteer Movement for Foreign Missions, 1920), 93-196.

11. Hopkins, *History of the Y.M.C.A. in North America*, 640.

12. Thomas Sharp, "The Student Council," *The Student Volunteer Movement Bulletin* IV (January 1923): 11-13.

13. This followed the realization that the major reason student volunteers were rejected by the mission boards was due to physical health. See Ester Shoemaker, "The Physical Examination," *The Student Volunteer Bulletin* IV (March 1923): 84.

14. Lucile Gibson, "Student Expression in the Student Volunteer Movement," *The Student Volunteer Movement Bulletin* IV (March 1923): 74-77.

15. "Report of the General Secretary of the Student Volunteer Movement to the Executive Committee, from September 1, 1919 to August 31, 1920," September 29, 1920, SVM Archives, Series V.

16. Robert F. Wilder, "Annual Report for the Year 1925-1926," (undated by about a month before the end of the fiscal year), SVM Archives, Series V.

17. See Minutes of the Executive Committee of January 27, 1923. See also "Report of Robert P. Wilder to the Student Volunteer Council," February 22-25, 1923; and "Report of the General Secretary to the Executive Committee Student Volunteer Movement," September 29, 1923, SVM Archives, Series V.

18. Hopkins, *History of the Y.M.C.A. in North America*, 211-220, 290-291, 472-475, 580-583, and 643.

19. Minutes of the Standing committee, June 5, 1920, SVM Archives, Series V.

20. Minutes of the Standing Committee, June 5, 1920, SVM Archives, Series V.

21. Minutes of the Executive Committee, February 24, 1923, SVM Archives, Series V.

22. No Study as yet exists of black American missionaries in Africa, but for an overview of the subject see Sylvia M. Jacobs, "The Historical Role of Afro-Americans in American Missionary Efforts in Africa," in *Black Americans and the Missionary Movement in Africa*, ed. Sylvia M. Jacobs (Westport, CT: Greenwood Press, 1982), 5-29, and Walter L. Williams,

Black Americans and the Evangelization of Africa 1877-1900 (Madison: The University of Wisconsin Press, 1982).

23. "Statement Concerning the Request of the Home Missions Council that the Student Volunteer Movement recruit for the Home Mission Boards at well as for the Foreign Boards," SVM Archives, Series V.

24. Minutes of the Standing Committee of the SVM, February 21, 1920, SVM Archives, Series V.

25. "Report of the Student Volunteer Movement for Foreign Missions," attached to the Executive Committee minutes, September 27, 1921, SVM Archives, Series V; and Minutes of the Standing Committee, February 24, 1922; Minutes of the Executive Committee, September 23, 1922; and "Report of the General Secretary to the Executive Committee, September 23, 1922, SVM Archives, Series V. See also "New Student Fellowship for American Service," *The Congregationalist* (16 March 1922), found in Robert P. Wilder Papers.

26. Wilder to Mott, Nov. 22, 1921, Robert P. Wilder Papers.

27. R.O. Hall, "The Price of World Federation, Peking, 1922," *The Student World* XV (January 1922): 143.

28. "Editorial," *The Student World* XVI (October 1923): 134-5.

29. Sherwood Eddy, letter to the Executive Committee, July 17, 1922, SVM Archives, Series V.

30. Minutes of the Executive Committee, September 23, 1922, SVM Archives, Series V.

31. Minutes of the Standing Committee, November 21, 1922, SVM Archives, Series V.

32. For more on Judd's life see Lee Edwards, *Missionary for Freedom: The Life and Times of Walter Judd* (New York: Paragon House, 1990).

33. Paul Blanshard, *Personal and Controversial* (Boston: Beacon Press, 1973).

34. Paul Blanshard, "Human Relationship and Modern Industrialism," in *Christian Students and World Problems*, ed. Milton Stauffer (New York: Student Volunteer Movement for Foreign Missions, 1924), 90.

35. Robert E. Speer, "The Relation of the Foreign Missionary Enterprise to the World Situation Today," in *Christian Students and World Problems*, ed. Milton Stauffer (New York: Student Volunteer Movement for Foreign Missions, 1924), 138-139.

36. S. Ralph Harlow, "The Indianapolis Convention," *The Intercollegian* 41 (February 1924): 5.

37. Ruth Bowles, "Student Impressions of Indianapolis," *The Student Volunteer Movement Bulletin* V (February 1924): 91.

38. "Conclusions and Proposals," in *Christian Students and World Problems*, ed. Milton Stauffer (New York: Student Volunteer Movement for Foreign Mission, 1924), 233-243.

39. T.H.P. Sailer, "A Study in Contrasts," *The Student Volunteer Movement Bulletin* V (February 1924): 119.

40.   Clemmy Miller, "The Road Ahead," *The Student Volunteer Movement* Bulletin V (March 1924): 139.
41.   A more radical version of this approach led to the concept of a "world religion" based on the contributions of Christianity, Buddhism, Hinduism, Islam and others. The assumption of the religious relativists who held this position was that all religions were fundamentally the same, derived from God, and contained at least a part of the truth. Therefore, a complete religion would not be attained until all cultures made their distinctive contribution. For a contemporary interpretation see A.K. Reischauer "Native Religions – a Liability or an Asset," *The Student Volunteer Movement* Bulletin VI (April 1926): 8-9.
42.   "The Findings of the Council," *The Student Volunteer Movement Bulletin* V (March 1924): 151.

Chapter Nine

1.   Reinhold Niebuhr, "Our World's Denial of God," *The Intercollegian* 44 (February 1927): 130. Niebuhr's article was originally given as an address at the 1926/27 National Student Conference held in Milwaukee.
2.   Van Wyck Brooks, *The Ordeal of Mark Twain* (New York: E. P. Dutton & Company, 1920), 1.
3.   Walter Lippmann, *A Preface to Morals* (New York: The Macmillan Co., 1929), 302.
4.   Marion E. Dice, "Broadening the Student Mind," *The Student Volunteer Movement Bulletin* II (October 1921), 157.
5.   "Students and Christianity To-day – A Symposium of Statements by Leaders in Many Lands," *The Student World* XIV (April 1921): 57-92.
6.   Ibid., 66.
7.   Ibid., 76.
8.   Robert Wilder, "Report of Robert Wilder [to the General Council]," 1927, Wilder Papers.
9.   Wilder, 9.
10. Wilder, 10, 13.
11. Wilder, 13, 15, 10.
12. Henry Van Dusen, "The Spiritual Tone of Indianapolis," *The Student Volunteer Movement Bulletin* V (February 1924): 104-107.
13. James Endicott, "Student Impressions of Indianapolis," *The Student Volunteer Movement Bulletin* V (February 1924): 92.
14. T.H.P. Sailer, "A Study in Contrasts," *The Student Volunteer Movement* Bulletin V (February 1924): 119-122.
15. J. Davidson Taylor, "The Spirit of the Council," *The Student Volunteer Bulletin* (February 1925): 7.
16. "Report of the Findings Committee," *The Student Volunteer Movement Bulletin* (February 1925): 8-10.

17. Dr. Walter H. Judd, "The Purpose of the Convention," in *Christian Students and World Problems*, ed. Milton Stauffer (New York: Student Volunteer Movement for Foreign Missions, 1924), 7.

18. Ibid., 8.

19. Sigmund Freud, "A Difficulty in the Path of Psycho-Analysis," *The Standard Edition of the Complete Psychological Works of Sigmund Freud* vol. XVII (London: The Hogarth Press and the Institute of Psycho-Analysis, 1955), 135-144.

20. Ibid., 143. For a further discussion of Freud's article and its importance for understanding American culture see Warren I. Susman, "'Personality' and the Making of Twentieth-century Culture," *Culture as History*, 271-285.

21. Paul Marrison, "The Future of the Student Volunteer Movement," *The Intercollegian* 41 (April 1924): 24.

22. T.T. Brumbaugh, "Convention Mistakes: By an 'Inside' Student Observer," *The Student Volunteer Movement Bulletin* V (February 1924): 122-124. For the unabridged version of the letter see the SVM Archives, Series V.

23. Stan Pier to W.P. McCulloch, April 27, 1926, Wilder Papers.

24. Wilder to J. Lovell Murray, November 1, 1925, Wilder Papers.

25. Wilder to Murray, November 1, 1925, Wilder Papers.

26. Minutes of the Standing Committee, October 31, 1925, SVM Archives, Series V.

27. Sharp to Wilder, November 5, 1925, Wilder Papers.

28. In addition to Murray and Speer the three other senior members included Leslie Blanchard, Francis Miller and Marvin Harper. The junior members included Ray Wilson, George Leeder, Dorothy Dunning, Chester Harlett and Lynda Goodsell. The Commission chose to include addition SVM members: J.C. Robbins, Fay Campbell, Virginia Prichard, and Wade Bryant. Three professors were also coopted by the committee to provide representation for the missionary and student point of view: E.D. Lucas of Forman Christian College, Lahore, India, D.J. Fleming of Union Theological Seminary, and Ralph Harlow of Smith College.

29. Report of Commission of Ten, 6, SVM Archives, Series V.

30. Ibid., 5.

31. W.P. McCulloch to Robert Speer, December 30, 1925, SVM Archives, Series V.

32. Pier to McCulloch, April 27, 1926, Wilder Papers.

33. Robert P. Wilder, "A Message to Volunteers," *The Student Volunteer Movement Bulletin* VII (October 1926): 3.

34. Reinhold Niebuhr, "Our World's Denial of God," *The Intercollegian* 44 (February 1927): 127-130.

35. Wilder to McCulloch, February 10, 1926, Wilder Papers.

36. "Sailed Volunteers for 1926," *The Student Volunteer Movement Bulletin* VII (May 1927): 287.

37. Robert E. Speer, "Abiding Values of the Student Volunteer Movement," *The Student Volunteer Movement Bulletin* VII (December 1926): 67.

38. "Youth and Missions," *The Christian Century*, 12 January 1928, 40.

Epilogue

1. William Ernest Hocking, *Re-Thinking Missions: A Laymen's Inquiry After One Hundred Years* (New York: Harper and Brothers Publishers, 1932), 44.

2. Milton Stauffer, "Contracts with Non-Christian Cultures," *The Intercollegian* 41 (October 1923): 16. D.J. Fleming, "Cultivating Christian World Mindedness," *The Student Volunteer Movement Bulletin* VI (October 1925): 12-12. D.J. Fleming, "A Long Look From Montevideo," *The Student Volunteer Movement Bulletin* VI (October 1925): 20-23.

3. SVM Archives, series I.

4. Martha L. Smalley, "Archives of the Student Volunteer Movement for Foreign Missions" (New Haven: Library of the Yale University Divinity School, 1980), 170-171, typewritten.

5. David M. Howard, "The Rise and Fall of SVM," *Christianity Today*, 6 November 1970, 17.

6. Herbert Reece Coston, Jr., "The World's Student Christian Federation as an Ecumenical Training Ground," (Ph.D. Diss., Northwestern University, 1963.)

7. Larry D. Pate, *From Every People: A Handbook of Two-Thirds World Missions with Directory/Histories/Analysis* (Monrovia: MARC Publications, 1989), 51.

8. Donald McGavran, "My Pilgrimage in Mission," *International Bulletin of Missionary Research* 10 (April 1986): 53-58. George G. Hunter, III, "The Legacy of Donald A. McGavran," *International Bulletin of Missionary Research* 16 (October 1992): 158-162.

9. Gerald H. Anderson, "American Protestants in Pursuit of Mission: 1886-1986," *International Bulletin of Missionary Research* 12 (July 1988): 110.

10. William Martin, *A Prophet With Honor: The Billy Graham Story* (New York: William Morrow and Co., Inc., 1991), 439-442.

11. Hutchison, *Errand to the World*, 176.

12. Anderson, 113.

13. Ralph Winter, "The Student Volunteers of 1886, Their Heirs, and the Year 2000," *International Journal of Frontier Missions* 2 (April 1985): 151-180.

14. H. Wilbert Norton, Sr., "The Student Foreign Missions Fellowship over Fifty-five Years," *International Bulletin of Missionary Research* 17 (January 1993): 20.

15. Ibid.

16. James M. Reapsome, "Great Commission Deadline," *Christianity Today* 33 (January, 15, 1988): 26-29.

17. David Barett and James Reapsome, *Seven Hundred Plans to Evangelize the World: The Rise of a Global Evangelization Movement* (Birmingham: New Hope, 1988), 41-43.

18. Robert T. Cooke, "Lausanne II and World Evangelization," *International Bulletin of Missionary Research* 14 (January 1990): 15-17.

19. David R. Hackett, ed., *The GCOWE '95 Declaration, AD 2000 & Beyond Movement* (Bellevue, WA: Presbyterian Frontier Fellowship, 1995), 3.

20. Anderson, 114.

21. Pate, 45-46, 51-52.

22. Hill, 167-174.

23. Edward Gilbreath, "Manhood's Great Awakening," *Christianity Today*, 39 (February 6, 1995): 22, 26. "Heavenly Promises" *U.S. News and World Report* 119 (October 2, 1995), 68.

24. Robert Bly, *Iron John: A Book About Men* (New York: Vintage Books, 1990).

25. F. Scott Fitzgerald, "Babylon Revisited" in Malcolm Cowley, ed., *The Stories of F. Scott Fitzgerald* (New York: Charles Scribner's Sons, 1951), 388.

26. William J. Bennett, *The Book of Virtues: A Treasury of Great Moral Stories* (New York: Simon and Schuster, 1993).

27. Shellby Steele, *The Content of Our Character: A New Vision of Race in America* (New York: Harper Perennial, 1990).

28. Allan Bloom, *The Closing of the American Mind* (New York: Simon and Schuster, 1987).

Selected Bibliography

General Works

Ahlstrom, Sydney E. *A Religious History of the American People*. New Haven: Yale University Press, 1972.

Allen, Frederick Lewis. *Only Yesterday: An Informal History of the 1920's*. New York: Harper and Row Publishers, 1931.

Anderson, Gerald H. "American Protestants in Pursuit of Mission: 1886-1986." *International Bulletin of Missionary Research* 12 (July 1988): 98-118.

Barett, David and James Reapsome. *Seven Hundred Plans to Evangelize the World: The Rise of a Global Evangelization Movement*. Birmingham: New Hope, 1988.

Beaver, R. Pierce, ed. *American Missions in Bicentennial Perspective*. South Pasadena: William Carey Library, 1977.

_____. *Ecumenical Beginnings in Protestant World Missions: A History of Comity*. New York: Nelson, 1962.

_____. "Missionary Motivation Through Three Centuries." In *Reinterpretation in American Church History*, ed. J.C. Brauer, 113-151. Chicago: University of Chicago Press, 1968.

Beaver, R. Pierce. *American Protestant Women in World Missions: History of the First Feminist Movement in North America*. Grand Rapids: William B. Eerdman's Publishing Co., 1980.

Beahm, William M. "Factors in the Development of the Student Volunteer Movement for Foreign Mission." Ph.D. diss., University of Chicago, 1941.

Bederman, Gail. "'The Women Have Had Charge of the Church Work Long Enough': The Men and Religion Forward Movement of 1911-1912 and the Masculinization of Middle-Class Protestantism." *American Quarterly* 41 (January 1993): 432-465.

Beecher, Lyman. *A Plea for the West*. Cincinnati: Truman and Smith, 1835.

Binfield, Clyde. *George Williams and the Y.M.C.A.* London: Heinemann, 1973.

Blanshard, Paul. *Personal and Controversial*. Boston: Beacon Press, 1973.

224

Braisted, Ruth Wilder. *In This Generation*. New York: Friendship Press, 1941.

Brauer, Jerald C., ed. *Reinterpretation in American Church History*. Chicago: University of Chicago Press, 1968.

Bruner, F.D. *A Theology of the Holy Spirit*. Grand Rapids: Eerdmans, 1970.

Butler, Jon. *Awash in a Sea of Faith: Christianizing the American People*. Cambridge: Harvard university Press, 1990.

Carter, Paul A. *The Spiritual Crisis of the Gilded Age*. DeKalb: Northern Illinois University Press, 1971.

Calder, Jenny. *The Victorian Home*. London: B.T. Batsford, 1977.

Cauthen, Kenneth. *The Impact of American Religious Liberalism*. New York: Harper and Row, 1962.

Carnes, Mark C. *Secret Ritual and Manhood in Victorian America*. New Haven: Yale University Press, 1989.

Chandler, Alfred D. *The Visible Hand: The Managerial Revolution in American Business*. Cambridge: The Belknap Press of Harvard University Press, 1977.

Coben, Stanley. *Rebellion Against Victorianism: The Impetus for Cultural Change in 1920s America*. New York: Oxford University Press, 1991.

Cooke, Robert T. "Lausanne II and World Evangelization." *International Bulletin of Missionary Research* 14 (January 1990): 15-17.

Comaroff, John, and Jean Comaroff. *Ethnography and the Historical Imagination*. Oxford: Westview Press, 1992.

Coston, Herbert Reece, Jr., "The World's Student Christian Federation as an Ecumenical Training Ground." Ph.D. Diss., Northwestern University, 1963.

Cross, Whitney R. *The Burned-Over District: The Social and Intellectual History of Enthusiastic Religion in Western New York, 1800-1850*. Ithaca: Cornell University Press, 1950.

Davis, Lawrence B. *Immigrants, Baptists, and the Protestant Mind in America*. Urbana: University of Illinois Press, 1973.

Dedmon, Emmett. *Great Enterprises: 100 Years of the YMCA of Metropolitan Chicago*. New York: Rand McMally, 1957.

Deighton, Lee C. ed. *The Encyclopedia of Education*. New York: The MacMillan Company and the Free Press, 1971. S.V. "Education of Women: History," by Kathryn Kish Sklar.

Douglas, Ann. *The Feminization of American Culture*. New York: Alfred A. Knopf, 1977.

Dickens, A.G. *The English Reformation*, 2nd ed. London: Batsford, 1989.

Edwards, Jonathan. *A Faithful Narrative of the Surprising Work of God*. In *The Works of Jonathan Edwards* Vol. IV., ed. Sereno E. Dwight, 17-74. New York: S. Converse, 1829-1830.

Edwards, Lee. *Missionary for Freedom: The Life and Times of Walter Judd*. New York: Paragon House, 1990.

Elsbree, Oliver Wendell. *The Rise of the Missionary Spirit in America 1790-1815*. Williamsport, Pa.: Williamsport Printing and Binding Co., 1928.

Emerson, Ralph Waldo. "Divinity School Address." In *Selected Writings of Ralph Waldo Emerson*. New York: Signet Classic, 1965.

Fass, Paula. *The Damned and the Beautiful: American Youth in the 1920s.* New York: Oxford University Press, 1977.

Findlay, James F., Jr. *Dwight L. Moody: American Evangelist, 1837-1899.* Chicago: University of Chicago Press, 1969.

Finney, Ross Lee. *Personal Religion and the Social Awakening.* Cincinnati: Jennings and Graham, 1913.

Fisher, Galen M. *John R. Mott: Architect of Co-operation and Unity.* New York: Association Press, 1952.

Franzen, Ruth. "The Legacy of Ruth Rouse." *International Bulletin of Missionary Research* 17 (October 1993): 154-158.

Geiger, Roger L. *To Advance Knowledge: The Growth of American Research Universities, 1900-1940.* New York: Oxford University Press, 1986.

Gordon, George Angier. "The Gospel for Humanity?" In *American Protestant Thought in the Liberal Era,* ed. William R. Hutchison. 2nd. ed. Washington, D.C.: University Press of America, 1984.

Hall, Mary Ross and Helen Firman Sweet. *Women in the Y.W.C.A. Record.* New York: Association Press, 1947.

_____. *A Christian America: Protestant Hopes and Historical Realities,* 2nd ed., revised. New York: Oxford University Press, 1984.

Harder, Ben. "The Student Volunteer Movement for Foreign Missions and Its Contribution to 20th Century Missions." *Missiology: An International Review* VIII (April 1980): 139-154.

Hardman, Keith J. *The Spiritual Awakeners: American Revivalists from Solomon Stoddard to D.L. Moody.* Chicago: Moody Press, 1983.

Hatch, Nathan. *The Democratization of American Christianity.* New Haven: Yale University Press, 1989.

Hersey, John. *The Call.* New York: Alfred A. Knopf, 1985.

Hill, Patricia. *The World Their Household.* Ann Arbor: University of Michigan Press, 1984.

Hofstadter, Richard. *The Age of Reform: From Bryan to F.D.R.* New York: Alfred A. Knoph, 1955.

Hofstadter, Richard. *Anti-Intellectualism in American Life.* New York: Alfred A. Knopf, 1963.

Hogg, W.R. *Ecumenical Foundations: A History of the International Missionary Council.* New York: Harper, 1952.

Hopkins, C. Howard. *History of the Y.M.C.A. in North America.* New York: Association Press, 1951.

_____. *John R. Mott, 1865-1955.* Grand Rapids: William B. Eerdman's Publishing Co., 1979.

Hopkins, C. Howard and Ronald C. White. *The Social Gospel: Religion and Reform in Changing America.* Philadelphia: Temple University Press, 1976.

Howard, David M. "The Rise and Fall of SVM." *Christianity Today,* 6 November 1970, 15-17.

Hunter, George G., III. "The Legacy of Donald A. McGavran." *International Bulletin of Missionary Research* 16 (October 1992): 158-162.

Hunter, Jane. *The Gospel of Gentility: American Women Missionaries in Turn-of-the-Century China*. New Haven: Yale University Press, 1984.

Hutchison, William R. "American Missionary Ideologies: Activism as Theory, Practice and Stereotype." In *Continuity and Discontinuity in Church History*, ed. F. Forrester Church and Timothy George, 351-362. Leiden: Brill, 1979.

_____. *American Protestant Thought in the Liberal Era*. 2nd ed. Washington, D.C.: University Press of America, 1984.

_____. *Errand to the World: American Protestant Thought and Foreign Missions*. Chicago: The University of Chicago Press, 1987.

Jacobs, Sylvia M. "The Historical Role of Afro-Americans in American Missionary Efforts in Africa." In *Black Americans and the Missionary Movement in Africa* ed. Sylvia M. Jacobs, 5-29. Westport, CT: Greenwood Press, 1982.

Johnson, Douglas. *Contending for the Faith: A History of the Evangelical Movement in the Universities and Colleges*. Leicester, England: Intervarsity Press, 1979.

Johnson, Paul E. *A Shopkeeper's Millennium: Society and Revivals in Rochester, New York, 1815-1837*. American Century Series. New York: Hill and Wang, 1978.

Johnson, R. Park. "The Legacy of Arthur Judson Brown." *International Bulletin of Missionary Research* 10 (April 1986): 71-75.

Jones, Charles E. *Perfectionist Persuasion*. Metuchen, NJ: Scarecrow Press, 1974.

Lautourette, Kenneth Scott. *A History of the Expansion of Christianity*, Vol. IV: *The Great Century: A.D. 1800 - A.D. 1914, Europe and the United States of America*. New York: Harper and Brothers, 1941.

_____. *A History of the Expansion of Christianity*, Vol. V: *The Great Century in the Americas, Australasia, and Africa A.D. 1800 - A.D. 1914*. New York: Harper and Brothers, 1943.

_____. *A History of the Expansion of Christianity*, Vol. VI: *The Great Century in Northern Africa and Asia A.D. 1800 - A.D. 1914*. New York: Harper and Brothers Publishers, 1944.

Leach, William R. *Land of Desire, From Department Store to the Department of Commerce: The Rise of America's Commercial Culture*. New York: Pantheon Books, 1993.

Lears, T. J. Jackson, *No Place of Grace: Anitmodernism and the Transformation of American Culture*, 1880-1920. New York: Pantheon Books, 1981.

Leuchtenburg, William E. *The Perils of Prosperity 1914-32*. Chicago: The University of Chicago Press, 1958.

Leverenz, David. *Manhood and the American Renaissance*. Ithaca: Cornell University Press, 1989.

Lotx, Denton. "The Watchword for World Evangelization." *International Review of Mission* LXVIII (April 1979): 177-189.

MacAloon, John J. *This Great Symbol: Pierre de Coubertin and the Origins of the Modern Olympic Games*. Chicago: University of Chicago Press, 1981.

MacMillian, Donald N. "The Presbyterian Who Invented Basketball." *Presbyterian Record* CXVII (January 1993): 20-22.

Marsden, George. *Fundamentalism and American Culture: The Shaping of Twentieth-Century Evangelicalism, 1870-1925.* New York: Oxford University Press, 1980.

Marty, Martin. *Modern American Religion: The Irony of It All, 1893-1919.* Vol. 1. Chicago: University of Chicago Press, 1986.

Mathews, Basil. *John R. Mott, World Citizen.* New York: Harper, 1934.

Matthews, Mary L. "The Story of Mount Holyoke Missionary Association, 1878-1884." *The Missionary Review of the World* LVII (December 1934): 565.

McDannell, Collean. *The Christian Home in Victorian America, 1840-1900.* Bloomington: University of Indiana Press, 1986.

Meyer, D.H. "American Intellectuals and the Victorian Crisis of Faith." In *Victorian America,* ed. Daniel Walker Howe. Philadelphia: University of Pennsylvania Press, 1976.

Miller, Perry. *Jonathan Edwards.* [New York:] William Sloane Associates, 1949.

Morgan, William H. *Student Religion During Fifty Years.* New York: Association Press, 1935.

Neill, Stephen. *Colonialism and Christian Missions.* New York: McGraw-Hill, 1966.

_____. *A History of Christian Missions.* Harmondsworth: Penguin, 1964.

Norton, H. Wilbert, Sr. "The Student Foreign Missions Fellowship over Fifty-five Years." *International Bulletin of Missionary Research* 17 (January 1993): 17-21.

Ober, Frank W., editor. *James Stokes: Pioneer of Y.M.C.A.'s.* New York: Association Press, 1921.

Pate, Larry D. *From Every People: A Handbook of Two-Thirds World Missions with Directory/Histories Analysis.* Monrovia: MARC Publications, 1989.

Patterson, James A. "The Legacy of Robert P. Wilder." *International Bulletin of Missions Research* 15 (January 1991): 26-32.

Pence, Owen E. *The Y.M.C.A. and Social Need.* New York: Association Press, 1946.

Phillips, Clifton. "The Student Volunteer Movement and Its Role in China Missions, 1886-1920." In *The Missionary Enterprise in China and America,* ed. John K. Fairbank, 91-109. Cambridge: Harvard University Press, 1974.

Phillips, Clifton. "Changing Attitudes in the Student Volunteer Movement of Great Britain and North America." In *Missionary Ideologies in the Imperialist Era: 1880-1920,* ed. Torben Christensen and William R. Hutchison, 131-145. Aarhus, Denmark: Aros Publishers, 1984.

Piper, John F. "Robert E. Speer: Christian Statesman in War and Peace." *Journal of Presbyterian History* 47 (September 1969): 208.

_____. "Robert E. Speer on Christianity and Race." *Journal of Presbyterian History* 61 (Summer 1983): 227-247.

_____. "Robert E. Speer: His Call and the Missionary Impulse, 1890-1900." *American Presbyterians: Journal of Presbyterian History* 65 (Summer 1987): 97-108.

Pollock, John Charles. *Moody: A Biographical Portrait of the Pacesetter in Modern Mass Evangelism.* Chicago: Moody Press, 1983.

228

Rabe, Valetin. *The Home Base of American China Missions, 1880-1920.* Cambridge: Harvard University Press, 1978.

Reapsome, James M. "Great Commission Deadline." *Christianity Today* 15 January 1988, 26-29.

Robert, Dana L. "The Legacy of Arthur Tappan Pierson." *International Bulletin of Missionary Research* 8 (July 1984): 120-125.

Rosenthal, Michael. *The Character Factory: Baden-Powell and the Origins of the Boy Scout Movement.* New York: Pantheon Books, 1986.

Rotundo, E. Anthony. *American Manhood: Transformations in Masculinity from the Revolution to the Modern Era.* New York: Basic Books, 1993.

Rouse, Ruth. *The World's Student Christian Federation: A History of the First Thirty Years.* London: Student Volunteer Movement Press, 1948.

Rouse, Ruth and Stephen Neill, ed. *A History of the Ecumenical Movement, 1517-1948.* London: Society for the Propagation of Christian Knowledge, 1954.

Ruether, Rosemary Radford. "Radical Victorians: The Quest for an Alternative Culture." In *Women and Religion in America*, Vol. 3, 1900-1928, ed. Rosemary Radford Ruether and Rosemary Skinner Keller, 1-47. San Francisco: Harper and Row, 1986.

Sandeen, Ernest R. *The Roots of Fundamentalism.* Chicago: University of Chicago Press, 1970.

Schneider, Robert A. "Royal G. Wilder: New School Missionary in the ABCFM, 1846-1871." *American Presbyterians: Journal of Presbyterian History* 64 (Summer 1986): 73-82.

Scott, Donald M. *From Office to Prfession: The New England Ministry, 1750-1850.* Camden, NJ: University of Pennsylvania Press, 1978.

Shedd, Clarence Prouty. *The Church Follows Its Students.* New Haven: Yale University Press, 1938.

_____. *Two Centuries of Student Christian Movements.* New York: Association Press, 1934.

Shedd, Clarence Prouty, et. al. *History of the World's Alliance of YMCAs.* New York: Fleming H. Revell, 1910.

Showalter, Nathan D. *The End of a Crusade: The Student Volunteer Movement for Foreign Missions and the Great War.* Ph.D. Diss., Harvard University, 1990.

Sims, Mary S. *The Natural History of a Social Institution: The Young Women's Christian Association.* New York: The Woman's Press, 1936.

Singleton, Gregory H. "'Mere Middle-Class Institutions'" Urban Protestantism in Nineteenth-Century America." *Journal of Social History* VI (Summer 1973): 489-504.

_____. "Protestant Organizations and the Shaping of Victorian America." *American Quarterly* XXVII (December 1975): 549-560.

_____. "Fundamentalism and Urbanization: A Quantitative Critique of Impressionistic Interpretations." In *The New Urban History: Quantitative Explorations by American Historians*, ed. Leo F. Schnore and Eric E. Lambard. Princeton: Princeton University Press, 1975.

Smalley, Martha L. "Archives of the Student Volunteer Movement for Foreign Missions." New Haven: Library of the Yale University Divinity School, 1980. Typewritten.

Smith, Timothy L. *Called Unto Holiness*. Kansas City : Nazarene Publishing House, 1962.

Starr, Harris E., ed. *Dictionary of American Biography*. Vol. XXI, Supplement One. New York: Charles Scribner's Sons, 1944. S.v. "Harland Page Beach," by Kenneth Scott Lautourette.

Steele, Shellby. *The Content of Our Character: A New Vision of Race in America*. New York: Harper Perennial, 1990.

Susman, Warren I. *Culture as History*. New York: Pantheon Books, 1984.

Taylor, Mary Geraldine. *Borden of Yale*, revised edition by David Bentley-Taylor. London: China Inland Mission, Newington Green, 1952.

Tawney, Richard H. *Religion and the Rise of Capitalism*. New York: Harcourt Brace & Co. Inc.,1926. Reprint Gloucester: Peter Smith, 1962.

Vance, Norman. *The Sinews of the Spirit: The Ideal of Christian Manliness in Victorian Literature and Religious Thought*. Cambridge: Cambridge University Press, 1985.

Veysey, Laurence R. *The Emergence of the American University*. Chicago: University of Chicago Press, 1965.

Weber, Timothy. *Living in the Shadow of the Second Coming: American Premillennialism, 1875-1982*. Grand Rapids: Academic Books, 1983.

Weisberger, Bernard. *They Gathered at the River: The Story of the Great Revivalists and Their Impact Upon Religion in America*. Boston: Little, Brown and Co. 1958.

Welter, Barbara A. "The Feminization of Religion in Nineteenth-Century America." In *Clio's Consciousness Raised*, ed. Mary S. Hartman and Lois Banner. New York: Harper, 1973.

_____. "She Hath Done What She Could: Protestant Women's Missionary Careers in Nineteenth-Century America." In *Women in American Religion*, ed. Janet Wilson James, 111-125. Camden, NJ: University of Pennsylvania Press, 1980.

Wheeler, W.R. *A Man Sent From God: A Biography of Robert E. Speer*. Westwood, NJ: Revell, 1956.

Wiebe, Robert H. *The Search for Order, 1877-1920*. New York: Hill and Wang, 1967.

Williams, Walter L. *Black Americans and the Evangelization of Africa 1877-1900*. (Madison: The University of Wisconsin Press, 1982).

Wilson, J. Christy, Jr. "The Legacy of Samuel M. Zwemer." *International Bulletin of Missionary Research* 10 (July 1986): 117-121.

Winn, William E. "Tom Brown's School Days and the Development of `Muscular Christianity.'" *Church History* XXXIX (March, 1960): 64-73.

Winter, Ralph. "The Student Volunteers of 1886, Their Heirs, and the Year 2000." *International Journal of Frontier Missions* 2 (April 1985): 151-180.

"Youth and Missions." *The Christian Century*, 12 January 1928, 39-40.

Works from the Era of the SVM

Barton, Bruce, *The Man Nobody Knows*. Indianapolis: Bobbs-Merrill, 1925.

Barton, James L. *Educational Missions*. New York: Student Volunteer Movement for Foreign Missions, 1913.

Beach, Harlan P. *The Cross in the Land of the Trident*. New York: International Committee of the YMCA, 1895.

_____. *Knights of the Labarum, Being Studies in the lives of Judson, Duff, MacKenzie and MacKay*. Chicago: Student Volunteer Movement for Foreign Missions, 1896.

_____. *Dawn on the Hills of T'ang; or Missions in China*. Revised edition. New York: Young People's Missionary Movement, 1907.

Brooks, Van Wyck. *The Ordeal of Mark Twain*. New York: E.P. Dutton & Co., 1920.

Brown, Arthur J. *The New Era in the Philippines*. New York: Student Volunteer Movement for Foreign Missions, Fleming H. Revell Co., 1903.

_____. *The Foreign Missionary: An Incarnation of a World Movement*. New York: Student Volunteer Movement for Foreign Missions, 1907.

Cary, Otis. *Japan and Its Regeneration.* New York: Student Volunteer Movement for Foreign Missions, 1899.

Chapman, J. Wilbur. *The Life and Work of Dwight L. Moody*. Philadelphia (?): J.C. Wilson(?), 1900.

Dennis, James S. *Social Evils of the Non-Christian World*. New York: Student Volunteer Movement for Foreign Missions, Fleming H. Revell Co., 1897.

Eddy, George Sherwood. *Suffering and the War*. London: Longmans, Green and Co., 1916.

_____. *Everybody's World*. New York: George H. Doran, 1920.

_____. *Religion and Social Justice*. New York: George H. Doran, 1927.

_____. *A Pilgrimage of Ideas: The Re-Education of Sherwood Eddy*. New York: Farrar and Rinehart Inc., 1934.

_____. *Pathfinders of the World Missionary Crusade*. New York: Abingdon-Cokesbury, 1945.

_____. *Eighty Adventurous Years: An Autobiography*. New York: Harper, 1955.

Eerdman, Charles R. "An Ideal Missionary Volunteer." *The Missionary Review of the World*. 36 (old series) 26 (new series) (August 1913): 567-577.

Ely, Richard T. *Social Aspects of Christianity*, and Other Essays. New York: Thomas Y. Crowell & Co., 1889.

Fosdick, Harry Emerson, *The Manhood of the Master*. New York: Association Press, 1913.

Foster, John, *Decision of Character*. Abridged, with an introduction by John R. Mott. New York: Student Volunteer Movement, 1907.

Freud, Sigmund. *The Standard Edition of the Complete Psychological Works of Sigmund Freud*. Vol. XVII. "A Difficulty in the Path of Psycho-Analysis." London: The Hogarth Press and the Institute of Psycho-Analysis, 1955.

Guinness, M. Geraldine. *The Story of the China Inland Mission*. London: The China Inland Mission, 1894.

Guinness, Lucy. *In the Far East: Letters from Geraldine Guinness in China*. New York: Fleming H. Revel, 1889.

Guinness, Joy. *Mrs. Howard Taylor: Her Web of Time*. London: China Inland Mission, 1949.

Glover, T.R. *The Jesus of History*. New York: Association Press, 1921.

Hocking, William Ernest. *Re-Thinking Missions: A Laymen's Inquiry After One Hundred Years*. New York: Harper and Brothers Publishers, 1932.

Hughes, Thomas, *Tom Brown's School Days*. Chicago: Rand, McNaily & Company, reprint, 1857.

_____. *The Manliness of Christ*. London: MacMillan & Co., 1880.

Jenks, Jeremiah W. *The Political and Social Significance of the Life and Teachings of Jesus*. New York: Young Men's Christian Association Press, 1908.

Kellogg, S.H. *A Handbook of Comparative Religion*. New York: Student Volunteer Movement for Foreign Missions, 1907.

Lippmann, Walter. *A Preface to Morals*. New York: The MacMillan Co., 1929.

Marsh, Dwight W. *The Tennessean in Persia and Koodistan*. Philadelphia: Presbyterian Publication Committee, New York: A.D.F. Randolph, 1869.

Mathews, Shailer. *The Social Teaching of Jesus: An Essay in Christian Sociology*. New York: Hodeder & Stoughton, George H. Doran Company, 1897.

Mateer, Robert M. "Theological Students and Foreign Missions." *The Missionary Review* III (March-April 1889): 131-133.

Montgomery, Helen Barrett. *Western Women in Eastern Lands: An Outline Study of Fifty Years of Woman's Work in Foreign Missions*. New York: MacMillan, 1910.

Morse, Richard C. *My Life With Young Men: Fifty Years in the Young Men's Christian Association*. New York: Association Press, 1918.

Mott, John R. *Strategic Points in the World's Conquest*. New York: Fleming H. Revell, 1897.

_____. "Our Responsibility for the Extension of Christ's Kingdom into the Regions Beyond." *The Churchman* 22 January 1898, 116-117.

_____. *The Evangelization of the World in This Generation*. New York: Student Volunteer Movement, 1900.

_____. *The Decisive Hour of Christian Missions*. New York: Student Volunteer Movement, 1910.

_____. *The Present World Situation*. New York: Student Volunteer Movement, 1914.

_____. "The Present World Conflict and Its Relation to Christian Missions." *The Outlook of Missions* VII (December 1915): 573-580.

_____. *The Future Leadership of the Church*. New York: Association Press, 1916.

_____. *The World's Student Christian Federation: Origin, Achievements, Forecast*. New York: World's Student Christian Federation, 1920.

_____. *Five Decades and a Forward View*. New York: Harper and Brothers, 1939.

Murray, J. Lovell. *The Call of a World Task*. New York: Association Press, 1918.

Ober, C.K. *The Association Secretaryship*. New York: Association Press, 1918.

_____. *Luther D. Wishard, Projector of World Movements.* New York: Association Press, 1927.

_____. *Exploring a Continent.* New York: Association Press, 1929.

Peabody, Francis Greenwood. *Jesus Christ and the Social Question.* New York: Grossett and Dunlap Publishers, 1900.

_____. *Jesus Christ and the Christian Character.* New York: The MacMillan Co., 1905.

Pierson, Arthur T., *Crisis of Missions; or, The Voice Out of the Cloud.* New York: Robert Carter and Brothers, 1886.

_____. "Student Volunteers' Convention." *Missionary Review.* XIV (May 1891): 352-360.

_____. *The Keswick Movement.* New York: Funk & Wagnalls Co., 1903.

Renan, Ernest. *The Life of Jesus.* Charles Edwin Wilbour, trans. New York: Carleton, Publisher, 1864.

Rauschenbusch, Walter. *Christianity and the Social Crisis.* New York: MacMillan, 1907.

_____. *The Social Principles of Jesus.* New York: Association Press, 1916.

Sheldon, Charles M. *In His Steps.* New Jersey: Barbour and Co., Inc. Westwood, 1984.

Smith, George Adam. *The Life of Henry Drummond.* New York: Double Day & McClure Company, 1898.

Speer, Robert E. *Studies of the Man Christ Jesus.* New York: Young Men's Christian Association Press, 1896.

_____. *A Memorial of Horace Tracy Pitkin.* New York: Fleming H. Revell Co., 1903.

_____. *Christianity and the Nations.* New York: Fleming H. Revell, 1910.

_____. *South American Problems.* New York: Student Volunteer Movement for Foreign Missions, 1912.

_____. "A Few Comparison of Then and Now." *Missionary Review of the World.* 51 (January 1928): 5-10.

_____. *"Re-Thinking Missions" Examined.* New York: Fleming H. Revell, 1933.

Soper, Edmund Davison. *The Faiths of Mankind.* College Volunteer Study Courses, Third Year Part II. New York: The Women's Press, 1920.

Strong, Josiah. *Our Country.* Cambridge: The Belknap Press of Harvard University Press, 1963.

The Student Volunteer Movement After Twenty-Five Years. New York: Student Volunteer Movement for Foreign Missions, 1911.

"This World's Evangelization not an Easy or Short Work." *The Foreign Missionary.* XXXV (January 1878): 230-233.

Thompson, A.C., et. al. *Modern Apostle of Missionary Byways.* New York: Student Volunteer Movement for Foreign Missions, 1889.

Thronton, Douglas M. *Africa Waiting: or the Problem of Africa's Evangelization.* London: 1897; reprint, New York: Student Volunteer Movement for Foreign Missions, 1906.

Wallace, Lew. *Ben-Hur: A Tale of the Christ*. New York: The Heritage Press, 1960.

Ward, Harry F. and Richard H. Edwards. *Christianizing Community Life*. New York: Association Press, 1919.

"Dr. [Gustave] Warneck on `The Modern Theory of the Evangelization of the World." *Missionary Record of the United Presbyterian Church*. XVIII (October 1897): 297-299.

Watson, Charles R. "The Gains, Losses, and Handicaps of Foreign Missions Occasioned by the War, A Contrast of the Missionary Situation in July, 1914, and January, 1919." In *Foreign Missions Conference of North America*, ed. Fennell P. Turner, 116-127. New York: Foreign Missions Conference, 1919.

Weatherford, Willis Duke. *Negro Life in the South*. New York: Young Men's Christian Association Press, 1910.

Wilder, Robert P. *The Great Commission: The Missionary Responses of the Student Volunteer Movements in North America and Europe*. London: Oliphants Ltd., 1936.

_____. *The Student Volunteer Movement for Foreign Missions: Some Personal Reminiscences of Its Origin and Early History*. New York: 1935.

Wilder, Royal Gould. "To Our Readers." I *The Missionary Review*. (January-February 1878): 3-12.

_____. "Who Will Go For Us?" *The Missionary Review*. I (January-February 1878): 12-19.

_____. "Answer to the Foreign Board Required by the General Assembly — Presented to the Board October 30, 1877." *The Missionary Review*. I (March-April 1878): 125.

Williamson, J. Rutter. *The Healing of the Nations: A Treatise on Medical Missions Statement and Appeal*. London: Student Volunteer Missionary Union, 1899.

Wilson, Elizabeth. *Fifty Years of Association Work Among Young Women 1866-1916*. New York: National Board of the YWCA of the USA, 1916.

Wishard, Luther D. *A New Programme of Missions: A Movement to Make the Colleges in All Lands Centers of Evangelization*. New York: Flemming H. Revell, 1895.

_____. "The Beginning of the Students' Era in Christian History." 1917. TMs. Yale Divinity School Library.

Year Book of the Young Men's Christian Associations of North America for the Year 1902. New York: International Committee, 1902.

Year Book of the Young Men's Christian Association of North America, May 1, 1915 to April 30, 1916. New York: Association Press, 1916.

Zwemer, Samuel M. *Islam, A Challenge to Faith*. New York: Student Volunteer Movement for Foreign Missions, 1907.

_____. *The Unoccupied Mission Fields of Africa and Asia*. New York: Student Volunteer Movement for Foreign Missions, 1911.

234

Pamphlets of the Student Movement

The Achievements of the Student Volunteer Movement for Foreign Missions During the First Generation of its History 1886-1919. New York: Student Volunteer Movement for Foreign Missions, 1919.

Bosworth, Dean Edward Increase. *The Present Crisis in the Kingdom of God: A Call for Character.* New York: The International Committee of Young Men's Christian Associations, 1907.

Campbell, Charles Soutter. *William Whiting Borden: A Short Life Complete in Christ.* (Found in the Miscellaneous Person Papers: William Whiting Borden, Yale Divinity School Archives.)

The Christian Enterprise Abroad: A Pre-Convention Study. New York: Student Volunteer Movement for Foreign Missions, 1923.

Clark, C.A. *An Appeal from Japan.* Student Volunteer Series, No. 11. New York: Student Volunteer Movement for Foreign Missions, ca. 1890.

The First Two Decades of the Student Volunteer Movement. New York: Student Volunteer Movement for Foreign Missions, 1906.

Eddy, George Sherwood. *The Supreme Decision of the Christian Student.* Chicago: The Student Volunteer Movement for Foreign Missions, 1893.

_____. *Horace Tracy Pitkin: Missionary Advocate and Martyr.* (Found in the SVM Archives, Series VII.)

_____. *The Maker of Men.* New York: Association Press, 1917.

Hull, William E. *The American Inter-Seminary Missionary Alliance.* Gettysburg: J.E. Wible Printer, 1886.

King, Henry Churchill. *How to Make a Rational Fight for Character.* New York: The International Committee of Young Men's Christian Associations, 1902.

Lyon, D. Willard. *The Volunteer Band for Foreign Missions.* The Student Volunteer Series, no. 4. New York: Student Volunteer Movement for Foreign Missions, ca. 1895.

Mott, John R. "The Beginnings of the Student Volunteer Movement." In *The Student Volunteer Movement After Twenty-Five Years, 1886-1911,* no editor stated, 10-11. New York: Student Volunteer Movement, 1911.

_____. *The Call of the Non-Christian World.* Laymen's Missionary Movement, 1907.

_____. *Modern World Movements: God's Challenge to the Church.* London: Student Christian Movement, 1908.

Speer, Robert E. *Things That Make a Man.* New York: Association Press, 1899.

_____. *How to Deal with Temptations: An Address to Young Men.* New York: Association Press, 1912.

The Student Volunteer Movement of South Africa. Lovedale Mission Press, 1916.

Turner, Fennell P. *A Year of the Student Volunteer Movement for Foreign Missions.* New York: Student Volunteer Movement for Foreign Missions, 1910.

Wilder, Robert P. *The Student Volunteer Movement: Its Origin and Early History.* New York: Student Volunteer Movement, 1935.

_____. *The Pledge of the Student Volunteer Movement for Foreign Missions.* New York: Student Volunteer Movement for Foreign Missions, 1890.

Published Reports of the Student Movement

Inter-Seminary Alliance Convention Report. Hartford, CT: The Case, Locwood & Brainard Co., 1880-1895.

Make Jesus King: The Report of the International Student's Missionary Conference, Liverpool, January 1-5, 1896. New York: Fleming H. Revell Co., 1896.

Moorhead, Max Wood, ed. *The Student Missionary Enterprise.* Boston: Press of T.O. Metcalf and Co., 1894.

Norton, Fred L. *A College of Colleges.* New York: Revell, 1889.

Pierson, Delavan L., ed. *Northfield Echoes.* East Northfield: Rastell & McKinley, 1894-1896; Northfield Echoes, 1897-1899; The Northfield Bookstore Store, 1900-1903..

St. John, Burton, ed. *North American Students and World Advance.* New York: Student Volunteer Movement for Foreign Missions, 1920.

Report of the First International Convention of the Student Volunteer Movement for Foreign Missions. Boston: Press of T.O. Metcalf and Co., 1891.

Shanks, T.J. ed. *A College of Colleges.* Chicago: Fleming H. Revell, 1887.

The Student Missionary Appeal. New York: Student Volunteer Movement for Foreign Missions, 1898.

Students and the Modern Missionary Crusade. New York: Student Volunteer Movement for Foreign Missions, 1906.

Students and the Present Missions Crisis. New York: Student Volunteer Movement for Foreign Missions, 1910.

Students and the World-Wide Expansion of Christianity. Ed. Fennell P. Turner. New York: Student Volunteer Movement for Foreign Missions, 1914.

Stauffer, Milton, ed. *Christian Students and World Problems.* New York: Student Volunteer Movement for Foreign Missions, 1924.

World Student Christian Federation Annual Reports, 1897-1926. In the Archives of the World Student Christian Federation, Yale Divinity School.

Contemporary Periodicals of the Student Movement

Association Men. Chicago: International Committee of the Young Men's Christian Association, 1894-1924. The official journal of the North American YMCA.

The Association Outlook. Toronto: Young Men's Christian Association of Canada, 1902-1920. The official organ of the city and college YWCA of Canada.

College Bulletin of the Young Men's Christian Association. New York: International Committee of the Young Men's Christian Association, 1878-1886. In 1887 it became the *Intercollegian.*

The North American Student. New York: Council of North American Student Members, 1913-1918. It temporarily replaced the *Intercollegian.*

The Student Movement. London: Christian Student Movement, 1898-1962. The journal of the SCM of Great Britain and Ireland.

The Student Volunteer. Chicago: Student Volunteer Movement for Foreign Missions, 1893-1897. the official organ of the SVM until *The Intercollegian* was jointed published by the SVM and YMCA, 1898-1912.

The Student Volunteer Movement Bulletin. New York: Student Volunteer Movement for Foreign Missions, 1915-1930. It then became *Far Horizons*.

The Student World. New York: World Student Christian Federation, 1980-1925. The official organ of the WSCF.

The Intercollegian. New York: Young Men's Christian Association, 1887-1891, 1898-1912, and 1918-1934. The journal of the YMCA, which followed the *College Bulletin*. Between 1898 and 1912 it was published jointly by the YMCA and SVM.

Archival and Manuscript Collections
at the Yale Divinity School Library

The Archives of the Student Volunteer Movement for Foreign Missions
The Archives of the World Student Christian Federation
The John R. Mott Papers
The George Sherwood Eddy Papers
The Robert Parmelle Wilder Papers

Index

□